The Origins and Course of Common Mental Disorders

The Origins and Course of Common Mental Disorders describes the nature, characteristics and causes of common emotional and behavioural disorders as they develop across the lifespan, providing a clear and concise account of recent advances in our knowledge of the origins and history of anxious, depressive, anti-social and substance related disorders.

Combing a lifespan approach with developments in neurobiology, this book describes the epidemiology of emotional and behavioural disorders in childhood, adolescence and adult life. David Goldberg and Ian Goodyer demonstrate how both genes and environments exert different but key effects on the development of these disorders and suggest a developmental model as the most appropriate for determining vulnerabilities for psychopathology. Divided into four sections, the book covers:

- The nature and distribution of common mental disorders
- The biological basis of common disorders
- The human life cycle relevant to common disorders
- The developmental model

This highly readable account of the origins of emotional and behavioural disorders will be of interest to behavioural science students and all mental health professionals including psychiatrists, psychologists, social workers, nurses and counsellors.

David Goldberg is Professor Emeritus at the Institute of Psychiatry, King's College London

Ian Goodyer is Foundation Professor of Child and Adolescent Psychiatry at the University of Cambridge

The Origins and Course of Common Mental Disorders

David Goldberg and Ian Goodyer

Routledge
Taylor & Francis Group

LONDON AND NEW YORK

First published 2005 by Routledge
27 Church Road, Hove, East Sussex BN3 2FA

Simultaneously published in the USA and Canada
by Routledge
270 Madison Avenue, New York, NY 10016

Routledge is an imprint of the Taylor and Francis Group

© 2005 David Goldberg and Ian Goodyer

Typeset in Times by RefineCatch Ltd, Bungay, Suffolk
Printed and bound in Great Britain by
TJ International Ltd, Padstow, Cornwall
Paperback cover design by Oxted Colour Printers,
Old Oxted, Surrey

This publication has been produced with paper manufactured to
strict environmental standards and with pulp derived from
sustainable forests.

British Library Cataloguing in Publication Data
A catalogue record for this book is available from the British Library

Library of Congress Cataloging in Publication Data
Goldberg, David P.
   The origins and course of common mental disorders/David Goldberg & Ian Goodyer.
      p. ; cm.
   Includes bibliographical references and index.
   ISBN 1-58391-959-7 (hbk)—ISBN 1-58391-960-0 (pbk) 1. Mental illness—
Epidemiology. 2. Psychiatric epidemiology.
   [DNLM: 1. Mental Disorders–etiology. 2. Mental Disorders–
      prevention & control.]
1. Goodyear, Ian M. II. Title.
   RC455.2.E64G655 2005
   616.89—dc22   2005001406

ISBN 1-58391-959-7 hbk
ISBN 1-58391-960-0 pbk

Contents

Figures

Tables

Foreword

I begin with the hope that *The Origins and Course of Common Mental Disorders* enjoys a large readership. That is not simply because I like and respect the authors. It reflects my belief that this book can inspire more medical students to choose psychiatry as a specialty because it makes clear the intellectual excitement at the frontiers of research; that it will provide house officers with an integrated view of a field typically fragmented by narrow partisanship; and that it will broaden the horizons of practitioners by effectively bringing together (without blurring) the genetic, biological, and psychosocial roots of behaviour. To the extent these predictions are correct, it may even improve the quality of patient care!

David Goldberg has managed to do what I had supposed to be impossible. He has made a superb book on *Common Mental Disorders* even better. During the 12-year interval since its first incarnation with Peter Huxley as its co-author, there has been very considerable progress in the sciences basic to psychiatry: neuroscience, molecular biology, genetics and social epidemiology. Treatment outcomes in psychiatry, both psychopharmacologic and psychotherapeutic, have been subject to more exacting tests. David, this time writing with Ian Goodyer, has integrated the new knowledge into an almost completely rewritten text, not in the form of updates or add-ons, but with the new concepts from the separate domains integrated into the exposition, insofar as it is possible to do so. David and Ian provide a remarkably concise account of what is reasonably well established about the genesis of mental disorders (it is the nature of science that 'truth' is approximated but never completely realised), what is probably true but less certain, and what must remain speculative in the absence of decisive evidence. They will forgive me if I call them what they are: sherpas who guide the reader safely in ascending the heights but ask for no credit when the ascent is successful.

The Origins and Course of Common Mental Disorders is written in a remarkably lucid style. I am tempted to call it 'deceptively lucid', at the risk of coining an oxymoron, because the style conceals the depth of scholarship and original thought that has gone into its composition. David Goldberg and Ian Goodyer strive for transparency. That is, they interpose nothing between reader and subject matter. They illuminate the issues rather than obscure them with displays of erudition.

Their monograph is informed by epidemiological intelligence. What makes this feature so noteworthy? *Intelligence* has two primary meanings in the *American Heritage Dictionary*: that is, as 'a faculty of thought and reason' and as 'received information; or 'news'. The third listed meaning is also particularly apposite: 'secret information'. Although the studies that David Goldberg and Ian Goodyer cite are all reported in the open literature, it is not much of an exaggeration to call them 'secret' because they have had so little influence on the delivery of mental health services. But why *epidemiological* intelligence?

The mode of analysis employed throughout this book is *population based*; it takes into account *denominators* (populations) as well as *numerators* (cases). The reader is alerted to the importance of the way 'caseness' is defined. Definitions, however arbitrary, can be made operational to attain reliability; however, their ultimate justification lies in the consequences they have for particular purposes. The authors employ epidemiological intelligence in an analysis of the distribution of illness in the community, the demographic and social correlates of that distribution, and causal inferences derived from the observed interrelations. The result is a lucidly presented, closely reasoned, and firmly data-based argument with major implications for health policy. Goldberg and Goodyer are concerned for the way care is – and should be – delivered in the community; their reference point is patient management.

Patients seen by psychiatrists, after referral from generalists, are so skewed a sample of ill persons in the population that psychiatric classification schemes provide a distorted account of problems in the community. Perhaps one in ten to one in fifteen individuals with symptoms of mental illness in the community reaches the psychiatric outpatient department. Some fail to come to the general practitioner's surgery in the first place; such persons are identified only when community surveys are undertaken. Others are not recognised as having psychiatric problems when they are seen by the generalist; still others are managed (more or less well) at this level in the system.

Less than 10 per cent of the symptomatic 'eligibles' make their way to the specialist. As would be expected, they are on average the sickest patients; they suffer from the less common ailments. Because traditional psychiatric studies are based on so unrepresentative a sample, it is not surprising that specialist nosology does not meet the needs of the generalist practice. It was not until research psychiatrists, taking their lead from Michael Shepherd (Shepherd *et al.* 1959, 1986), undertook to examine patients in the GP's consulting room that psychiatrists became aware of how far short our classification schemes fall in dealing with the more common mental illnesses.

Patients do not arrive in the doctor's office neatly packaged and presorted. It is not only that each patient exhibits unique particularities; it is also that the patient's idiosyncrasies shape his illness manifestations. This interaction between a unique history and a shared biology is both the bane and the joy of general medical practice: the bane in that the variability in the ways similar illnesses present necessitates a meticulous search for the commonalities underlying remarkably different complaints; the joy is that each new encounter is a challenge to the practitioner's ingenuity. Medical practice, conscientiously undertaken, defies routinisation!

Making the diagnosis (that is, identifying the diabetes or the depression underlying the complaint of weight loss) only starts the process. The goal is to help *this* patient to understand the nature of *his or her* problem and to weigh the benefits and the costs of the available therapeutic alternatives. It demands of the doctor a sensitivity to the nuances of cultural meaning as they are refracted through individual experience; it demands the flexibility and the imaginativeness to tailor standard regimens to fit the particularities of the patient's situation.

Naming the problem matters to the patient as well as the doctor. Patients seek more than remission of their symptoms; they search for relief from the anxiety aroused by the threat to their integrity. They want the doctor to interpret the meaning of their misfortune. The medical label given and the explanation provided not only legitimate the illness experience but shape its very expression (Eisenberg 1999).

For the doctor, 'making the diagnosis' matters insofar as it informs treatment and forecasts the likely course of the illness. At least, that is what should matter. The process can become an academic exercise, pursued without regard to the hazard for the patient or the likelihood it will lead to benefit. For the dedicated clinician, the purpose of diagnosis and classification is to enhance the physician's ability to help the patient. That is, its goals are both pragmatic and compassionate. The doctor wants a guide to action, one whose elegance and tightness of logic are far less important to him than its utility in guiding management. Goldberg and Goodyer provide just such a structure for evaluating mental illness. The simplicity and straightforwardness of their scheme make it easy to underestimate the profundity of the insights they provide.

All too often, dimensional and categorical models of illness are counterposed as though they were mutually exclusive and demand the choice of one or the other. To the contrary, the one to be preferred depends upon the conditions to which it is to be applied and the purposes of its use. Goldberg and Goodyer grant the utility of categorical models for psychotic conditions, even though existing models are imperfect. For the less severe but more common complaint patterns seen in office practice, they demonstrate quite convincingly that a dimensional model provides a far more comprehensive account of clinical reality.

Let us not forget is that 'caring has been central to medical practice in all cultures throughout history ... trade-offs between caring and technical expertise are not rational, necessary, or inevitable, provided that health services pursue human rather than commercial goals' (Hart and Dieppe 1996). Goldberg and Goodyer guide readers through this thicket as well. I trust it is now abundantly clear why I wish this book a large readership.

Leon Eisenberg, MD
Maude and Lillian Presley Professor of Social Medicine and
Professor of Psychiatry, Emeritus
Harvard Medical School
Boston MA 02115

Introduction

The model for conceptualising common mental disorders using the terms vulnerability, destabilisation and restitution was proposed in a book written jointly with Professor Peter Huxley in 1992. Since it was written, there has been an explosion of new knowledge in psychiatric genetics, and great advances in both neuroscience and child development. The earlier model survives into this book, but it is beginning to look rather different.

The effects of our genes are now seen as being modified by the social environment in which we find ourselves, so that in some environments the gene will manifest itself, but be silent in others. We speculate that genes are related both to the tendency of many individuals to be resilient in the face of life stress, and to the vulnerabilities of others. We explain that the apparent influence of genes on such 'soft' aspects of our lives as whether we have social support, or how many stressful life events we experience, is moderated by dimensions of our personality – themselves partly under genetic control. Most importantly, we emphasise that the vulnerability which we have at birth is only a potential vulnerability – it can be made worse or better by life experiences. The social factors that were discussed in the earlier book all make their reappearance in this one, as their salience has been in no way reduced by the advances in genetics.

In previous books 'common mental disorders' referred only to the disorders now referred to as 'internalising disorders'. No account was taken of the equally important externalising disorders – including conduct disorders and hyperactivity disorders in childhood, as well as anti-social personality, drug and alcohol abuse in adult life.

Acknowledgements

Professor Philip Cowen looked through Chapter 4 on the brain, and made valuable comments. Mr Alan Hervé of the Office of National Statistics very kindly made data available for some of the tables that appear in Chapter 2. Dr Rob Stewart undertook to carry out special analyses of the differential effects of different kinds of life event throughout the adult lifespan, using data made available by the Office of National Statistics, and these are reported on in Chapter 8. We are grateful to Leon Eisenberg, one of the giants in our field, for providing the Foreword to our book.

David Goldberg
Ian Goodyer

Part I

The nature and distribution of common mental disorders

Chapter 1

Competing models for common mental disorders

Categorical models of common mental disorders

The conventional taxonomy of mental disorders is that set out in the fifth chapter of the World Health Organisation's *International Classification of Disease*, tenth edition (WHO 1988: ICD-10). This is broadly comparable to the fourth edition of the American Psychiatric Association's (1994) *Diagnostic and Statistical Manual*, fourth edition (DSM-4).

These classifications are arrived at by consensus meetings of distinguished psychiatrists, either in Geneva or in Washington. They are essentially arbitrary, 'top-down' classifications – and they are necessarily revised at regular intervals, as new treatments become available, as new mental disorders emerge, or as research findings indicate heterogeneity within diagnostic entities.

Inevitably, it is easier to reach consensus about major, severe disorders that are worldwide in their distribution – like dementia, mental retardation, schizophrenia and bipolar disorder. It is far more difficult to achieve consensus about the common mental disorders, where cultural factors and differing diagnostic habits dictate different patterns of common symptoms of mental distress.

Thus, 'brain fag' (Africa), 'kidney weakness' (China), 'Jibyo' (Japan), 'burn-out' (USA), 'chronic fatigue' (UK) or 'neurasthenia' (Asia) are all ways of referring to syndromes of disordered function in various parts of the world that have no known organic pathology. One solution to this otherwise intractable problem is to impose the diagnostic concepts that have been agreed by senior psychiatrists upon general physicians in the rest of the world. These concepts are heavily influenced by American and European psychiatrists, and may do less than justice to the forms of disorder in other parts of the world.

It should cause no surprise that different diagnostic systems assign quite different diagnostic labels to the same patients, or even to distinguish between cases and normals. In community surveys that have used more than one categorical system to classify people, Surtees *et al.* (1983) found agreement in only 61 per cent in Edinburgh; Grayson *et al.* (1990) in only 65 per cent in Manchester; and in only 72 per cent in the Netherlands.

Within the group of cases by both systems, agreement about diagnosis was even worse: for example, Surtees found agreement in only 16.7 per cent of 'anxiety' patients, and 56 per cent of 'depressed' patients, Grayson and his colleagues found agreement in 25.6 per cent and 50 per cent in Manchester, UK, and van den Brink and others (1990) found agreement in 47.5 per cent and 57.5 per cent of these groups. Those investigators using a single categorical system, triumphantly produce figures of specious accuracy.

A further problem is that these categories do not occur on their own, but in combinations with other disorders: thus Angst and Dobler-Mikola (1985) calculated that combinations were nine times more likely than chance in depression, five times in panic, and 3.5 times for anxiety. American investigators solve this problem by portentously announcing that different disorders are 'co-morbid' with one another: thus, a person who has sufficient symptoms of both anxiety and depression is declared to have 'major depressive disorder co-morbid with generalised anxiety disorder'. Thus, the National Co-morbidity study in the USA shows a 'co-morbidity' between depression and anxiety over 12 months as 57.5 per cent (CI 53–61.7) (Kessler *et al.* 2003).

It is also of interest that many of the social characteristics of anxious and depressive states overlap with one another: Eaton and Ritter (1988) using the Diagnostic Interview Schedule in the Epidemiologic Catchment Area survey in Baltimore found that the socio-demographic characteristics were similar, the associations between the scale scores and the presence of alcohol problems, drug abuse, schizophrenia and anti-social personality were the same, and so were the associations between scale scores and stressful life events.

A final problem with categories of common disorders is that they do not exhibit consistency over time. Cases of morbid anxiety may be mingled with episodes of depression, may be complicated by predominant obsessional symptoms or hypochondriacal preoccupations at some times but not others: such longitudinal changes in common mental disorders have been documented by numerous investigators over the past 25 years (Eaton and Ritter 1988; Lee and Murray 1988; Andrews *et al.* 2001; Angst 1990; Goldberg *et al.* 1998).

A somewhat different approach to internationally agreed diagnostic rules is to use a kind of multivariate analysis called 'Grades of Membership analysis'. In this approach, subjects who report two of the core symptoms of depression are recruited to study the natural grouping of symptom clusters that emerge in that particular population. An example of this approach would be Blazer and others (1988) examination of 406 people complaining of at least two depressive symptoms, selected from a much larger population in North Carolina. Five 'fuzzy' types of patient emerged:

1   A mild dysphoric group   197
2   An elderly cognitively impaired group   83

3   A predominantly depressed group   44
4   A predominantly anxious group   43
5   A group of women with premenstrual symptoms   39

This is an interesting approach since pattern of symptoms found in one country is not being applied, willy-nilly, to another setting. The fuzzy categories that emerge can indeed be cross-tabulated with conventional categorical diagnosis. Notice that a 'predominantly anxious' group emerges despite the fact that subjects were selected because of depressive symptoms. However, to adopt this approach internationally would substitute a cacophony of different 'fuzzy' groups for the Esperanto of internationally agreed diagnostic rules.

Faced with these apparently unsolvable problems, it may be wondered why categorical models live on. They live on because they are needed. Public health physicians need to compare the health of one population with another, and health managers need to plan mental health services. Working clinicians who wish to offer a structured psychological intervention or a pharmacological intervention must decide whether the individual who has sought their help needs one, or some other, intervention. Also, the diagnostic label frequently justifies the intervention offered; and many people like to know what the clinician thinks is wrong with them if they are to collaborate with a treatment programme. Arbitrary diagnostic labels fulfil this function admirably.

The rules adopted to justify categories are on the whole fairly arbitrary, but then they always are in medicine where a continuously distributed quality is concerned – blood pressure, anaemia or body mass index are all examples – morbidity and mortality increase as one ascends the scale, but the cut-points adopted are determined by the resources available in the health system to investigate and subsequently treat the patient. In 1960, for example, we tolerated a diastolic blood pressure of up to 110 mm mercury in a man, and 120 mm mercury in a woman. It is now possible to treat any diastolic blood pressure above 90 mm: the cost and difficulty of the investigations has decreased and more effective drugs are available – but the phenomena of hypertension have not changed.

The ICD-10 classification allows an interesting modification to a simple dichotomous diagnosis, by dividing depression into four categories: not depressed, mild, moderate and severe depression. This is sensible if there is evidence that different treatment regimes are effective with depression at various levels of severity. In the case of depression, there is accumulating evidence that this is indeed the case.

Dimensional models of common disorders

Aubrey Lewis (1934) wrote that anxiety was a common, and probably integral, part of the depressive reaction, and this accords both with clinical experience and with many different data sets dealing with the distribution of common symptoms in general populations. Adolf Meyer (1955) taught that the individual patient is unique, and can neither be broken down into separate aspects nor categorised into categories of disease entities. His emphasis on understanding the sick individual is called the *idiographic* method, in contrast to approaches which concentrate on how groups in sick individuals resemble one another, called the *nomothetic* approach.

It should not be thought that clinicians should be obliged to adopt one approach or the other: the former is indispensable for understanding what Karl Jasper (1963) had earlier referred to as 'the whole man in his state of sickness', while the latter is essential if knowledge is to advance concerning the advantages of one treatment over another.

Syndromes, symptoms and dimensions of symptoms

It is important to distinguish between categorical notions of mental disorders, which are themselves *syndromal*, in that they consist of collections of symptoms observed by clinicians, and dimensional models which are exploring the relationship between *individual symptoms*, without reference of collections of symptoms. Dimensional models arrive at *dimensions of symptoms*, which are obtained by 'bottom-up' analysis of sets of symptoms in large sets of respondents – the dimensions representing sets of symptoms which characteristically occur together. These clearly bear some relationship to the syndromes of clinicians, but are not identical with them, and are arrived at in a different way. Furthermore there is no assumption that possession of one set of symptoms will make possession of another set unlikely – as is the case with syndromes. Thus there is a much stronger relationship between anxious symptoms and depressive symptoms than there is between 'generalised anxiety disorder' (GAD) and 'major depression' (MD), both themselves syndromes. There are two reasons for this. A concept like GAD assumes that everyone with fewer than the critical number of symptoms required for diagnosis is treated as a 'non-case', whereas symptom counts are measuring the relationship over the whole range. The other reason is that different categorical disorders have different time requirements: GAD requires symptoms for six months, while MD only requires them for two weeks. Some of the very real differences between the two categories therefore refers to chronicity – those with GAD have not remitted, during a time when many depressive episodes will have terminated.

Diagnostic categories assume homogeneity within each category, while dimensional approaches assume that there are certain underlying dimensions of sickness which are themselves defined in terms of collections of symptoms which regularly occur together, and which may (or may not, of course) correspond to the biological processes that underpin our mental life.

Symptoms of common disorders – if alcohol and drug use, and somatic symptoms are excluded – tend to fall into two major groups which may be called anxious and depressive symptoms. These dimensions are correlated with one another, the size of the correlation depending on the population studied and the particular research interview or questionnaire being used.

Thus Eaton and Ritter (1988) found a correlation of +0.42, while work using the General Health Questionnaire consistently shows correlations even higher than this, usually between +0.65 and +0.75. Goldberg *et al.* (1987) using a modified version of the Present State Examination in Manchester found that the two symptom axes correlated +0.70 with one another.

Clark and Watson (1991) conducted a conventional factor analysis on 90 items dealing with common mental disorders and produced three factors: one associated with somatic arousal and anxiety, another with symptoms specific to depression, and a third representing general distress. In a later paper Watson and others (1995) demonstrated factor invariance across students, adults in the community and patients in several different centres. They argued for a 'mixed anxiety depression' assessment to capture these results.

Latent trait analysis

This is a form of statistical analysis developed in the field of education by Rasch (1960) to study results of attainment tests. Different test items differed from one another in how difficult students found them, and how well they distinguished between students at the difficulty level at which 50 per cent of students were successful with them. It assumes there is an underlying dimension of difficulty, and assesses the probability of their endorsement at various levels of difficulty. It is a simple matter to transfer this model to mental disorders: the level of difficulty becomes the point on the underlying severity axis at which 50 per cent of patients will complain of the symptom. Duncan-Jones and his colleagues were the first to apply this model to psychopathology in 1986, and were attracted to it because no assumption is made (as in 'latent class analysis') that there are categories underlying the symptoms.

Goldberg and colleagues used this approach in 1987 with a series of research interviews among primary care attenders, and produced a two dimensional space defined by symptoms, as shown in Figure 1.1.

Some symptoms are loaded mainly on one axis, while others are intermediate and load on both. Thus, abnormal fatigue, loss of concentration, neglect due to brooding, thoughts of death, poor appetite and depressed mood are intermediate between the axes. Symptoms such as worry, subjective nervous tension, muscular tension, poor sleep, tension pains and free floating anxiety characterise anxiety; while loss of interest, poor energy, loss of libido, loss of appetite, self-depreciation, diurnal variation of mood, hopelessness, early waking and slowness characterised depression. The ratings by the interviewing doctor of observed anxiety and observed depression loaded on each axis, appropriately.

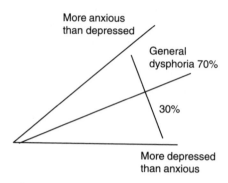

Figure 1.1 Dimensions of symptomatology for internalising disorders

Latent trait analysis furnishes three characteristics of each symptom: the severity level at which 50 per cent of those taking the test are likely to endorse the symptom (the '*threshold*'), the '*direction*' of the symptom which refers to the inclination of the symptom towards one axis or the other, and the ability of the symptom to discriminate between individuals at the point in two-dimensional space at which it appears (the '*slope*', or discrimination of the symptom). In other words, at the threshold of the symptom, how rapidly does the probability of endorsement rise? A good symptom will have a steep slope.

Simon and his colleagues (2002) compared the symptom pattern and latent structure of symptoms across all 15 centres in the WHO's study of mental disorders in primary care settings in order to account for cross-national differences in the prevalence of depression. The symptom pattern and latent structure were found to be strikingly similar across the centres, and true differences in prevalence were described. It was of interest that in high prevalence centres depression was associated with lower disability. At these centres there were higher rates of depression onset, as well as depression resolution, and the use of same international standard for diagnosis identified patients with less illness and less severe impairment.

Ormel and his colleagues (1995) extended the range of symptoms to include various phobic symptoms – these had been excluded in the original work. Patients in Manchester, Groningen and rural Holland were compared and a three-dimensional model was found to provide the best fit for each population studied: phobic symptoms now appearing as a separate dimension from anxious symptoms – albeit highly correlated with them.

Internalising and externalising disorders

Of course, if different symptoms are put into the analysis, different dimensions can emerge. Kendler and his colleagues (1997) analysed data from the

National Co-morbidity study in the United States, and produced two major dimensions – internalising and externalising. *Internalising* corresponds to the two correlated dimensions of depression and anxiety, and can be thought of as the 'general dysphoria' dimension in Figure 1.1. Externalising by contrast refers to disorders manifested by altered behaviour, such as alcohol-related disorders, drug dependence and anti-social behaviour.

It is tempting to suppose that 'internalising' is the opposite of 'externalising', but alas, this is not so. Indeed, they have a weak correlation with one another. That reflects the fact that it is possible to have an externalising disorder, like, say, alcohol dependence, and also to be depressed. But they are two groups of disorders whose aetiologies are different – both in the genetics and the effects of the environment. They are also associated with different personalities who are most at risk: internalising with high neuroticism, introversion and conscientiousness; externalising with extraversion, low neuroticism and low conscientiousness (Krueger *et al.* 2003).

Dimensional models of internalising disorders

Kendler and others (1995) studied genetic and environmental risk factors in six common mental disorders in women: phobias, generalised anxiety disorder, panic disorder, bulimia, major depression and alcoholism. Genetic influences were best explained by postulating two factors – one responsible for both depression and anxiety, the other for panic, phobias and bulimia. The genetic influence on each disorder was found to be only moderate, with specific influences on alcohol. Common environment appeared only in bulimia, and disorder specific non-shared environmental influences on panic, phobias and alcoholism. In an earlier paper (1993) he had shown substantial co-morbidity between major depression and various types of phobia – a relationship strongest for agoraphobia and absent for animal phobias. However, all these phobias were found to be mainly determined by non-shared environment – but the factors in the non-shared environment between agoraphobia and depression correlated moderately, with two-thirds of the variance held in common.

Krueger and his colleagues (1998, 2003) analysed a study of the general population in New Zealand and found the same dimensions using the Diagnostic Interview Schedule (DIS). The WHO international study of mental disorders in general medical settings (Ustun and Sartorius 1995) applied the primary care version of the Composite International Diagnostic Interview (CIDI-PC, Robins *et al.* 1988). There was no measure of drug dependence or anti-social behaviour, so the alcohol-related items (measured by the WHO's AUDIT questionnaire (Babor *et al.* 1989) provided the only measure of 'externalising'. In the later paper these data were converted to a set of current symptom counts for each person: these were current depression (25 items), somatisation (41 items), hypochondriasis (6 items), neurasthenia (4 items), anxious worry (5 items), anxious arousal (21 items), and hazardous use of alcohol from the AUDIT.

The investigators compared four competing models: a one-factor model, with all items loading on a single general factor; a two-factor model with all items except the AUDIT on a single factor, and the AUDIT on the other; a set of different three-factor models, one with depression/anxiety, somatisation/hypochondriasis/neurasthenia and alcohol use; the remaining one depression/anxiety/neurasthenia, somatisation/hypochondriasis and alcohol use. The various models were suggested by exploratory analyses on the different participating centres.

When the data were compared for each centre, in Berlin, Mainz and Seattle, three-factor solutions provided the best fit to the data, although neurasthenia loaded with anxious/depression in the German centres, while it loaded on somatisation in the USA. In the remaining 12 centres the two-factor model provided the best fit.

When the data for all 15 centres was combined, the best fit was obtained with the two-factor model, with all the internalising symptoms on one dimension, and the sole externalising measure on the other.

These findings have been broadly confirmed in the 'Nemesis study' in a large community sample in the Netherlands: once more the three factors that emerged were alcohol and drug disorders on an externalising factor, and two correlated internalising factors: one for anxious depression, the other for phobias and panic disorder. This paper analysed the same population one year later and demonstrated substantial stability between the dimensions of the model (Volleberg *et al.* 2001).

Krueger and Finger (2001) have used the same interview – the CIDI – on the National Co-Morbidity study, confining their attention to the 251 people (only 3.1 per cent of the total sample!) who said they were seeking professional help for a mental disorder. Because all these patients were internalising, a single latent trait was extracted representing this mode of disorder. All of the DSM-4 diagnoses loaded heavily on this factor, although oddly, depression and dysthymia had weaker loads than the various phobic diagnoses.

Dimensional models and externalising disorders

Krueger and his colleagues (1998, 2002) have applied the symptoms that are used to make the diagnoses of their conduct disorder, adolescent anti-social behaviour (AASB), alcohol and drug dependence and 'constraint' to the Minnesota twins, and finds a common 'externalising' dimension running through this symptom pool. This is largely genetically determined, but the individual diagnoses have own specific variance. For AASB, for example, there is no additional genetic variance, but a strong environmental component. For alcohol and drugs on the other hand, there is some additional genetic component, but once more the effects of the environment are stronger. A similar study on the Colorado twins used the diagnoses of conduct disorder, attention deficit hyperactivity disorder and substance abuse, together with the personality dimension of novelty seeking (Young *et al.* 2000). This also found a latent 'behavioural disinhibition' variable which related to all the diagnoses, which was highly heritable (h^2 = 82 per cent).

In a separate study, Krueger and colleagues (2004) have applied latent trait modelling to four sets of symptoms (110 in all!) that have been used in categorical research criteria for *alcohol dependence* (Feighner criteria, RDC, DSM-3 and DSM-3R). A single latent trait of severity was found to run through these symptoms – and, as usual with latent trait methods, each symptom can be assigned an exact severity level at which 50 per cent of the population will endorse it, as well as a measure of that symptom's discriminatory ability. Taken together, the symptoms are providing maximum discrimination at a severity level of about 1.8. Symptoms such as having had 5 or more drinks on one occasion, for example, is a highly discriminating symptom, but at a very low severity, well below that required for alcohol dependence by any of the criteria. Reducing one's activities in order to drink more than once each month is also highly discriminatory – but this time at about the severity level at which the diagnosis can be made. Having withdrawal symptoms after cutting down is a highly discriminatory symptom well above the severity level. Many of the symptoms are shown to have poor discriminatory ability and should probably be dropped in preference for a set of highly discriminatory symptoms, across a wide range of severity. In this way diagnostic criteria can be improved in the future.

The findings about internalising and externalising are in a sense inevitable, when one recalls that many mentally distressed people do not have an alcohol problem, and many with an alcohol problem are not emotionally distressed. There are, it is true, some patients with both disorders, but they are in a minority. On the other hand there is a non-specific common core of symptoms which all common mental disorders have in common: so that two major factors representing alcohol and drug disorders, and anti-social behaviour on the one hand, and common mental disorders on the other, are bound to arise when multivariate analysis is applied to large data sets.

Dimensional models of personality

Personality in adults refers to a set of fairly stable ways in which people differ from one another in functioning in their social world and thinking about themselves. There have been many different methods of classifying these ways and giving them names. Adult personality is preceded in childhood by variations in temperament, which refers to demonstrable differences between children in aspects of functioning such as emotional reactivity, sociability and level of motor activity. The latter differences between children have been shown to have a fairly strong genetic component – and indeed, we shall see that the various dimensions of adult personality also have a substantial genetic component – although by the time adult life is reached the environment will also have had a strong influence in determining adult personality.

If dimensional models of symptoms succeed in simplifying the over-complex categorical systems of adult mental disorders, at first glance the same can hardly be said of dimensional models of personality. One seems to have swapped the fairly simple categorical models of personality for the Tower of Babel. Each new team of psychologists producing of a personality scale makes their own selection of test items, and performs their own favourite multivariate analysis before producing a set of scales to which they give their own idiosyncratic names.

In the past quarter century the production of large numbers of scales nested within a large questionnaire has fallen out of favour. Most designers now appear to prefer between three and five scales. However, the advantage of fewer scales is that it becomes possible to discern rough equivalence between the various instruments. Indeed, it would be surprising if the numerous scales were really describing different things, since trivially reworded items are typically being offered to large data sets, and higher order factors are being examined.

Table 1.1 shows three recent scales with the equivalent terms used to describe them. Clark's 'neuroticism' is not only markedly similar to Eysenck's (1947) neuroticism, but bears the same similarity to Tellegen's 'negative affect' and Cloninger's (1987) 'harm avoidance'. The robust nature of this scale is important, as it is of great significance where internalising disorders are concerned. We pointed out above that internalisation is not the converse of externalisation: the same applies to positive and negative affect, which are by no means bipolar scales. Indeed, the terms themselves are not that helpful and alternative names should be sought.

The other scale that appears in common between the scales is conscientiousness, which unaccountably did not appear in Eysenck's EPI, although his scale 'psychoticism' may possibly have unwittingly reflected this quality. It is an important scale because it typifies those with externalising disorders.

Dimensional models clearly fit the data better than categorical models, as

Table 1.1 Three recent classifications of personality, showing rough correspondence

The 'big five' Widiger and Costa (2002)	SNAP Clark (1993)	MPQ Tellegen (2003)
Harm avoidance	Neuroticism	Negative emotionality
Agreeableness	(–ve affect)	
Extraversion	Extraversion	Positive emotionality
Openness	(+ve affect)	
Conscientiousness	Conscientiousness	Conscientiousness
	(disinhibition)	

they are 'bottom-up' rather than 'top-down' – that is to say, derived from an examination of the patterns of symptoms encountered in the community rather than the experiences of senior clinicians working in specialised practice. Nevertheless, they do have their own limitations as well. Different dimensions will be obtained with interviews covering different symptom areas – as the discrepancy between the Present State Examination (dealing with anxiety, depression and neurasthenic symptoms) and the CIDI-PC/ AUDIT (which deal with somatic symptoms and alcohol problems in addition) clearly illustrate. Furthermore they are not of much help to the practising clinicians who like, rightly or wrongly, to think that they have a 'case' of some specific disorder to treat, ideally with a specific remedy.

However, for purposes of relating symptom patterns to social and interpersonal variables they have undoubted advantages over categorical models, and we will return to them in later chapters.

Kleinman (1988) has asked why anxiety disorders should be distinguished from depressive disorders, since they share the same social origins:

> Demoralisation and despair owing to severe family, work or economic problems trigger syndromes of distress that have biological as well as social correlates. These correlates are often labelled psychiatric disorder, but they have been reconceived by social scientists as the psycho-biological sequelae of social pathology and human misery generally.
>
> (Kleinman 1988: 59)

Those espousing a dimensional model see this as an empirical question, both concerning the social variables correlated with each dimension, and the question about how often individuals score in the abnormal range in only a single dimension.

Mental illness and disability

Mental disorders account for as much of the total disability in the population as physical disorders (Ormel and Costa e Silva 1995), and there is a clear dose-response relationship between illness severity and the extent of disability (pp. 338–40). Moreover, depression and disability show synchrony of change (Ormel et al. 1993), and onsets of depression are associated with an approximate doubling of both social and occupational disability (Ormel et al. 2004). In places where there is a high prevalence of emotional symptoms people appear to learn to function normally despite experiencing symptoms which would cause disability in another culture (Simon et al. 2002), so that the relationship between illnesses and the associated disability is a relative one. Associated disability is not usually a defining quality of a categorical illness, but a good case might be made for considering whether it should be.

Vulnerability, destabilisation and restitution

Vulnerability and resilience

The main aim of this book is to disentangle the factors that lie behind the fact that some individuals are remarkably vulnerable to minor life stresses, while others can be extraordinarily resilient. We will describe what is known about the genetic factors that lie behind both vulnerability and resilience, and the way in which life experience can either increase or reduce vulnerability to common mental disorders.

We will consider the genetics of common disorders, and explore what is known about how genes operate, and how they influence our hormones, our neurotransmitters, and our immune functions.

We will explore the factors that lie behind gender differences, as there is convergent evidence that females appear to have a greater vulnerability to common disorders.

We will pass on to factors in early life, and consider the role of maternal neglect and the various forms of abuse to which children are vulnerable.

Destabilisation

Individuals vary in the amount of life stress that is necessary to release an episode of illness. In general terms, even major mental disorders like schizophrenia and mania are more common after life stressors, but these disorders can also occur without discernible external stress. In contrast, common disorders are usually released by stressors. Such stressors are by no means always psychological. They can also be social and cultural, as well as new episodes of physical disease which can themselves sometimes be implicated in the causal nexus. We will devote a chapter to these processes and show that different personalities will tend to experience different kinds and different amounts of stressors, so that personality, itself partly controlled by genes, must also be included in any consideration of how genes affect our vulnerability to common illnesses.

Restitution

Finally, we will address those factors that appear to hasten recovery. Clinicians like to suppose that recovery is mainly a matter of exposing the sick individual to an appropriate treatment – but only a minority of disorders will fail to improve given sufficient time for spontaneous recovery, and social and interpersonal factors are of great importance in determining course of illness. Indeed, biomedical treatments should really be evaluated on two criteria: first, are they effective in shortening the length of episode or the severity of episode; second, are they effective in preventing relapse?

Relapse prevention is especially important since many disorders may resolve either spontaneously or facilitated by a psychological or biomedical intervention, yet relapse on many occasions after recovery. We will describe the factors that favour restitution of an episode and consider evidence that some clinical interventions may also have effects in this respect.

Take-home messages

- Categorical models will live on because doctors prescribing medications need them, public health physicians use them in monitoring services, they allow communication between countries, they facilitate research projects, and insurance companies base reimbursement upon them.

- Categorical models often use arbitrary cut-points to define allegedly homogeneous disorders, ride roughshod over subtle differences between cultural expression of distress, and impose cut-points on what are essentially disorders of different degrees of severity. They tend to be reified by unwary clinicians, who seek different explanations for essentially similar types of disorder.

- Dimensional models allow comparison between cultures, and a study of the relative importance of groups of symptoms which tend to occur together. For some research purposes, it is more powerful to express a quality as a graded dimension rather than as a single dichotomous entity.

- Dimensional models allow one to measure the degree of similarity between groups of different disorders, and so convert an essentially impossible task into one permitting at least a partial solution.

- Common mental disorders may usefully be thought of in two large classes – 'externalising' disorders which manifest themselves in observed behaviour, and internalising disorders that are disorders of inner experience.

- In the book that follows, we distinguish between *vulnerability and resilience* (those factors that precede episodes of mental disorder and serve either to increase or reduce the individual's likelihood of becoming ill), *destabilisation* (the processes by which an episode is released at a particular time); and *restitution* (the factors related to recovery from episodes of emotional ill health).

Chapter 2

The distribution of common mental disorders

The filter model updated

In 1980, Goldberg and Huxley put forward a model for relating mental morbidity in the community to that in primary care, and this in turn to morbidity as treated by the specialist mental illness services. This had not previously been attempted, since the various rates are not really comparable. Thus epidemiological surveys in the community were typically concerned with morbidity at a point in time (point prevalence), while those treated by the mental illness services were reported as annual rates (period prevalence). Rates in general medical practice were sometimes reported as annual rates (Shepherd *et al.* 1966) but more often as rates per 100 consecutive attenders. However, point prevalence could be converted to annual period prevalence rates, provided that the number of new illnesses each year (annual inception rates) could be either estimated (Goldberg and Huxley 1980) or measured more accurately (Goldberg and Huxley 1992) – simply by adding one to the other. Since that time surveys often report annual period prevalence by asking people to remember their health over the previous year: this may cause some under-reporting due to the tendency to forget unpleasant material – but it is more accurate than the best guesses that were made about inception rates.

Rates per 100 consecutive attenders in primary care can also be converted to annual rates, provided that the annual consultation rate is known, simply by multiplying one by the other.

Five levels and four filters

When these calculations were carried out, we obtained a model at five levels:

1   The community.
2   Total rates of mental disorder among those attending primary care.
3   Morbidity detected by medical officers or GPs.
4   Total rates of mental disorder treated by the mental health services.
5   Rates for mental disorders admitted to hospital.

It must be appreciated that mental disorders are by no means homogeneous: they differ in both form and severity.

Many of the disorders seen in community settings are relatively mild, and states of anxious depression predominate. These disorders will be the principal focus of this book, provided they achieve severity levels that merit international diagnosis. In medical settings combinations of anxious depression with somatic symptoms are the commonest form of disorder, with alcohol-related disorders coming second. Patients seen by the mental illness services are more likely to have severe disorders, such as schizophrenia, drug-related psychotic illnesses, and dementia. The only forms of depression common in this setting are bipolar disorders and treatment-resistant depression.

In those countries where medical officers – either in primary care or in hospital accident and emergency departments – are gatekeepers to mental health care, it is approximately true that between each of these levels there is a filter. In order to go from community to general medical care one must display illness behaviour (the first filter); in order for the mental disorder to be noticed by the doctor he or she must have detection skills (second filter); in order to be seen by the mental illness services the doctor must be willing to refer (third filter); if the patient is to be admitted to a psychiatric bed the psychiatrist must be willing to admit (fourth filter).

In countries where people can refer themselves directly to mental health professionals the third filter is of course far less important – and rates at level four are correspondingly higher.

The rates at these five levels are shown in Table 2.1, from which it can be seen that in the UK the first filter is not holding back that many of the distressed people in the community, but the second filter most certainly is doing so. Once detected, most disorders will be treated in primary care, only a small minority being referred on to mental illness services. Of those treated by specialist services, only a minority are admitted to psychiatric beds. This demonstrates the crucial importance of primary care in the organisation of mental illness services.

Whereas in England GPs are the gatekeepers to psychiatric care, it is possible for those in the Netherlands to go directly to the outpatient mental

Table 2.1 Annual period prevalence rates for mental disorders at five levels in three cities

	Manchester[1]	Groningen[2]	Seattle[3]
1 Community	250–315	250–303	221–281
2 All attenders	210–230	224	164
3 CPM	101	94	78
4 Referral	20.8	34	58
5 Beds	3.4	10	9

Notes: 1 = Goldberg and Huxley (1992); 2 = Giel et al. (1990); 3 = Goldberg (1995).

illness services, and access to mental health professionals in the USA is limited only by the patient's ability to pay for care. Whereas the rates in the community are not greatly different in the three countries, the rate in primary care in the USA is somewhat reduced, and that in mental health sector increased.

The community: Level one and first filter

In recent years major epidemiological surveys of mental disorder have been conducted in the UK, the USA, Australia and the Netherlands. Generally speaking, these surveys have not altered the rates computed by earlier more limited surveys to any great extent (see Table 2.2). The best source of data in Great Britain is the OPCS survey of psychiatric morbidity (Meltzer *et al.* 1995a, 1995b; Gill *et al.* 1996), which was based on a sample of 10,000 people randomly chosen living in private households. This survey was based on standardised interviews by trained interviewers, and has been repeated by the Office of National Statistics in 2000.

They have been valuable in drawing attention to the variation between rates in town and country, between the sexes, between social classes and the covariation of rates with social conditions.

In the Census of 2001 mental disorders occurring during childhood were included. The results are summarised in Table 2.3(a) and compared with the rates for adults obtained by the Office of National Statistics (2000) in Table 2.3(b).

It can be seen from Table 2.3(a) that total rates for common mental disorders are somewhat higher in boys, because of their very much higher rates for externalising disorders. Rates for 'emotional disorders', combinations of symptoms of shyness, tearfulness and anxious symptoms, are similar before puberty, but the rate in girls becomes higher than the rate in boys after the age of 11. The female excess at this age range is very much smaller than that which occurs after puberty.

When these figures are compared with the adult figures in Table 2.3(b) it is at once apparent that there is an enormous increase in the rates reported,

Table 2.2 Revised figures for annual period prevalence rates per 1000 for all mental disorders in the community based on large probability samples, compared with earlier estimates

	Earlier estimate	Revised figure
USA	221–252[1]	281–295[2]
UK	250–315	about 270[4]
The Netherlands	250–303	224.3[3]
Australia	n/a	227[4]

Notes: 1 = ECA study; 2 = Kessler *et al.* (1994); 3 = Bijl *et al.* (1998); 4 = Andrews *et al.* (2001).

Table 2.3(a) Rates for common mental disorders in children and adolescents per thousand at risk, England and Wales 2001 (source: Office of National Statistics website)

		Ages	*5–10*	*11–18*
Internalising disorders	Emotional disorders	Females	3.3	6.1
		Males	3.3	5.1
Externalising disorders	Conduct disorder	Females	2.7	3.8
		Males	6.5	8.6
	Hyperactivity disorder	Females	0.4	0.5
		Males	2.6	2.3

Table 2.3(b) Rates per thousand, past month for internalising disorders, past year for externalising; rates for mild and above alcohol dependence; all drugs illegal (source: Office of National Statistics, adults in private households, 2000)

		Ages	*20*	*30*	*40*	*50*	*60*	*70*
Internalising disorders	Anxiety	Females	200	210	210	217	162	133
	Depression	Males	93	141	158	177	140	58
	Phobias							
	OCD							
Externalising disorders	Alcohol	Females	73	42	21	15	7	4
	dependence	Males	217	163	139	69	33	25
	Drug use	Females	67	28	12	4	4	4
		Males	163	94	26	20	5	1

mainly due to the rather different ways of measuring common disorders. All the survey measures are quite different in adult life. It is likely, for example, that some of the children included in the 2001 survey were taking alcohol and recreational drugs before the age of 18, but these questions were not included. Similarly, 'emotional disorder' in childhood is certainly the nearest equivalent to anxiety and depression in adult life, but is by no means identical with it.

Nonetheless, at all ages there is a heavy male preponderance for externalising disorders, and after puberty the female excess in internalising disorders is also substantial.

Reasons for the gender differences: internalisers and externalisers

Females have higher rates for depression and all anxiety-related disorders, while males have higher rates for alcohol dependence, as well as drug dependence and delinquency. The first group of disorders is characteristic of those who introspect about how they are feeling, which we will call *internalisation*, while the latter are characteristic of those who act out or *externalise* their problems. Just because a problem can be described in psychological terms it does not necessarily mean that the explanation for it is necessarily psychological. In subsequent chapters we will consider genetic and hormonal explanations as well as psychological ones and we will bring our arguments together in Chapter 11.

Some of the gender differences in depression are because men tend to forget unpleasant symptoms, whereas women seem to remember them pretty well. Thus when Angst and Dobler-Mikola (1984) asked young Swiss about symptoms experienced either in the past four weeks or the past three months there was no difference between males and females, but when asked about the previous year there was a 2:1 difference. Many of the national epidemiological surveys do indeed ask about the previous year, so this tendency needs to be remembered. Psychiatric geneticists ask their subjects to remember their entire lifetime, where this effect seems likely to produce even greater differences. However important this effect, it is unlikely to explain the entire difference, since the OPCS and ONS surveys in the UK ask about symptoms in the previous month, in a large probability sample containing the whole age range, and does find consistent gender differences (Melzer et al. 1995a, 1995b). Women are also more likely to acknowledge illness, more likely to make contact with a doctor, and to present psychological symptoms having consulted a doctor. There is thus definitely something else to explain, and we will return to this topic in later chapters.

Depression

In the UK, the commonest disorder in the community is depression, and here the female rates greatly exceed the male rates during early and middle adult life. The OPCS survey showed that the overall point prevalence (illness at a given time point) of depression defined by ICD-10 is 21/1000 (males 17, females 25). If the less specific and milder concept of 'mixed depression and anxiety' is included, these figures rise dramatically to 98/1000 (males 71, females 124). Much of the female excess is accounted for by a mild disorder called 'mixed anxiety-depression' (Meltzer et al. 1995a, 1995b; Gill et al. 1996).

In the USA, depression defined by DSM-4 has a one-year prevalence of 66/1000, and what is quaintly called the 'lifetime prevalence' of 162/1000 (Kessler et al. 2003).

The prevalence of depression in the UK is highest among the separated (56/1000 female, 111/1000 male), next highest among widowed males (70/1000) and divorced females (46) with lowest prevalences among the married (17/1000 and 14/1000 respectively). Female prevalences are higher among the single and cohabiting than among the married, but male rates are low for all of these.

There are clear trends for years of education for males, with those finishing education later having progressively lower rates for depression; these effects are less for females. Social classes three and below have higher rates than classes one and two for both sexes. Lone parents have the highest rates, and couples with children higher rates than those without them.

In the UK, rates for depression are higher in town than country, with 'semi-rural' intermediate. Those living in rented accommodation have high rates, with owner occupiers the lowest. Unemployment has a marked effect on females, with rates being 56/1000 for the unemployed compared with 11/1000 for those at work: once more, part-time employment is intermediate (22/1000). For males 'the economically inactive' have even higher rates than unemployment – 37/1000 vs 27/1000, to be compared with 12/1000 for those in full-time work.

Rates for depression for the homeless living in leased accommodation and hostels are also high, 130/1000 for ICD depression, 270/1000 for all forms of depression. A screening questionnaire with the roofless homeless showed 60 per cent in the high range of the instrument (Gill *et al.* 1996). Those who are depressed consume no more alcohol than the non-depressed, but their cigarette consumption is higher (Meltzer *et al.* 1995b).

Kessler and others (2003) have calculated that the mean duration of episode is 16 weeks in the USA, to be contrasted with a duration of six months in Switzerland (Angst and Preisig 1995).

Anxiety disorders

These often occur alongside depressive disorders, but also occur on their own. The commonest are generalised anxiety disorder (GAD), phobic disorders and panic disorder. They are similar to depressive disorders in being more common in adult females than males; in town than in country and in unemployed people than among the employed.

There are interesting differences. Whereas depression becomes rarer in females over the age of 55, anxiety disorders do not. GAD and panic disorder are common among widows, but not among widowers. Ethnic group has little effect on either depressive or anxiety disorders, except that Asian females have high rates of depression, and West Indian or African males have high rates of GAD, compared with the white population.

Angst and Vollrath (1991) showed that individuals who later develop panic disorder or anxiety disorder have displayed symptoms of anxious disorders usually beginning during childhood, and have more family problems in early life compared with those who develop depressive disorders. Anxiety disorders usually begin between the ages of 20 and 30, and are similar to depression in being triggered by life events. Co-morbidity with depression is very common (Angst and Dobler-Mikola 1985).

Alcohol dependence

Male rates are very much higher than female rates (75 versus 21/1000) and are maximal in the 20 to 25 year age group, becoming less prevalent thereafter. Among males, it is much more common among the separated (200/1000) and single (144/1000) than among the married (39/1000), but females do not show this effect. Rates are higher among the unemployed than those in employment (117 vs. 74/1000) (Meltzer *et al.* 1995a, 1995b).

People with disorders who do not attend their doctor: failure to pass the first filter

Those with more severe disorders with many symptoms of mental disorder are more likely to consult a doctor than those with milder disorders (Bebbington *et al.* 2000a); indeed, the more severe disorders pass more readily through all the filters in the model. People are more likely to consult after severe stressful life events. Lonely people – including the single, separated and divorced – are more likely to attend, and unemployment also increases the tendency to attend.

One of the advances made by the recent national study of mental disorder is that it has allowed a far more accurate assessment of the numbers of people with 'neurotic disorders' (in practice, depressions and anxiety states) who do not consult their doctor. Bebbington and his colleagues (2000b) report that about one-third of 'neurotic' patients made contact with their doctor with a mental health problem, and of these less than one-third were receiving treatment. These figures are dramatically lower than those given by Goldberg and Huxley 1992; the reason for the discrepancy being that many of these patients will consult their doctor but not for a mental health problem. They consult because of somatic symptoms accompanying their mood disorder.

Meltzer and his colleagues (2000) have studied the reasons why people did not consult a doctor at times when they or their family thought that they should have done so. The commonest reason was 'not thinking that anyone could help with the problem' or that one should be able to cope with such a problem oneself. Less common reasons were thinking the problem would get better by itself, being too embarrassed to discuss the problem with anyone, and being afraid of what one's family and friends would think.

Andrews and his colleagues (2001) in the Australian Co-Morbidity Study defined illnesses warranting treatment as those with multiple co-morbidity in the past year, or with moderate/severe disability from their disorder in the past month. About 23 per cent of the population reported at least one disorder in the past year, and 14 per cent a current disorder. Of this group 35 per cent consulted their doctor for a mental health problem, and most of these had seen their GP. Only half of those who were disabled or who had multiple disorders had consulted. Of those who did not, half said they did not need treatment.

Attenders at primary care: level two and the second filter

The arrival of standardised, fairly brief research interviews for mental disorders in the past 50 years has meant that there are now many reports of the total rates for such disorders in both primary care and general medical settings. One of the problems in comparing these rates is that the various interviews, and varying research methods, may be a cause of differences in the reported rates. Here we will rely on the World Health Organisation's Study of Mental Disorders in General Medical Settings, since identical methods were used in 15 different cities across the world, and a total of 25,916 attenders at general medical clinics were screened with the General Health Questionnaire (GHQ) (Ustun and Sartorius 1995). A stratified sample of 5438 people were assessed with the Composite International Diagnostic Interview (CIDI-PC, Primary Care Version) and various disability scales, and the physicians seeing them completed a detailed assessment form.

It can be seen that overall prevalence of mental disorders among attenders at general medical clinics is very considerable, ranging from 52.5 per cent in Santiago de Chile, to 7.3 per cent in Shanghai; the overall mean prevalence being 24 per cent. The commonest diagnoses across the 15 centres are depression, generalised anxiety disorder and alcohol dependence. In 11 of the centres, depression is the most common disorder. However, it should be noted

Table 2.4 Rates for three commonest mental disorders; for any mental disorder; and the detection rate for any disorder; in 15 centres. Centres are in descending rank order of the prevalence of mental disorder; only the three most common disorders are shown; patients may have multiple diagnoses (after Ustun and Sartorius, 1995)

Centre	Depression %	General anxiety %	Alcohol dependence %	Any mental disorder %	Detection rate by doctor %
Santiago	29.5	18.7	2.5	52.5	74.1
Rio de Janeiro	15.8	22.6	4.1	35.5	37.8
Paris	13.7	11.9	4.3	26.3	46.8
Manchester	16.9	7.1	2.2	24.8	62.9
Groningen	15.9	6.4	3.4	23.9	51.2
Mainz	11.2	7.9	7.2	23.6	60.0
Bangalore	9.1	8.5	1.4	22.4	40.4
Athens	6.4	14.9	1.0	19.2	19.0
Berlin	6.1	9.0	5.3	18.3	56.0
Ankara	11.6	0.9	1.0	16.4	24.1
Seattle	6.3	2.1	1.5	11.9	56.9
Verona	4.7	3.7	0.5	9.8	76.1
Ibadan	4.2	2.9	0.4	9.5	55.1
Nagasaki	2.6	5.0	3.7	9.4	18.3
Shanghai	4.0	1.9	1.1	7.3	15.9
All centres	10.4	7.9	2.7	24.0	48.9

that the CIDI-PC may make multiple diagnoses on a single patient, and many patients had both anxiety and depression. Other common diagnoses (not shown here) were somatisation disorder, 'neurasthenia' (or chronic fatigue syndrome) and harmful use of alcohol. Four other mental disorders were also assessed.

In the UK and the Netherlands, over 95 per cent of patients with diagnosable disorders will go directly to their GP; in other European centres and in Seattle about 20 per cent will have seen other doctors before arriving at the doctor being seen (Ustun and Von Korff 1995).

In this study, the results for all doctors working in a particular centre were pooled to obtain an overall detection rate for mental disorders (the second filter). It can be seen that across the 15 centres, just under one half of the disorders were detected by the physicians, with detection rates varying from a high of 76.1 per cent to a low of only 15.9 per cent. It is known from previous work (Goldberg and Huxley 1992) that individual physicians are even more variable in their detection rates than this. Countries where GPs have a more 'personal' style of service – where they know their patients, where they have an appointment system and where they arrange follow-up visits – detect most.

The more detailed results for Manchester are shown in Table 2.5, which shows the full range of ICD-10 mental diagnoses. The greater recognition rates for 'somatisation disorder', generalised anxiety and dysthymia (a form of mild chronic anxious depression) are related to the fact that there are longer requirements for minimum duration than other disorders, and detection rates increase the more often a patient has been seen.

Table 2.5 Results for disorders among patients attending their GP in Manchester, by prevalence among consecutive attenders and recognition rates by the GP

	Estimated prevalence %	Recognised by GP %
Depression	16.9	69.6
Neurasthenia	9.7	49.8
Generalised anxiety	7.0	72.3
Agoraphobia	3.8	69.6
Alcohol problems	3.6	66.1
Panic disorder	3.5	70.6
Dysthymia	2.0	80.9
Hypochondriasis	0.5	60.3
'Somatisation disorder'	0.4	100
One or more	26.2	62.9
Two or more	14.1	67.4

Ability to detect emotional disorders: failure to pass the second filter

The ability of a particular doctor to detect disorders is made up of two components: the overall *accuracy* with which non-cases are declared normal and cases are seen to be disordered; and the tendency to assess many fewer or many more cases than there are. This latter tendency has been called '*bias*', so that a doctor with a high bias will make many correct guesses, at the expense of many incorrect assessments that non-cases are disordered. In contrast, a low bias doctor will rarely accuse a non-case of being a case, but will miss many cases of disorder. It has been shown that 'high bias' doctors are psychologically minded and ask many questions with a psychological content, whereas the reverse is true of low bias doctors (Goldberg and Huxley 1980).

The centres with high detection rates in Table 2.4 are Verona, Santiago, Manchester and Groningen: of these, only Verona has doctors with a very high bias, since they identify 4.8 times as many cases as are actually present. Centres with low detection rates are Shanghai, Nagasaki, Athens and Ankara, and of these all except Shanghai have a low bias.

The more interesting quality is the ability to make accurate diagnostic assessments. This has been shown to be influenced partly by the doctor's personality, but mainly by the way in which the interview is conducted (Marks *et al.* 1979; Goldberg *et al.* 1991). The behaviours shown below are those which allow patients to release the cues that will make it easy for the doctor to diagnose emotional distress. Conversely, doctors who do not demonstrate such behaviours will have patients who suppress these cues, thus making detection more difficult (Goldberg *et al.*. 1991).

- Make eye contact with the patient.
- Make empathic comments.
- Pick up verbal cues.
- Pick up non-verbal cues.
- Ask directive questions with a psychological content.
- Do not read notes or look at their computer while the patient is speaking.
- Deal with over-talkativeness.
- Deal with today's problem.

It has also been shown that doctors who possess these behaviours are better communicators about all aspects of the medical encounter. They give clearer information to their patients and better advice (Millar and Goldberg 1991).

The failure to detect emotional distress is not necessarily embarrassing to primary care. Many patients are consulting for physical reasons and would be scandalised if they were told they were mentally ill, despite having the symptoms which justify a diagnosis. There are two reasons for taking the emotional disorder seriously: if a real physical disease is present it is likely to be exacerbating the symptoms; if there is no demonstrable physical disease present, it may be the cause of the presenting symptom.

As a group, patients with unrecognised mental disorders do not have a worse prognosis than those with recognised disorders. Their illnesses are milder and had a more recent onset, and they are younger. However, recognised patients often do not receive adequate treatment, so the question remains open. There are also undoubtedly individuals within the unrecognised group who would benefit from recognition and treatment (Goldberg *et al.* 1998).

Detected mental disorders in primary care: level three and third filter

The extent to which the assumptions of the model are obeyed can be assessed with a 'pathways diagram' such as Figure 2.1, from which it can be seen that in European countries of those referred to the specialist mental health services, between 66 and 81 per cent went directly to their GP, and between 8 and 18 per cent went directly to their Accident and Emergency Department; direct referrals from the community were uncommon (between 0 and 15 per cent) (Gater *et al.* 1991). Data for Manchester were published by Gater and Goldberg (1991) where more detailed results peculiar to a particular centre are presented.

The arrival of better defined diagnoses may possibly be responsible for the apparent decline in rates reported by GPs themselves. Whereas they reported that approximately 10.2 per cent of Londoners suffered from a mental disorder in the course of a year (Shepherd *et al.*. 1966), and that 10.1 per cent had such

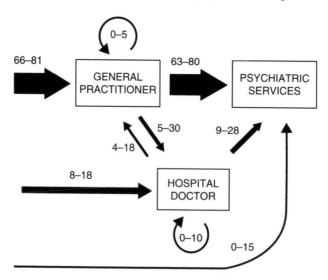

Figure 2.1 Pathways to care in the European centres. Source: Reproducted from Goldberg, D. P. and Huxley, P. J. (1992) *Common Mental Disorders – A Bio-social Model*, Figure 3.1 p. 31. With permission of Routledge.

Table 2.6 Mental rates per 1000 at risk for adult mental disorders (from the 1992 National Morbidity Survey, 1991–1992, Series MB5 No. 3, London: Office of National Statistics)

GP diagnosis	Males %	Females %	Both sexes %
'Neurosis' unspecified	20.2	48.1	34.4
Anxiety disorders	13.6	48.1	21.4
Depression	9.3	25.2	17.3
Neurasthenia	3.6	10.3	7.0
Alcohol problems	2.1	0.6	1.3
Phobias	0.4	1.6	1.0
Any mental disorder	**50.3**	**94.4**	**72.8**

disorders in their third national study (HMSO 1986), by the time the study was repeated in 1992 the figure had dropped to 7.3 per cent (Table 2.6).

In general, GPs only refer some 20 per cent of the mental disorder recognised by them, accounting for a decline in rates from around 10 per cent to about 2 per cent. It must be emphasised that GPs selectively refer psychotic and demented patients to mental illness services, and that the mean severity of the illnesses referred is greater than those treated in the practice. However, with increasing numbers of mental health workers offering sessions within group practices, the prevalence of mental disorders treated by the mental health professions may increase in the future. Thus, the community mental health service centred on primary care described by Jackson and her colleagues in 1993 saw a great increase in treated prevalence. Often, however, the specialist clinics in primary care have been concentrated on patients with established mental illnesses, which have previously been treated in psychiatric units.

Now that the Department of Health no longer funds psychiatric case registers, which used to provide unduplicated counts of treated rates at levels four and five, it is necessary to revert to previously published material in order to document this filter.

Practices in urban areas are more likely to refer patients to mental illness services than those in rural areas, perhaps because travel times are shorter, and because of the somewhat higher rates seen in urban areas in the UK (see Goldberg and Huxley 1980). The reason most frequently given by GPs for referral is that the patient has failed to respond to treatment from themselves. After this, there has been a need for further assessment, or the request has come from the patient or his family. Less common reasons are the wish for the specialist to take over treatment, or to deal with suicidal thoughts.

Level four and fourth filter

The absence of case registers and the increasing tendency of mental illness services to provide clinics in primary care has meant that firm statements about total numbers of patients seen by the mental illness services are now hard to come by. In the past, they saw somewhere between 1.5 and 3.0 per cent of the population in the course of one year, with 2.0 per cent being a median estimate. The figure may now be very slightly higher. The diagnoses of those seen by the services are given in Table 2.7.

It can be seen from Table 2.7 that the population rates for dementia, schizophrenia and personality disorders are in fact higher at level four than at level three, so that failure to detect these disorders is probably responsible for the lower rates reported by GPs. However, the mental illness services are only seeing half of the affective psychoses and alcohol problems known to the GPs, only 18 per cent of the depressives, and only 7 per cent of 'other neuroses'. In terms of percentages of the various disorders seen by the two services, it can be seen that levels of dementia, schizophrenia, personality disorders and alcohol-related problems form a much greater part of the work undertaken by the mental illness service. The cases seen predominantly by primary care services are those of 'other neurosis' (predominantly anxiety disorders), adjustment disorders and depression.

Psychologists are more likely than psychiatrists to see new cases of disorder in their primary care clinics, with anxiety disorders, post-traumatic stress disorders and depression being among the common problems seen. In contrast, psychiatrists are more likely to be seeing cases of more severe mental disorders, frequently among those already known to their service. Most cases of schizophrenia are now followed regularly in the community by psychiatric nurses, with the opinions of psychiatrists only being sought when medication has to be altered or if admission to hospital is sought.

Admission to psychiatric beds is now mainly confined to those cases where there is a risk to the health or safety of the patient or others, or where there is a problem needing further assessment with the need for close observation, or special investigations cannot readily be done as an outpatient.

Table 2.7 Mental illness rates/1000 adult population at risk for the UK in 1986 (level 3) and Salford in 1983 (levels 4 & 5) Salford data from Malcolm Cleverly (Goldberg and Huxley 1992)

Diagnostic group	Level 3 Primary care	Level 4 Mental illness services: all	Level 5 Mental illness services: inpatients
Dementia, organic	2.2 (2.2%)	2.75 (13.2%)	0.50 (15.3%)
Schizophrenia	2.0 (2.0%)	4.08 (19.6%)	0.72 (22.1%)
Affective psychosis	3.0 (3.0%)	1.47 (7.0%)	0.41 (12.6%)
Depression	28.0 (27.6%)	5.35 (25.6%)	0.69 (20.3%)
Other neurosis	35.7 (35.2%)	2.46 (11.8%)	0.17 (5.1%)
Alcohol, drugs	2.7 (2.7%)	1.37 (6.6%)	0.39 (11.9%)
Personality disorder	1.1 (1.1)	1.62 (7.8%)	0.30 (9.2%)
Adjustment, other	26.7 (26.3%)	1.74 (8.4%)	0.30 (9.2%)
All diagnoses	101.4 (100%)	20.9 (100%)	3.3 (100%)

Level five: admissions to hospital beds in psychiatric units

Since 1950, the number of beds in mental hospitals has been falling steadily and dramatically. There were 142,000 in 1977, and only 55,000 in 1994. This corresponds to a rate of 1.56/1000 in 1982, which had fallen 0.9/1000 in 1994, and despite protests to the contrary from Ministers, fell from 0.58 in 2001 to 0.52/1000 in 2002. During a similar period the number of patients detained in hospital against their will has risen, from 21,000 in 1991, to 27,915 in 2002 (Department of Health 2003). This is probably due to several factors: the shortage of beds means that average length of stay has fallen dramatically, since the decline in the number of admissions is much smaller than that in the number of beds, as shown in Table 2.8. This has had the effect of making the wards much more disturbed places than they were, and the situation has been exacerbated by the arrival of many patients with psychotic illnesses induced by drugs. Added to this, in many hospitals there has been a decline in numbers of nurses on the wards necessitated by the formation of community mental health teams, so that the emphasis is often on crisis resolution and custodial functions, to the detriment of good nursing care.

Although these developments have not produced a better atmosphere on the wards, the trend towards shorter stays has probably been beneficial to patients. Early work on the effects of shortened length of stay suggested that disabilities and defect symptoms accumulate the longer the stay (Wing and Brown 1970), and comparisons between units with lengths of stay of different duration showed better social adjustment, more active life and fewer defect symptoms in those with shorter stays (Goldberg 1991).

It can be seen from Table 2.8 that annual admissions to inpatient units have been falling steadily between 1999 and 2002, with a steady decline in the intermediate years (not shown). The only exceptions to this have been bipolar disorders and eating disorders, where the number of admissions has hardly changed.

Table 2.8 Admissions for all mental disorders by broad diagnostic group, England and Wales, for 1999 and 2002 (Department of Health 2003)

Diagnostic group	1999	2001
Dementia	27,601	22,649
Other organic brain	4,193	4,133
Alcohol and drugs	40,497	36,398
Schizophrenias	34,179	32,170
Mood disorders	52,456	47,618
Neurotic and personality disorders	30,965	26,807
Mental retardation	21,886	16,143
Total for year	227,727	185,918

Stepped care

The increasing importance of primary care, together with the increasing availability of mental illness services in this setting, has necessitated a new model to take account of the relationships between the two services. The prevailing model is now called 'stepped care', which attempts to address three questions:

- Who gives the treatment?
- Which treatment do they give?
- Where does treatment take place?

Inevitably these questions do not always lend themselves to neat answers, but since some treatments are only offered by mental health professionals, and since the economic cost of their treatments tends to be much higher than those treatments available in primary care, the problem is a very practical one.

Figure 2.2 was produced by the Guideline Development Group for the National Institute for Clinical Effectiveness (NICE) and addresses the problem of depression. The bottom step, equivalent to level two in the present model, acknowledges that many depressions are not detected by GPs – typically because the patient is asking for help with a somatic symptom and does not always mention their mood disorder unless asked directly about it.

The next step deals with detected depression, but is confined to those

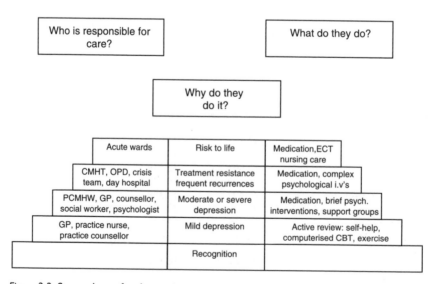

Figure 2.2 Stepped care for depression

depressions which are of mild severity. Here the range of interventions available is wide, drugs probably have only a minor part to play, and many members of the primary care team can help the patient. However, depressions of moderate or severe intensity should attract a specific intervention, and both drugs and specialised forms of psychotherapy have demonstrable effects on the course of the illness. Level three of this model corresponds to all of steps two and three, as well as some of step four.

Mental health professionals are most likely to be involved with the next step four, which is concerned with those who respond poorly or not at all to the usual interventions, and those suffering from recurrent episodes over a fairly small period of time. Here more specialised treatments are offered, and treatment may be either in primary care or in a specialised setting. It is approximately the same as level four.

Finally, those whose life is at risk or who cannot be managed at home may have to be admitted to the top level, which is level five of this model. Thus, the model takes account of the greatly increased cost of ascending the model, as well as the need for (often scarce) professional training.

Take-home messages

- Most people in the community with mental disorders diagnosable using international criteria are not seen by the mental illness services. These common, high prevalence disorders are not homogeneous, but consist of two groups of disorders where females have a preponderance of mood disorders and disorders in which anxiety is a prominent feature, and males form the largest group of those with alcohol-related disorders.
- Many cases are not detected by clinical services, but on average these are milder disorders and often self-limiting.
- Most of those whose disorder is detected are seen and treated in primary care services. Disorders characterised by anxiety and depression form by far the largest group.
- Those disorders seen by the mental illness services form two substantial groups: those whose disorder has not responded to interventions given by primary care staff, and more severe disorders requiring special assessment. Disorders seen by the mental illness service are more likely to be accompanied by personality disorders, and more likely to occur among marginalised people – those who are divorced or separated, unemployed or living below the poverty line. They are also much more likely to be longstanding disorders.
- Most disturbed psychotic people and most whose mental state poses a risk to life of either themselves or others are seen by the specialist services.

- The problems dealt with by the two services are different, and require different skills and different treatment strategies. It is unwise of psychiatrists to suppose that the problems which they see are the same as those seen in primary care, or respond in an identical way to treatment strategies.

Part II

The biological basis of common disorders

Chapter 3

Genes and environment

The set of genes that each individual inherits from their parents at the time of conception is referred to as the *genotype*, while the observable manifestation of these genes during life are referred to as the *phenotype*. Not all genes that we have will manifest themselves in the phenotype, and some characteristics of the adult individual may be quite independent of genotype. Many have been tempted to try and partition the variation in the adult into inherited and acquired characteristics, but the task is complicated and only crude approximations can be offered. Indeed, Eisenberg (2002) has written that 'to ask how much of the phenotype is due to nature and how much to nurture is as useless as to ask how much of the area of a rectangle is due to its length and how much to its width. Every phenotypic trait reflects genes expressed in particular environments'. He goes on to say that to produce another Wolfgang Amadeus Mozart, we 'would need not only Wolfgang's genome, but mother Mozart's uterus, father Mozart's music lessons, Wolfgang's sister Nannerl, his wife Constanze, the state of music in eighteenth-century Austria, Papa Haydn's sponsorship, the patronage of Emperor Joseph II, on and on, in ever-widening circles. Without his unique genome, the rest would not have sufficed. But we cannot make the assumption that his genome, cultivated in another world at another time, would result in an equally creative musical genius' (Eisenberg 2002).

The fact that several major illnesses of interest to psychiatrists – such as Huntington's chorea and phenylketonuria – are caused by genetic abnormalities of known location, has prompted psychiatric geneticists to search for the 'genes for schizophrenia, depression, anxiety and phobias'. No such genes will ever be found, since genes do not control man-made abstractions like psychiatric illnesses, but the biological processes that underlie them. The psychiatric geneticists of course know this perfectly well and the 'genes for specific illnesses' is really just a psychiatric shorthand. Unfortunately unsuspecting people often take it literally.

They also go well beyond the mental disorders and study the genes for stressful life events, for social support and for parenting. Nor is this all. The genetic basis for style of parental discipline is also sought, although here the genetic basis is found to account for only between 17 and 27 per cent of the variance. Those who had supposed that the decision to punish their child in a particular way was a parental choice are naturally dampened by the air of genetic triumphalism that informs these studies, and perhaps awed by the apparent accuracy with which variance is partitioned between additive genetic, common environmental and unique environmental variables.

How variance is partitioned between genes and environment

This is done by measuring the degree of similarity between a set of identical (monozygotic, MZ) twins and comparing this with similar figures for a set of non-identical (dizygotic, DZ) twins. The analysis proceeds by assuming that the genes are indeed identical in the MZ twins and that therefore they have perfect correlation for variance due to genetics, but since they only share half their genes in the case of the DZ twins, it is assumed to be 0.5. Variance due to common family environment is also assumed to be perfect for both MZ and DZ twins. Anything left over is attributed to a residual term covering unique (or non-shared) environment, plus measurement error (the latter is often conveniently forgotten when results are reported). The similarity between the MZ twins is now considered to be due to the sum of the effects of genetic factors and shared environment, while the similarity between the DZ twins is due to half the genetic factor, plus the shared environment. Comparisons of the within-pair correlations for the two sets of twins will thus result in rough estimates of the variance due to genes (a), shared environment (c) and unique environment (e). Once these assumptions have been made, a set of analyses are performed to estimate (a), (c) and (e) together with their standard errors.

Problems with partitioning the variance between genes and environment

The first point to make is that such partitioning is an intrinsically peculiar task, involving the application of mathematical models to data concerned with mental disorders in identical and non-identical twins, and does not typically involve the researchers in actually measuring any genes. The simplistic separation of factors between genes and environment is complicated by the following facts:

1   *The assumption that the environment is the same for each twin (sometimes referred to as the equal environments assumption, EEA) is not correct.* Each of us has a 'unique environment' and even in identical twins this will cause each one of us to experience life differently. It is never true to assume that a 'shared family environment' is ever truly shared (i.e. has

perfect correlation). Even a pair of MZ twins may try to ensure that they have different clothes and are perceived as separate individuals, and will in turn perceive their parents in somewhat different ways. Such different experiences may cause different genes to become active. Therefore it is not justifiable to attribute all of the differences between identical and fraternal twins to genetic causes.

2 *Genes often manifest in the phenotype by interaction with the environment and estimates of 'the variance due to heredity' include this 'G×E inter-action'.* This expression concerns itself with genes which may or may not manifest themselves in the phenotype, depending upon the environment to which the organism is subjected. We already have several important examples of this phenomenon which are relevant to the aetiology of depression (described in the next section).

3 *Genes may also manifest themselves by partially causing a phenotype (such as a personality type) which is itself associated with an increased rate of illness. This 'gene-environment correlation' will also be attributed wholly to genes.*

4 *Sometimes factors that might be assumed to be genetic turn out to be environmental.* This can be demonstrated in experimental animals by cross-fostering (Francis *et al.* 1999; Meaney *et al.* 2001). Some rat mothers can be bred who display much maternal licking, grooming and nursing behaviour and arched back nursing (high LG-ABN mothers), while others can be bred who display such behaviours only rarely. The high LG-ABN mothers produce offspring that have dampened hypothalamo-pituitary axes (HPA) in adult life, and will show dampened responses to stress. The low LG-ABN offspring show the opposite – hyper reactivity and increased stress responses in adult life. Yet if neonates of high LG-ABN mothers are given to low LG-ABN mothers, and the latter's off-spring are given to high LG-ABN mothers, the phenomenon is just as strong. It is the environment, not the genes, that produces the anxious adult rat. Even more impressive, when females (from low LG-ABN mothers) who have experienced high LG-ABN mothering have their own litters, they continue to manifest high LG-ABN behaviours. Good mothering is being transmitted without the presence of altered genes, but which alter subsequent gene expression. Their offspring will have increased hippocampal glucocorticoid receptor mRNA expression, higher central benzodiazepine receptor levels in the amygdala, and lower corticotropin releasing factor mRNA in the paraventricular nucleus of the hypothalamus.

5 *Environmental variables can affect the adult phenotype.* This can be observed both in bees and in rats. Worker bees are genetically identical to queen bees, which are larger and have large ovaries capable of producing thousands of eggs a day, while workers often have no ovaries at all. Yet the difference between them is due to the future queen being fed royal

jelly by nurse bees. In rats, Weaver and others (2004) have shown that high LG-ABN behaviour permanently alters the development of HPA responsiveness to stress through tissue-specific effects on gene expression. They go on to show that control of gene expression 'epigenetic effects' can both be established through behavioural programming, yet is potentially reversible.

6   *Experience may construct brain anatomy* (Eisenberg 1995). The ground plan of brain structure may be encoded in the genome, but precise connectivity between neurons results from stimulus-driven competition among axons. Thus in professional violinists, finger representation for the left hand (the hand that fingers the strings) is larger than it is in the motor cortex of non-musicians (Elbert *et al.* 1995). In auditory cortex, representation for piano tones, but not for pure tones of similar fundamental frequency, is enlarged by about 25 per cent in pianists in comparison to controls who have never played the piano. Moreover, the enlargement is correlated with the age at which the pianist began to practise (Pantev *et al.* 1998).

7   *Contribution of 'shared' environment decreases with time: not so genetic factors.* An illustration of this is if we compare the data for intelligence reported by Plomin (1990), where common environment is important at early assessments, but during adolescence becomes very small. One's genes are always there, but effects of each individual's unique environment overrides the effects of shared environment and memories become mistier and highly selective.

8   *Adoption studies fail to confirm an important genetic component in childhood depression.* One might have expected a higher correlation between biological mothers and childhood measures of depression than between adoptive mothers and their adoptive children: in fact both correlations are close to zero (van der Oord *et al.* 1994; Eley *et al.* 1998).

Interaction between genes and the environment (G×E interaction)

One of the genes that is responsible for the transport of serotonin (a neurotransmitter implicated in depressive phenomena) is called the 5HTT gene on chromosome 17 (17q11.2). It can both be long, both short, or heterozygous. This gene may well moderate the serotoninergic response to stressful events.

Those with the homozygous long version (31 per cent of this population) are relatively resilient in that they tend not to develop depression even when they have experienced several stressful events. Heterozygous people (51 per cent) are more likely to become depressed if they experience events, while those who are homozygous short (17 per cent) have a very strong relationship. Without stress, the gene does not manifest itself, but in the presence of stress

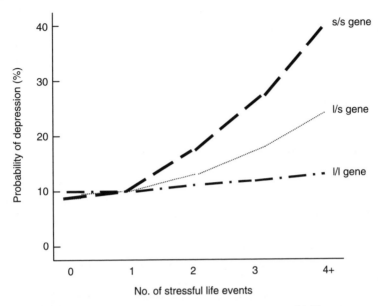

Figure 3.1 Relationship between 5HTT transporter gene, stressful life events and the probability of a depressive episode (after Caspi *et al.* 2003)

one's genetic make-up will determine how likely you are to become depressed (Caspi *et al.* 2003). See Figure 3.1.

Another example of the 5HTT transporter gene having important interactions with the environment is seen in rhesus monkeys that have an equivalent gene, which can be heterozygous or homozygous. Those with the short version of the gene (heterozygous) have more affective responding whether they had been reared with their mothers or in a nursery, but only those reared in the nursery showed lower orientation scores (Champoux *et al.* 2002). Monkeys who had poor early rearing experiences also had high levels of the metabolite of 5HT in their cerebro-spinal fluid if they were homozygous, but low levels if they were heterozygous. In contrast, those were reared by their mothers had similar levels irrespective of their zygosity (Bennett *et al.* 2002). Thus, the gene is exerting a disadvantageous effect only if the early rearing experience has been poor.

The gene responsible for encoding the enzyme which metabolises several neurotransmitters, monoamine oxidase A (the 'MAO-A gene'), is related to anti-social behaviour. An abnormality of this gene results in an individual with high levels of all the transmitters metabolised by this enzyme – noradrenaline, dopamine and serotonin. In mice, deletion of this gene results in an aggressive animal, but if MAOA activity is restored the aggressiveness disappears. In humans, a null gene at this location has been linked to anti-social behaviour (Brunner *et al.* 1993).

Caspi and his colleagues (2002) have shown that while abnormalities of this gene are related to anti-social behaviour, the manifestation of the gene in later life depends upon the environment. As we shall see in a later chapter, one of the environmental risk factors for anti-social behaviour is parental mal-treatment. Children who are maltreated but have normal MAO-A activity are only slightly more likely to develop anti-social behaviour than those who have not been maltreated. But if the gene is abnormal, then the risk of anti-social behaviour increases greatly with increasing degrees of maltreatment. This relationship holds true for all later measures of anti-social behaviour: anti-social personality disorder, conviction for violent offences, childhood conduct disorder and an index of 'disposition towards violence'.

Finally, Henquet *et al.* (2004) have shown that the increased rates of schizophrenia among cannabis users is not because future schizophrenics are more likely to have abused cannabis (the 'self-medication' hypothesis) but because those with an increased genetic risk for schizophrenia have much higher rates of phenotypic illness if they use cannabis.

In summary, some genes only manifest themselves in the presence of particular environments, so that simple linear model of 'gene leading to manifestation in the individual' is quite simply incorrect. However, tra-ditional genetic analysis assigns all such effects to genetic causes, without acknowledging the importance of particular environments.

The genetics of internalising

The genetic control of depression and anxiety

Most studies use bivariate genetic modelling to partition variance between A, C and U, as above (Kendler *et al.* 1987; Kendler and Prescott 1999; Thapar and McGuffin 1998). These studies all show the same thing: shared family environment has no contribution whatever, genetic factors account for around 40 per cent of the variance, and environment unique to the individual accounts for a large part of the rest. In their report on nearly 4,000 Australian twins, Kendler and his colleagues concluded that there was:

> no evidence for genes affecting depression which did not also affect anxiety. Genetic factors act to influence general level of symptoms, whereas the environment has specific effects, since some features of the environment strongly influence anxiety while having little influence on depression.
>
> (Kendler *et al.* 1987)

Subsequent studies have confirmed this conclusion. Kendler and others (1992a) used bivariate genetic analysis with his female Virginia twins to esti-mate the overlap between the genes responsible for depression and those for anxiety. The association between the two sets of genes was not significantly different from unity – in a word, they are the same or almost the same genes. These genes were thought of as being responsible for 'general distress' and the rest of the variance was due to the environmental variables unique to the individual. Some of these were common between depression and anxiety, but others were specific for each disorder.

Andrews *et al.* (1990a) used the Australian twins to examine six 'neurotic' disorders: depression, generalised anxiety, dysthymia, obsessive compulsive disorder, agoraphobia/panic and social phobia. They found them all to be influenced by the same genetic factors. Kendler and others did much the same with the Virginia twins and found that genetic influences on common disorders were best explained by two factors: one dealing with panic, phobias and bulimia, the other on generalised anxiety and depressive episodes. Hariri and others (2002) have argued that abnormalities of the 5HTT gene are responsible for increased fear and anxiety-related behaviours, and have related this to greater activity in a part of the brain called the amygdala in the presence of two short alleles of the 5HTT gene.

For all disorders, the genetic influence is only 'moderate' and the 'unique environment' is important for all disorders. The same group has also studied the relationship between alcoholism and depression but now including men in their twin sample (Prescott *et al.* 2000). Over two-thirds of women who had both disorders said that their depression ante-dated the alcohol abuse, whereas 61 per cent of men said the reverse. The correlation between the two disorders was low but positive in each gender (+0.31 for males, +0.37 for females), with genetic factors contributing to 61 per cent of the variance in males, but only 51 per cent in women. The factors responsible for the combination were found to be different for each gender.

Eley and Stevenson (1999a) in a twin study in London managed to reduce the correlation between depression and anxiety to only +0.3 by careful item selection and confirm that the same genetic factors are responsible for most of the correlation between them. Bivariate genetic analysis, which decomposes the covariance between two factors and separates them into additive genetic (A), common (shared) environment (C) and unique (non-shared) environment U, produces different results for anxious and depressive symptoms. Whereas depressive symptoms are largely related to genetic and unique environment, anxious symptoms are related to the two environmental factors. It is of interest that common environment is approximately as important as genetic factors, when symptoms in childhood and adolescence are being considered. In a further study of the same data set (1999b) these authors found that as boys move from childhood to adolescence there is an increase in the importance of genetic factors, while as girls move the common (shared) environment becomes more important. However, the unique (non-shared) environment is also important in both genders and in both life eras.

Are the genes controlling particular illnesses or controlling health?

If we consider results reported by Kendler and Prescott (1999), where the contribution due to genes is found to be 39 per cent, the data reported can readily be converted as shown in Table 3.1.

The genetic component depends on the discrepancy between MZ and DZ twins for discordant twin pairs. There are two observations about Table 3.1. First, most of the discordance is due to discordance for health, not discordance for illness. Second, the concordance for health is very much greater than the concordance for illness. Thus, while no one can quarrel with the assertion that genes are extremely important and do indeed account for around 40 per cent of the total variance, it seems unlikely that these genes are all controlling illness. They are more likely to be controlling health or resilience. Geneticists will argue that this is mere hair splitting, since vulnerability and resilience are two sides of the same coin. But if we are referring to genes responsible for perhaps relatively unstable biological systems, then they may well be operating at the healthy end of the health–sickness continuum.

A related study makes this possibility more likely. Rijsdijk and her colleagues (2003) examined the hereditability of the scores on the GHQ-28, which is a scaled version of the questionnaire that was administered to the London twins on two occasions, five years apart (Table 3.2).

This is a truly amazing result – since the amount of variance accounted for is approximately the same as that for 'neuroticism' which claims to be a stable personality trait, while the GHQ is an illness measure, with high scores only

Table 3.1 Where UU are twin pairs concordant for health: AA are pairs concordant for illness; UA are discordant pairs (after Kendler and Prescott 1999)

		UU %	AA %	UA %
Males	MZ	74.7	4.6	20.5
	DZ	70.2	4.2	25.4
Females	MZ	53.2	14.5	32.1
	DZ	43.7	15.2	41.0

Table 3.2 Hereditability of the GHQ-28. Where AG are additive genetic factors, UE are unique environment, and CE are common environment: the scales measure somatic symptoms (A); anxiety and insomnia (B); social dysfunction (C); severe depression (D)

	%	
A scale	42	AG, UE
B scale	46	AG, UE
C scale	33	CE, UE
D scale	45	AG, UE
Total score	52	AG, UE

Table 3.3 Scores of the normal UK population, tested with the GHQ on two occasions (personal communication, Pevalin 2003, derived from Buck 1990)

	%
Score low both occasions	55
Score low once, high once	36
Score high both times	9

at times of disorder. Thus, the heritability of the GHQ would have been predicted to be much lower than that for 'neuroticism'. The explanation can be found in normative data for the GHQ (Table 3.3), when the same normal people are tested on two occasions, some years apart (data from the British Household Survey, Buck 1990).

It can be seen from Table 3.3 that the largest group of people always have a low (potential normal) score, with a very much smaller group being consistently high. These two groups together account for the heritability of the questionnaire, and it can be seen that the heritability spreads across the entire score range (Figure 3.2).

If the result in Figure 3.2 is taken alongside Caspi *et al.'s* (2003) findings on resilience, it is possible that the genetic contribution to those who score consistently low on the GHQ is partly or wholly determined by the presence of a homozygous long 5HTT gene.

In summary, the genes for 'major depression' are largely or entirely shared with those for 'generalised anxiety disorder', and may overlap with genes responsible for panic and phobias. However, there appear to be separate genes controlling fear responses. The former genes are likely to control the level of emotional reactivity – a quality partially captured by personality measures of 'neuroticism' and 'negative affectivity'.

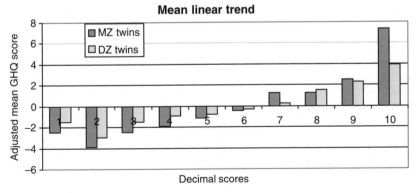

Figure 3.2 Distribution of MZ/DZ discordancies across the entire score range of the GHQ-28, decile scores (after Rijsdijk *et al.* 2003)

The genetics of externalising disorders

McGuffin and Gottesman (1984) combined seven twin studies of adult criminality and five of juvenile delinquency to produce an MZ concordance of
51 per cent, and a DZ concordance of only 22 per cent, suggesting that there
is an important genetic contribution to criminality. However, environmental
influences are also very important. This can be shown in adoption studies,
where the cross-fostering element allows some disentangling of the two contributions. Hutchings and Mednick (1975) found that having an adoptive
father with a police record did not increase likelihood of the adopted child
acquiring one (12 per cent, to be compared with 11 per cent when neither
adoptive nor biological parents had a record). If the biological father had a
record this increased to 21 per cent and if both biological and adoptive
fathers had one this increased to 36 per cent. Other adoption studies show the
same phenomenon. This suggests that some genetic loading towards criminality is necessary for environmental factors to become important, and we
have seen an example of this in Caspi's work already quoted.

Eley (1997) has studied a large series of twins based at the Institute of
Child Health in London, aged between 8 and 16. She argues that in her study
'general genes' are responsible for the correlation between anxiety and
depression. Indeed, genes are responsible for a massive 80 per cent of the
shared variance. She extends her argument to anti-social behaviours and
asserts that these same genes may also be responsible for some anti-social
behaviours. In her formulation, there are three components to anxiety and
depression:

- symptoms of 'negative affectivity' like crying, sadness and worry that is
  largely genetically determined
- symptoms of somatic arousal such as palpitations, sweating, tremor
  which are associated with anxiety
- symptoms of 'low positive affect' such as absence of enjoyment in life,
  low self-esteem, and self-blame which are associated with depression.

She showed that genetic factors are much more important in the aggressive
forms of anti-social behaviour than in the non-aggressive forms (e.g. lying,
truancy, stealing). It is in these latter forms that shared family environment is
almost as important as genetic factors (30 per cent versus 40 per cent),
whereas shared family environment seems relatively unimportant in aggressive
forms (5 per cent versus 65 per cent).

In a later paper comparing Swedish and British twins, Eley et al. (1999c)
show that there is an interesting gender difference: for non-aggressive ASB
shared family environment is greater for boys than girls, while genetic factors
are greater for girls. For aggressive ASB, genetic factors are once more
important for girls and for them shared family factors are negligible –

although they account for about one-fifth of the variance for boys. O'Connor and colleagues (1998) have also argued that about 45 per cent of the variance for internalising disorders is shared with that for externalising disorders.

Kendler and his colleagues (1995) analysed data on six major common disorders and found that the genetics of alcohol dependence were distinct from that for common mood disorders. In a later paper (1997b) they analysed data from the US National Co-morbidity study and showed that family aggregation for internalising disorders (depression and anxiety) separate from externalising disorders (alcohol, drugs and anti-social personality) transmitted across generations, with internalising disorders having somewhat higher path coefficients than externalising disorders (+0.36 vs +0.21). The gender of the parent influenced all disorders – with fathers more likely to have externalising and mothers internalising disorders. Depression in the mother was related to depression in the child more than depression in the father.

Young and his colleagues (2000) were interested in a personality dimension called 'novelty seeking'. They studied the relationship between this and symptoms of externalising disorders (conduct disorder, attention deficit hyperactivity disorder and drug dependence) in a series of adolescent twin pairs. Using latent trait analysis they found a single latent trait running through these symptoms and found that genetic factors were responsible for 84 per cent of the variance.

Krueger and others (2002) carried out a broadly similar study with the Minnesota twins, using a personality dimension called constraint. They studied a different but comparable set of symptoms, including those of conduct disorder, adolescent anti-social behaviour, alcohol abuse and use of illicit drugs. Once more a latent trait ran through these symptoms, with 81 per cent of the variance due to heredity. It should be emphasised that the earlier studies were concerned with medical diagnoses and this study was confined to externalising disorders.

In summary, there may possibly be a small overlap between the genes responsible for internalising disorder and those for externalising disorders seen in childhood, but studies of adults suggest that other genetic pathways are involved as well. There appears to be a strong genetic influence on the symptoms which make-up the disorders, but in general the associations between the tendency to externalise and the individual disorders is not so strong as it is for internalising. Just as 'neuroticism' and 'negative affect' are associated with internalising, 'novelty seeking' and lack of 'constraint' are associated with externalising. It is likely that some of the genes responsible for the common factor between these disorders help to determine these traits.

Genetics of personality disorders

The assertion that social variables such as life events, social support and styles of parental discipline may have a genetic component, as Foley et al. (1996)

argue, is intrinsically disturbing to a social scientist. However, there is no reason why it should be. No one, we hope, seriously supposes that a gene directly controls any of these phenomena. However, the causal line may well be indirect, so that a process which is known to be partly controlled by genes itself influences the occurrence of these phenomena.

A way that such control may be exerted genetically is the genetic control of personality variables. For example, one's emotional reactivity, which itself relates to one's habitual symptom level. This is typically estimated crudely by questionnaire measures such as Eysenck's 'neuroticism' or Hirschfeld's 'harm avoidance'. There is evidence that people with high 'neuroticism' scores are more likely to experience unfavourable life events (Headey and Waring 1989; Poulton and Andrews 1992), thus providing a direct link.

People with a depressive illness are more likely to have experienced loss events, so that if there is a genetic component to depression, there will also be one for loss events. Indeed, in the Caspi *et al.* study there was a direct relationship between the 5HTT gene and the number of stressful life events experienced: those with the double short version of the gene had on average experienced more stressful life events than those in the other groups.

Personality is partly determined by one's genes (Torgersen *et al.* 2000), partly by early life experience (Modestin *et al.* 1998). Yet one's personality also determines the kinds of life event one will experience in adult life. So personality characteristics like novelty seeking, extraversion, harm avoidance and openness will themselves determine the kinds of risk and the kinds of life situation to which a given individual is likely to be exposed.

Headey and Waring (1989) showed that unfavourable life events are related to 'neuroticism' and 'openness'. Saudino and her colleagues (1997) studied elderly Swedish twins and found that the heritabilities of various kinds of life event were substantial (in the range of 41 to 53 per cent) for females, although near zero for males. They showed that to the extent that there is a genetic influence on life events in women, it is entirely mediated by personality. Billig and others (1996) argue that genetically influenced individual differences in (lack of) *constraint* play a substantial role in life events whose occurrence is not independent of the individual's behaviour.

These are early preliminary results. We may expect later studies to throw further light on the ways in which genes can assert control over events that at first glance appear totally controlled by the environment.

Torgersen and others (2000) report a twin study of personality disorders using the DSM-3R classification, using the Norwegian twin register. High values of heritability are reported for narcissistic (0.79) and obsessive compulsive personalities (0.78); rather lower for borderline (0.69) histrionic (0.67) schizotypal (0.61) self-defeating (0.54) and lowest of all for schizoid (0.29), paranoid (0.28) and avoidant (0.28). However, there may be some contamination of these data, as the same person interviewed both members of each pair and may well have guessed the zygosity of the twins – thus possibly overestimating heritability.

Ono and his colleagues (2002) have examined the relationship between the 'big five' personality dimensions and depression on a symptom scale in a series of 251 twins in Tokyo. They found that there was a strong relationship between harm avoidance (= 'neuroticism'), and also a negative relationship between reward dependence and depression. However, the effects of unique environment were found to be greater than genetic variables, as might have been expected. There were no differences between males and females and the pattern of these relationships.

Kendler and Prescott (1999) reported that the genetic contribution to depression in adults was exactly the same – 39 per cent in both men and women. Jang and others (2000) on the basis of a small twin study using the 'anxiety sensitivity index' have claimed that girls are more sensitive than boys to such symptoms. This tendency is heritable only in females, with genetic factors accounting for about 44 per cent of the total variance. Possible non-genetic reasons for the difference will be described in later chapters.

What genes for common mental disorders probably do

A speculative summary

It is very likely that genetic control of the common mental disorders is effected by multiple recessive genes. However, they appear to be the same genes in the case of depression and generalised anxiety disorder. Such genes may well be controlling the general emotional reactivity of the organism. If this were so, the genetic control for mental disorders would largely (but not entirely) be concerned with the genetic determination of anxiety. This would be a fairly parsimonious explanation for the evidence, presented above, that genes are controlling resilience (i.e. low emotional reactivity) rather than being specific for particular illnesses. We will later consider evidence that depression needs both cognitive changes, low self-confidence, self-blame and so on, and is often triggered by certain kinds of loss event, while anxious symptoms are more often in response to stress. All of these are largely determined by the unique environment in which individuals find themselves. However, many personality characteristics are also largely genetically controlled, and these will help to determine the kinds of stressful life events experienced in adult life since individuals create their own environments.

The tendency to internalise covers a wider range of disorders than these two and there appear to be separate genes controlling panic and phobic disorders, in addition to those controlling the general tendency to internalise.

The genetic control of externalising disorders is on the whole weaker than that for internalisng, so that environmental influences are correspondingly more important, as we shall see. The externalising disorders are associated with the personality dimensions of lack of constraint or novelty seeking, and these are at least partly genetically determined. A basic point is that 'gene x environment' interaction is involved in the way that heredity affects disorders. The way in which this occurs is because genes can be switched on or switched off during adult life, depending on the environment.

Take-home messages

- Mathematical models can give approximate assessments of the importance of genetic factors in mental disorders, but such estimates include effects of the environment in assisting genes to manifest themselves in the phenotype.
- The almost universal finding that shared family environment can be ignored is unimpressive – as shared environment can be important in early life even though it becomes hard to detect as non-shared environmental influences accumulate in an individual.
- 'G×E interactions' are important for both depression and anti-social behaviour: loss events exert only a small relationship to depression unless a particular abnormality is present, and anti-social behaviour is associated strongly with childhood maltreatment only if another genetic abnormality is present.
- The assessments of the importance of non-shared environmental factors are always overestimates, as measurement error is included in the assessment.
- The genetic factors responsible for depression appear identical with those for anxiety, and most probably control emotional reactivity in the individual – assessed to some extent by measures of 'neuroticism' or in childhood 'emotionality'.
- It is likely that there are some genes specific for fear disorders, but such disorders also share genes with internalising disorders.
- Personality is partly determined by genes and will in turn largely determine the kinds of non-random stressful events experienced in later life. To the extent that this is so, there is another pathway by which our genes affect later disorders.
- Externalising disorders have only a modest overlap with internalising disorders and appear to have separate genetic pathways. These are partly related to a personality dimension variously measured by 'novelty seeking' and behavioural disinhibition: the latter being the polar opposite of 'constraint'.

Chapter 4

The brain, neurochemical codes and immunity

Three independent systems – the central nervous system (CNS), the neuro-endocrine system and the immune system – are responsible for the adaptation of the individual to the environment. In order to maintain a homeostatic balance, these three systems are in balance with one another at various levels. The CNS is of course the major controller, translator and integrator of environmental stimuli, and it largely controls adaptive responses of the body to the outside world.

Neurochemical codes, behaviour and social adversity

The impact of social adversities on the risk for psychiatric disorders cannot be understood without considering the biological basis of behaviour. How does the brain itself 'cope' with negative life events and chronic difficulties? Are social adversities as diverse as personal disappointments in relationships, child maltreatment, persistent poverty and chronic marital disharmony all translated into the same neurochemical codes that subserve moods, thoughts and behaviours over the lifespan? Ascertaining the neural basis of the psychological processes that play a role in the onset, maintenance, persistence or recovery of psychopathology is a major task for future research.

Experimental studies using animals, and rodents in particular, can be critical in delineating specific candidate processes in the brain that inform us about the likelihood of such mechanisms operating in humans. Such studies often involve altering neural pathways and chemical processes directly in the brain and observing changes in behaviour. Alternatively manipulations of animal environments can help us to understand crucial behaviours such as eating, sleeping and reproduction. Separations of maternal–infant pairs or siblings will give us information about the effects of removal of a critical environment on the development of neurochemical systems and behaviour.

Considering the animal as a biological entity and a survivor of a multiplicity of demands from the environment, requires an understanding of how biological systems at the neurochemical and behavioural level act in concert to bring about adaptive responses to a hostile environment. The complexity of this task cannot be underestimated even for rodents. How much more difficult then for an animal such as *homo sapiens* who brings a range of behavioural options more complex than any other into the social environment.

Man creates as well as reacts to social environments. When faced with demands, good or bad, from the environment the brain must not only possess the means for expressing adaptive behaviours but also decide on the priority and appropriateness of distinct behavioural response patterns that will allow the person to continue to function equally as well following exposure to life difficulties. This clearly requires a clear and fundamental understanding of how individuals and groups function prior to adversities. We know surprisingly little about normative adaptation at the level of the brain to social adversities.

Common mental disorders can be thought of as indicating a failure in personal adaptive mechanisms to adversity. These may come about because the individual does not possess the neurochemical and behavioural repertoire to respond adaptively or that he or she is impaired in their abilities to deploy those tools in an adaptive way.

Homeostasis and allostasis

All mammals engage in behaviours that must be tailored to demands and ensure the success of the animal's behavioural strategy for survival (fitness). Behaviours that are recruited to increase fitness and adaptation to demands have been classically defined as homeostatic processes (Cannon 1929). *Homeostasis* consists of three components:

- the necessity to confine some parameter within defined limits (high and low) a physiological example would be blood pressure, a psychological example would be attention
- a mechanism to know when these limits are exceeded (e.g. feeling faint with low blood pressure or distracted from a task due to low attention)
- the means to deploy a behavioural strategy to rectify the negative effect of demand (e.g. lying down when feeling faint or changing task when no longer attending).

Not all adaptive processing is confined within defined limits: in some cases the requirements for adaptation will vary with demand. This more dynamic adaptive processing is termed *allostasis*. Under these conditions there is a titration of the adaptive mechanism to ensure that fitness is retained. For example, comprehension of a textbook is likely to vary from one section to another. Thus the degree of attentional processing required may vary from high to moderate or even low dependent on the content. Individuals in order to stay on task will vary their level of attention. Multitasking abilities may vary according to the amount of 'work' the brain is doing, being greater perhaps when low levels of attention and working memory are being used in the task. Adapting to such a demand requires anticipation as well as response. Allostasis is both an anticipatory and response process.

The physiological environment is the key milieu for investigating maladaptation to social adversity. Genetic structures determine the control of that environment. Individual variations in genetic structure may give rise to functional differences in physiological abilities to respond to social adversity. But the interplay between genes and environment is complex and not static. Thus some environments will moderate the effectiveness of genes to exert their functional effects. Serious disruptions of key social environments such as maternal deprivation may alter the neural substrates such that functional genes coding for adaptive responses to homeostatic and allostatic demand may be less effective and increase the risk for maladaptation in the face of social adversity.

A key issue is to remember that the social environment is a persistent feature of our lives, one that we make as well as respond to. This social environment is seldom fully optimal and we are constantly titrating behavioural resources to minimise homeostatic and allostatic demands. How efficient we are at doing that is the key fundamental process in the risk for the common emotional and behavioural disorders across the lifespan. Thus the degree of psychiatric risk may well depend *on the extent to which the individual can remain functional and adaptive during the period of exposure* to social adversity. This resilience in the face of adversity will vary according to a variety of personal attributes and the presence of moderating social environments. A key issue here is the *extent to which chemical signals are effective in alerting the brain and mind to adversity* and how a response is mounted at the neurobiological level leading to a concerted and coherent behavioural adaptive response. Equally important is *how responses are turned off once adaptation following demand has been reached*. Psychiatric responses are likely when one or more of these three components is inefficient or ineffective.

Neural systems

The concept of a neural system is well established and recognises the anatomical fact that there are parts of the brain that specialise in defined subsets of neural function. A wealth of experimental data in animals and more recently from human neuro-imaging studies has shown that different areas of the brain are activated dependent on the demand or task that has been initiated. Three areas of an interconnected distributed neural circuit have been a particular focus of study in relation to emotion and cognition: the limbic system, the pre-frontal cortex and the orbito-frontal cortex.

The limbic system

The limbic system refers to a defined area of brain that consists of a series of interconnected anatomical structures with key functions involving emotion recognition, emotion response and cognitive activation (conscious thoughts) to the external stimulus. The system co-ordinates emotion-cognition processes to ensure switching on behavioural action and subsequently co-ordinating responses to switch off such actions. A feature of the limbic neural system is its rich connectivity with other parts of the brain. This indicates theoretically a high likelihood of a comprehensive involvement of neural circuits in adaptation to stress or at least the importance of the whole brain receiving, recognising and responding to signals located predominantly in one or more areas.

Since the overall feature of brain–mind functions is to effect a coherent and holistic adaptation all brain regions should remain in communication even where there are regions of specialisation. If the limbic system is not in communication with the speech and motor system then the chemical messages that become translated into a need for movement adaptation or language adaptation might not occur. A highly specialised but non-connected brain would be at serious risk for maladaptation at times of homeostatic and allostatic overload.

There are also functional distinctions within the limbic system. When these are closely associated with distinct neuroanatomical features this is considered a modular neural system. For example, a structure known as the *amygdala* is associated with emotion recognition and processing. Damage to the amygdala or blocking its connections to other parts of the limbic system interferes markedly with an individual's ability to recognise and mount an emotional signal to a social stimulus that is known to contain fearful, sad or happy stimuli (Calder *et al.* 2001). By contrast damage to other limbic structures, the hippocampus or hypothalamus impairs an individual's ability to organise a response to emotional stimuli even though their emotional content is recognised, probably through profound impairments in memory and recall of experience (Eichenbaum 1999).

The pre-frontal cortex

The pre-frontal cortex is the newest part of the brain and uniquely large in humans compared to all other animals. It is another brain system critically involved in emotional and cognitive processing (Roberts *et al.* 2000). Damage to this area of the brain is associated with poor judgement, impaired planning and problem solving and social disinhibition. The anatomical structure of the pre-frontal cortex is also highly differentiated and there are modular components here too. In humans the dorsal (top of the brain) and ventral (bottom of the brain) surfaces of the pre-frontal cortex show regional specialisation of function. The dorsolateral-pre-frontal cortex is known to be associated with deficits in planning, cognitive flexibility and decision making. By contrast the ventro-lateral pre-frontal cortex is associated with impairments in emotional sensitivity and social disinhibition. There are also some skills that appear to be carried out by a number of different regions of the pre-frontal cortex indicating perhaps a key general process termed 'response inhibition' and referring to the importance of filtering incoming information so that the brain can select and mount a response to stimuli.

Orbito-frontal cortex

The other part of the frontal cortex known to be crucial in emotion and cognition functions is the orbito-frontal area. Damage and deficits in this area lead to failures of emotion processing and emotion learning (Rolls 2000) indicating that an important co-operative interplay between cortical and limbic system elements is required to mount a coherent response to the emotional components of a social stimulus. For example, damage to the orbito-frontal cortex blunts the normal emotional reactions and behavioural responses to external stimuli. Monkeys show decreased aggression to humans, no longer reject foods they usually avoid or show a low preference for (Rolls 2000). In humans damage to this area results in increased social disinhibition, inappropriate euphoria and aggression together with social irresponsibility (DaMasio 1995). These effects indicate that the orbito-frontal cortex and its neurochemical codes are a key part of the social brain. Damage to this area impairs learning and/or remembering which social stimuli are rewarding (maintaining social networks and friends, selecting foods, and so on).

Overall these descriptions show how neuro-anatomical regions of the brain subserve emotions and cognitions that are the essential psychological elements required for behavioural adaptation to the environment. Unless you 'feel' you will not bother to adapt. Whilst regional specialisation of functions clearly occurs indicating modularity of certain brain systems, it also appears that some general principles are so important that they are part of the functional apparatus of many parts of the brain. A key issue here is the ability of the brain to filter information from the external world so that adaptive responses can be arrived at through a variety of regions working in concert. This complex continuous process is mainly non-conscious, occurring without the need for effortful thinking. This is presumably just as well as it is clear that our conscious abilities to process demands have limits, dependent on executive skills such as attention span, working memory capacity, speed of information processing. Breakdown in these functions is discussed in detail in Chapter 9 (destabilisation).

For example, a comprehensive response to a social stimulus that is likely to induce fear, sadness or happiness will require co-operation between the limbic-orbito-frontal and pre-frontal regions and the psychological functions they subserve. What do negative life events and chronic difficulties actually do to these systems? Are there some areas of the brain more than others that are likely to 'fail' in their functions under high social demand in the population at large, even if they have not undergone 'damage' as a result of head injury, infection or disease?

Before we tackle these psychiatric questions there is one further and crucial brain-based issue that requires some discussion. The brain communicates within itself via electrical and chemical signals. The latter are diverse and crucially vary in their distribution within the brain. It is increasingly apparent that it is this neurochemistry that acts in a large part as the language of the brain.

Neurochemical coding of adaptive responses to the environment

We will focus on four major classes of chemicals in the brain: amino acids; monoamines; peptides and steroids that we know are involved in emotion, cognition and behaviour. It is almost certain that there are other chemistries of relevance to psychological functioning but these have been the major focus in brain-behaviour research. After a brief description of each we will focus in detail on monoamines and steroids for which there is evidence for a clear-cut role in psychopathology and as moderators of the impact of social adversities on brain and mind.

Amino acids

There is considerable evidence that these simple compounds are used throughout the brain as transmitters. They play a role in how the nervous system learns via chemical processing. Gamma-aminobutyric acid (GABA) and glutamate are two amino acids which are particularly prevalent in brain regions with a very clear topographical anatomical structure. This is more prominent in the cortex than in the limbic system. There are few studies as yet of these chemical switches in humans under differing forms of stress. In rodents however there is considerable evidence that stress in early life, such as maternal separation, results in significant changes in chemical systems in the brain including amino acids (Francis *et al.* 1999; Caldji *et al.* 2000).

Neuroactive peptides

The manufacture of peptides in the brain is altogether more complex chemically than neurotransmitters derived from amino acids, and involves the synthesis of proteins which are subsequently cleared. Peptides are generally released in concert with other neurotransmitters and hence have a modulatory role in synaptic signalling. The limbic system has the highest concentration of peptides of any neural system but they are found throughout the brain. Like other neurotransmitters, peptides have a number of different signalling roles. For example, corticotrophic releasing factor (CRF) regulates the output of the steroid cortisol (see below), but also acts as an important neurotransmitter in brain circuitry involved with the behavioural response to demand. There is some evidence for the role of CRF in the onset of major depression (Nemeroff 2002). It is unclear how specific an association there is between a complex peptide and a particular form of psychopathology. As noted earlier peptides are involved in a large number of signalling functions within the brain in response to variable levels of demands. Thus tying down specificity without reference to the environmental context of the function subserved by CRF may lead to spurious associations. For example, whether the level of CRF varies with real life negative experiences leading directly to onset of depression is not known.

Monoamines

The monoamines represent a family of chemical systems that have pervasive effects on behaviour. The three main amino acids, *noradrenaline, serotonin, dopamine*, are all amines that have both anatomical and chemical features distinguishing them from peptides and other chemical transmitters. The distinguishing features are that these amines are located in comparatively small groups in the basal lower part of the brain but have an extensive network of fibres that spread to many parts of the brain including the limbic system and the cortex. Furthermore they are quite discrete fibres and only partially overlap. Functionally therefore activation in one monoamine system will introduce a distributed pattern of response in the brain that is widespread but not identical to that induced by the others. The monoamines are considered in more detail below.

Steroids

Steroids are an extensive family of chemical agents distributed widely in the brain. They include *cortisol*, the classical stress hormone, *oestradiol, testosterone, progesterone*, collectively the sex hormones, and *aldosterone* and *dehydroepiandrosterone* (DHEA). Cortisol and DHEA are the most implicated in the response to demand. Both have a high density in the limbic system but are also found in the cortex. Circulating levels of steroids can be relatively easily measured in the periphery from blood, urine and saliva. These peripheral levels are correlated with levels in the cerebrospinal and ventricular fluid in the brain (Guazzo *et al.* 1996). There is now clear-cut evidence that certain steroids are manufactured in the brain and play a key role in brain development and plasticity (Baulieu *et al.* 2004). These include DHEA and its sulphate DHEAS. Within the brain these neurosteroids modulate the effects of other transmitters including GABA and glutamate. Neurosteroids can therefore alter neuronal excitability throughout the brain very rapidly by binding to receptors for inhibitory or excitatory neuro-transmitters at the cell membrane. Their possible role in psychopathology is discussed below.

Physiological studies of social adversity

In contrast to the extensive investigations on the relations between the social environment and psychopathology, the physiological risk and response states have been an infrequent target for investigation. For example, the monoamine systems dopamine, serotonin and noradrenaline are seldom considered together within the same research investigation. Whilst considerable amounts have been learnt about changes in one or other of these systems in adaptation to stress, we know virtually nothing of the overall 'brain state' of an individual (or animal) which depends on their actions in concert. Further the effects of one brain system on another are also frequently ignored. For example, there is a wealth of information charting significant relations between the steroid cortisol and the monoamine serotonin, yet cortisol/serotonin interplay is seldom investigated when either one of these systems is under scrutiny in psychiatric research. This is a fundamental theoretical point that needs to be remembered as we turn our attention to the 'biological studies' of social adversities in humans.

Physiological components of risk for psychopathology

Monoamines

It is nearly 40 years since Coppen suggested that levels of brain serotonin are decreased in association with a depressive episode (Coppen 1967). More recently a causal process has been suggested whereby depression-prone subjects with a vulnerable serotonin system increase the liability for a depressive episode (Maes et al. 1995). Serotonin depletion in the brain and peripheral circulation can be achieved physiologically through removing the amino acid tryptophan from the diet (Sargent et al. 2000). This amino acid is a precursor for the biosynthesis of serotonin and dietary depletion lowers the circulating levels in the blood by some 20 to 30 per cent. Acute total tryptophan depletion will lower blood levels up to 90 per cent within 4 to 6 hours. Normal levels are rapidly restored on reintroduction of a normal diet. Depletion of brain serotonin effectively lowers mood in some but not all individuals but particularly those with past history of recurrent depression (Bell et al. 2001). Both these depressive disorders run in families and it appears that a positive family history as well as a personal history of depression is associated with lowered serotonin (Riedel 2004). Thus family history can cause small mood changes but a personal history of recurrent depression is associated with a larger mood lowering (Booij *et al.* 2002, 2003).

Acute tryptophan depletion is also associated with impairment in memory consolidation and attentional processing in healthy volunteers and recovered depressives (Klaassen *et al.* 2002; Murphy *et al.* 2002). This provides support for the serotonin vulnerability hypothesis but specifically in those with a familial predisposition to depression. A personal history of depression clearly has consequences for the serotonin system and its related functions being associated with the largest changes in tryptophan levels and associated cognitive impairments. In a nutshell, depression is bad for your brain and mind and your serotonin system may be compromised following this mental disorder.

But how do lower tryptophan levels occur in the community at large? Strickland and colleagues (2002) have recently shown that there is an abnormality in serotonin function in women in the community with a new onset of major depression that has been brought about by recent life events and difficulties. These findings support the theoretical proposition from Deakin and colleagues that a particular set of the serotonin receptors in the brain (the post-synaptic $5HT_{2c}$ ones to be exact) are activated by social adversity and mediate the symptoms of anxiety and depression (Deakin 1988, 1998). The ascending 5HT neural system originates deep in the brain and sends projections to the amygdala and frontal cortex. Deakin and Graeff (Graeff *et al.* 1996) have suggested that this pathway facilitates the onset and maintenance of conditioned fear. A different pathway but arising from the same area innervates a separate neural system the peri-ventricular and peri-aqueductal grey matter. Deakin and Graeff proposed that serotonin activation of this latter system inhibits inborn fight/flight reactions to impending danger, pain or asphyxia. Deakin has proposed that depletion of serotonin provides a unitary explanation for impairments in the two key coping systems processes: loss of sensitivity to fearful stimuli and blunted flight/fight reactions. It has also been shown that enhancing tryptophan levels increases the sensitivity of the fear system in both animals and man (Attenburrow *et al.* 2003). This theory awaits confirmation. In addition it is somewhat unitary and as we have already noted brain-mind states are unlikely to be explained by focusing on only one chemical system. Deakin and colleagues further posit overactivity in one of the 5HT pathways (dorsal raphe-amygdala) at the same time as underactivity in another (median raphe hippocampus) to explain functional changes of increased inhibition of fearfulness and loss of restraint to panic.

But what components trigger this loss of serotonin synchrony? It seems likely that environmental stressors increase cortisol which in turn lowers plasma tryptophan a bit – perhaps through indirect effects on daily diet. In a vulnerable person, say with a family history of emotional disorders, a small lowering of tryptophan availability over time plus 5HT1A receptor down-regulation produced by cortisol could lead to depression.

Investigating the relationship between neural systems and chemical codes has become increasingly possible with the using of neuro-imaging techniques to capture brain activity before, during and after a chemical challenge such as tryptophan depletion (Grasby 1999; Sargent *et al.* 2000). These experimental approaches have been highly successful in confirming directly that depletion of monoamines in the brain is associated with lowering mood (Berman *et al.* 2002; Bhagwagar *et al.* 2002). Another major monoamine, noradrenaline, has also been studied using challenge tests and depletion studies with similar findings (Berman *et al.* 2002). Indeed lowering of both 5-HT and noradrenaline can cause depression in those predisposed.

Neuro-imaging studies have located key areas in the frontal cortex rich in serotonin as those most susceptible to poor functioning when individuals are dysphoric and/or thinking negative thoughts about themselves or the world (Mayberg 1997; Mayberg *et al.* 1999, 2000). The mediating neurochemical components for the formation of a psychiatric state following social adversity are not confined to the cortex. The amygdala and hippocampus as well as the pre-frontal cortex are compromised in these studies showing the importance of co-operation between neural systems and chemical codes in regulating mood and thoughts. The mechanisms in everyday life may be that psycho-social adversities alter mood and cognitions and evoke a neurochemical response in monoamines and serotonin in particular in 'serotonin vulnerable' individuals. The precise social mechanism that leads to dysphoria is discussed elsewhere in Chapter 10.

Hormones

Cortisol and DHEA

Over the past 30 years it has become increasingly apparent that hormones have key functions in the brain. We will focus on the hormone *cortisol*, often considered the stress hormone because of its reactivity to external events. This hormone is critically involved in homeostasis and allostasis and is essential for survival when the body has to mobilise metabolic resources following an event, such as acute illness, physical trauma or social change. We will also discuss the role of *dehydroepiandrosterone* (DHEA). The functions of this hormone are not yet fully understood but it is involved in two key processes. One is in maintaining healthy blood vessels (vascular integrity) and the other in protecting the brain from deleterious effects of cortisol. The latter appears important when the levels of cortisol in the brain are high for days. In those circumstances parts of the limbic system (notably the hippocampus) may be damaged. DHEA may act as a neuroprotective agent in such circumstances (Kimonides *et al.* 1998, 1999). In addition to adrenal steroids having direct effects on brain and mental functions they have interactions with the monoamines. Cortisol in particular has powerful bidirectional effects on serotonin systems in the brain. During development absence of cortisol results in serotonin down regulation and depletion indicating a potentially important set of relations between these two systems and perhaps a more complex role in the chemical adaptation to social adversity than considered hitherto (Chalmers et al. 1993; Wissink et al. 2000).

A great deal is known about the control of cortisol secretion in relation to stressful environments. The hypothalamic-pituitary adrenal axis is the neuro-chemical system through which the release of cortisol is regulated. There is a negative feedback between the level of circulating cortisol in the periphery and the receptor regulation at the level of the hippocampus in the brain. Cortisol enters the brain via the blood-brain barrier and attaches to glucocor-ticoids receptors therein. These are located in a number of brain regions but are densely packed in the limbic system and in the hippocampus and amygdala in particular. The degree of receptor occupancy acts as a control signal on the whole axis. High occupancy levels increase inhibitory signals to the hypothalamus diminishing the release of a peptide, corticotrophin releas-ing factor (CRF) which is the chemical signal going to the pituitary and regulating the release of a second peptide adrenocorticotropin hormone (ACTH). Diminished ACTH in response results in the adrenal gland dimin-ishing the release of cortisol. This negative feedback system operates in a loop. Thus as lower cortisol levels enter the brain occupancy diminishes, CRF is upregulated (due to loss of inhibition from the hippocampus) and the system releases more cortisol. This is a highly dynamic physiological process, shown as Figure 4.1.

The glucocorticoid receptor shows polymorphic variation whose func-tional significance remains to be fully determined but appears to be in part controlling individual variations in circulating levels (Rosmond et al. 2000, 2001). Allelic variations also occur in the CRF peptide that controls the release of ACTH and hence cortisol. These receptors may be a target for preventing cortisol hypersecretion found in a significant proportion of depressive illnesses (Nemeroff 2002). There is some preliminary evidence that if polymorphisms are present in both the GC receptor and the CRF peptide, then cortisol levels will be markedly different dependent on the inherited characteristics of these variants (Rosmond et al. 2000, 2001; Smoller et al. 2003). Thus there are individual differences in cortisol levels not only due to reactivity to events but also to genetic differences. Further it is receptor sensi-tivity that is most likely to determine the impact of high steroid levels on the tissues in the brain and the subsequent physiological and psychological events. It may be that allelic variation leads to differences in receptor sensitivity and therefore variations in response to corticoids. Thus the genetic structure of the receptor itself may contribute to modulating the risk for psychiatric disorder via its sensitivity to circulating cortisol levels. Finally

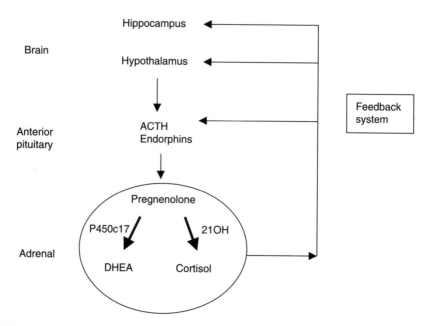

Figure 4.1 The hippocampal-pituitary-adrenal axis

allelic variations of corticotropin releasing hormone may be associated with a very wide variety of behavioural characteristics. These include the psychological process of behavioural inhibition, a measure of impulse control (Smoller *et al.* 2003) and high body mass index indicating excess weight gain (Challis *et al.* 2004). This indicates the complex and manifold functions of large peptide molecules in functional activity within an individual.

HPA axis development, dysfunction and psychiatric disorder

In the first nine months of life the HPA axis is rather irregular in its function and cortisol levels fluctuate rather markedly with no discernible pattern or rhythm. Minor perturbations, such as being picked up, feeding and clothes changing, result in significant alterations in cortisol levels. By 12 months of age there is a marked bio-behavioural shift in the HPA axis control of cortisol (Gunnar and Donzella 2002). Social regulation of the axis is now occurring and a rhythm is clearly established with higher morning levels rising within the first hour after awakening and reaching a maximum apex over the first few hours of the day followed by a decline over the second half of the day to a low nadir from early evening. This diurnal rhythm remains in this form throughout life.

Recent investigations of diurnal rhythm in twins show that the early morning levels are significantly more alike in monozygotic than dizygotic twins whereas evening levels show no such similarity (Bartels *et al.* 2003). Other studies have shown genetic influences persist over the 24-hour cycle and may affect the timing of the nadir as well as the apex (Meikle *et al.* 1988; Linkowski *et al.* 1993). This suggests that there is marked genetic control over the switching on of the axis in the morning but environmental factors exert increasing effects on levels as the day proceeds although genetic factors remain an influence.

As well as diurnal rhythm levels show reactivity to events. These episodic movements in levels generally show a rapid rise in the presence of a stimulus regardless of its salience indicating that this change is related more to surprise or novelty than personal meaning. Levels can remain quite high in relation to the behavioural requirements demanded by the stimulus: for example, to engage in social conversation with a surprise visitor or deal with an unpleasant event like a car crash. Cortisol levels lower gradually as the consequences of the event pass. In general levels return to baseline about 40 minutes after the cessation of the behavioural response. This rise and fall can occur at any time of the day and appears to be independent of the stage of the diurnal rhythm that an individual may be at.

Cortisol and depression

Studies of the HPA axis in psychiatric patients began some four decades ago with the observation that severely depressed patients showed a sustained elevation of their evening cortisol levels leading to a loss of the expected diurnal rhythm. Such patients showed a sustained high level invariably from around 8 pm through to 4 am. This observation has been repeated many times but it is now clear that this dysregulation occurs in no more than about half of depressed patients and perhaps even somewhat fewer (Plotsky *et al.* 1998). Until relatively recently these evening alterations in HPA axis function were considered to be a consequence of being depressed. Thus the HPA axis dysregulation has been considered a consequence of depressive illness. Two prospective studies have now established that morning cortisol hypersecretion precedes and predicts the onset of major depression in both adult women and adolescents of both sexes (Goodyer *et al.* 2000a, 2000b; Harris *et al.* 2000). There was no difference in evening cortisol levels between those who became depressed over the next 12 months and those who did not. Interestingly this change in cortisol cannot be accounted for by recent undesirable events or difficulties so it does not appear to be a reactivity effect to immediate or recent negative social experiences.

A further community study failed to establish a direct association between higher cortisol and depression in adult women but noted a strong link between cortisol levels and an increase in negative life events (Strickland *et al.* 2002). Depressed patients with higher cortisol levels are significantly more likely to experience further negative life events than depressed individuals with normal cortisol levels (Goodyer *et al.* 2001a). These depression-dependent negative life events increase the liability for persistent disorder. Thus the pathological process that arises from high cortisol levels in depressed patients is one which disturbs some aspects of affective-cognitive function that disrupts interpersonal behaviour.

There is increasing evidence that cortisol hypersecretion is also correlated with disturbances in memory (Newcomer *et al.* 1999; Lupien *et al.* 2002a). A range of factors may influence this cortisol–memory relationship including social adversity and a previous history of cortisol hypersecretion (Lupien *et al.* 2000, 2001, 2002b; Lupien and Lepage 2001). Thus a key cortisol function in the brains of healthy humans is to modulate learning and memory (Young *et al.* 1999; Lupien and Lepage 2001; Lupien *et al.* 2002b). This modulation process may have its key focus in the limbic system but is likely to exert an influence on general brain state involving many regions including the pre-frontal and orbito-frontal cortex.

Overall the neurochemical coding for responses to social events and the subsequent liability for anxiety and/or depression may be as follows. Occupancy of steroid receptors in the hippocampus and the amygdala triggers a complex cascade of cellular events leading to subjectively altered mood and organisation of the appraised experiences. Activation and modulation of these affective processes occurs through changes in the level of serotonin (and probably other monoamines systems) in the pre-frontal and orbito-frontal cortex. These interrelated physiological changes in the brain with changes in monoamines as the last chemical step lead to activation of cognitive controls and behavioural actions. Serotonin vulnerable individuals will react poorly to the corticoid driven affective signals arising from deeper in the brain. High cortisol will therefore not be adequately responded to and may lead to abnormal psychological processes and psychiatric disorders. As yet there are no methodologically sound studies in the community determining how cortisol and serotonin systems interact to cause common anxiety and depressive disorders.

Perhaps there will also be further advances in understanding the neurochemical basis of response to stress and the onset of psychiatric disorders via modern neuro-imaging procedures. Combining this technique with functional activation of brain and chemical systems using chemical and psychological challenge has already shown considerable interplay between the limbic and frontal cortex in volunteers and depressed patients (Mayberg 1997; Drevets 1998, 1999; Mayberg *et al.* 1999). These studies are only in their first decade and much will be learnt rapidly in the near future.

DHEA

DHEA shows a very different developmental history to that of cortisol (Kroboth *et al.* 1999). Unlike cortisol, concentrations of DHEA and its sulphate DHEAS vary with age (Parker 1999). DHEA is made by the placenta, so the foetus is exposed to its action. Concentrations decline from the first few months of life until 5 years of age and then rise rapidly from age 7 in girls and around 9 in boys (this is called *adrenarche*), until levels reach their peak between 20 and 30. Adrenarche is separable from puberty, since gonadotrophins and oestrogen have no effect on DHEA levels and the two events are not linked across time. After age 20 to 30, levels begin to decline in both sexes. By the ages of 70 to 80 years, levels are approximately 10 to 20 per cent of a 20 year old (Labrie *et al.* 1997). Unlike cortisol there is no clear-cut notion of how DHEA is regulated. It is not under the tight control of the HPA axis however. Thus although levels can vary somewhat with the rise and fall of cortisol as the adrenal is stimulated to secrete glucocorticoids, there are clearly other factors involved. DHEA has been shown to act as an antagonist to cortisol at the level of the glucocorticoid receptor (Kimonides *et al.* 1999). There is also evidence that DHEA promotes neurogenesis (Karishma and Herbert 2002). This ability to promote new neuronal growth if replicated could be a key neural feature of this hormone. Since as we have seen high cortisol persisting over days is associated with an increase in depression, DHEA may have neuroprotective effects in the brain diminishing the liability for cortisol to damage neurons and thereby decreasing the risk for psychopathology.

There is also evidence that increasing DHEA levels lower cortisol in the periphery providing further support for an anti-glucocorticoid effect of DHEA (Kroboth *et al.* 2003). If this was the action of DHEA then subjects at risk for psychiatric disorders and showing high cortisol levels would also be expected to show high levels of DHEA. This was demonstrated in a prospective study of adolescents. Those who subsequently developed major depression over the next 12 months had significantly higher levels above that expected for their age and sex; in normals levels are significantly greater in girls compared with boys (Goodyer *et al.* 2000b). The possibility that this rise is an attempt to offset the increase in cortisol activity is attractive but requires much further investigation before firm conclusions can be drawn. For example, from the adolescent study there is no clear-cut evidence that higher DHEA decreased cortisol in some at risk youth and thereby lowered the liability for subsequent depression. What is clear is that DHEA is not passively indicating a maturational effect of age but is involved in some active process. The finding requires replication but DHEA is a promising candidate as a neuroprotective agent at times of acute social adversity.

There is also some evidence that whilst DHEA levels rise during the early phase of a major depression they may then fall if the disorder persists. Two longitudinal studies of depressed patients, one from clinically referred patients and the other from a community based study, have both shown that higher cortisol/DHEA ratios occur due to a decline in DHEA levels during the illness and predict persistent disorder (Goodyer *et al.* 2001a, 2003). These findings support the notion that DHEA is rather vulnerable to chronic illness effects and that its decline is associated with a poor short-term outcome. The reasons for this decline in a potentially helpful neurosteroid are not clear. It may reflect the severity of the metabolic strain that a severe illness can produce. Similar findings have been noted in critically medically ill patients where low DHEA levels predict a poor response to treatment and a higher mortality (Bhagwagar *et al.* 2003; Marx *et al.* 2003).

A further difference from cortisol is the absence of any clear-cut associations with psychological processes. DHEA does not appear to be related to memory or learning nor to measures of self-evaluation (Huppert and Van Niekerk 2001). By contrast there is now good evidence that DHEA enhances positive mood and may act as an antidepressant (Wolkowitz *et al.* 1999; Hunt *et al.* 2000; Van Niekerk *et al.* 2001; Strous *et al.* 2003). Interestingly DHEA does not appear to exert effects via testosterone even though it is in the same metabolic pathway of androgen production. Rather it appears to possess direct effects on brain perhaps via its anti-glucocorticoid actions in the amygdala and hippocampus thereby modulating the neuro-affective rather than the neuro-cognitive system. Whilst definitive studies of sufficient sample size are required to confirm these observations, the evidence that DHEA has mood-enhancing effects is compelling. With the recent discovery of a receptor for DHEA it may not be too long before we are able to describe the physiology of this compound. From the psychiatric perspective DHEA looks potentially an important modulator of disorder mood states and deserves to be studied in detail as an adjunct to current treatments, particularly in persistent mood disorders.

Prematurity

Premature birth and low birth weight have been linked to adverse developmental outcomes in childhood. Follow-up studies of such children have noted a marked increase in cognitive difficulties compared with controls born at term or of the correct weight for dates. These include lower general intelligence, poorer attention and greater distractability, more behavioural difficulties and lower levels of educational attainment (Bhutta *et al.* 2002). There is also a tendency for these infants to have high circulating glucocorticoids in the weeks after birth suggesting a dysfunction in general foetal and infant programming of neurodevelopment (Leon 2001). This has led to the suggestion that there is an acquired general metabolic syndrome as a consequence of being born too light and/or too soon that carries persistent risks at least until mid-life.

A recent study has shown that prematurity and/or low birth weight is significantly associated with adolescent depressive disorder with the liability for depression increased some 11-fold in such infants. The cumulative risk for depressive episodes over the first two decades of life is 15.2 per cent in the premature/low birth weight group compared with 1.8 per cent in the controls

(Patton *et al.* 2004). The authors argue convincingly that this adverse mental health outcome may be due to the deleterious effects on the HPA axis as a consequence of interference in normal foetal programming of the brain. Interestingly the cumulative rates for depression were substantially higher in premature/low birth weight females compared to premature males suggesting a sex difference in the effects of prematurity/low birth weight for subsequent depressions. These findings are potentially very important as indicating infant vulnerabilities for child and adolescent depression. The study was not designed as a sex-differentiated investigation and the rates of depressions in males were very low. The impact on other psychiatric disorders, especially behaviour difficulties in males, was not reported. Thus the sex-differentiated observation requires further confirmation. In addition the genetic and acquired influences on the liability for being born too soon or too light are not taken into account. Whilst these are unlikely to remove the findings in their entirety different genetic influences on intrauterine stability, placental function and the possible role of acquired effects such as maternal well-being during the last trimester of pregnancy need to be taken into account in further studies. Overall this is very important longitudinal evidence for a significant infant risk on the developing brain and subsequent emotional psychopathology probably through deleterious effects on the developing hypothalamic axis.

Specific social adversities, steroids and monoamines

Infant stress

Recent research has implicated a role for infant experiences in the formation of HPA axis sensitivity. Animal studies have reported a substantial non-genetic effect of adverse maternal rearing practices on the development of chemical coding systems for behaviour including hypothalamic-pituitary-adrenal axis, hypothalamic and extra-hypothalamic corticotropin releasing hormone, monoaminergic, and gamma-aminobutyric acid/benzodiazepine systems (Kaufman *et al.* 2000). Loss of maternal care through separation leads to a potential change in the chemical signalling processes between the limbic system and the frontal and pre-frontal cortex. There are few studies in humans but a recent report of a prospective study of adolescents exposed to postnatal depression and difficult early maternal experiences as a result, showed significant increases in morning cortisol levels at 13 years of age in these offspring compared with those with no such early adversities (Halligan *et al.* 2004). This long-term association remained even when current adolescent depressive symptoms, puberty and current parental well-being were taken into account. This certainly suggests that early adversities may exert long-term effects on HPA axis function and might indicate one familial pathway that results in an increased vulnerability for psychopathology.

The extent to which these early effects on brain systems can be moderated via subsequent positive developmental pathways in the environment (such as good peer relations in the pre-school and school years) and/or genetic variations in behaviourally sensitive gene pathways is not known. Animal studies on monkeys have shown that offspring who carry the 's' allele of the serotonin transporter gene and are subject to maternal separation are indeed more likely to show abnormal brain chemistry. These animals have been reported as being more fearful and less pro-social than their mother-reared counterparts with the same genetic make-up (Champoux *et al.* 2002). This suggests an important gene–environment interaction in early infancy that leads to a vulnerable animal. These findings are complementary to those reported by Caspi and colleagues discussed previously showing a significant interaction between the same allelic variation and the increased liability for life events predicting the onset of major depression (Caspi *et al.* 2003).

Deprivation, maltreatment and traumatic experience

As childhood proceeds two major negative experiences are unfortunately more common than any society would like. First, *general deprivation* frequently results in low emotional stimulation, a poverty of social experiences required for normal cognitive development and often overlooked poor nutrition. Many studies have demonstrated that these privation experiences are associated with an increase in common emotional and behavioural disorder in the school age years. Severe chronic privations, such as being brought up in an orphanage since birth, are also associated with changes in the sensitivity of the HPA axis with cortisol hypersecretion frequently reported (Gunnar *et al.* 2001). The multiplicity of factors in chronic deprivation prevents any specific associations being made from such studies. Whether social and emotional neglect, poor nutrition, high rates of infection and poor hygiene act separately or in concert to produce HPA axis abnormalities is not clear.

A second major set of events in childhood to influence the HPA axis is that of child *maltreatment*. Here the negative experience is focused on physical and/or sexual abuse of children. Invariably in these studies overt maltreatment is associated with emotionally abusive experiences, such as persistent critical comment, narrow and restricted social opportunities and a lack of a secure emotionally consistent confiding relationship. Unfortunately it has become increasingly apparent that these experiences have significant biological consequences for neural systems and chemical codes for behaviour. Child maltreatment is associated with cortisol hypersecretion in some studies but also with cortisol hyposecretion in others (Gunnar and Donzella 2002). The latter observation is particularly puzzling but is not confined to maltreatment experiences. Some patients exposed to severe traumas, including war injuries and road traffic accidents and diagnosed as suffering from post-traumatic stress disorder, also show cortisol hyposecretion. This apparent suppression of HPA axis activity may not arise solely from the recent focal experience but also be connected either to prior experience or perhaps genetic vulnerabilities for low cortisol activity. We do not yet know but it is clear that we cannot assume that for some individuals very severe trauma has a direct and relatively instant suppressive effect on HPA function (Yehuda *et al.* 2004).

Severe conduct disorders

There is a small but increasing literature suggesting that an entirely different group of behaviour disorders also hyposecrete cortisol, even at times of stress. Children, adolescents and adults with *severe* conduct disorders have been shown to have remarkably suppressed cortisol levels compared with controls (McBurnett *et al.* 2000; Pajer *et al.* 2001). These individuals are known to have high levels of chronic psychosocial adversities but it is not yet clear if the reported low levels of cortisol, suggesting a suppressed HPA axis, are related to a history of adversity, or particular form of adversity, in this group of behavioural disorders. Indeed about 10 per cent of the population at large may have flat cortisol levels over the 24-hour period rather than the more common diurnal variation (Stone *et al.* 2001). The implications of a flat cortisol level in the population at large and finding this to occur in some individuals with markedly different disorders such as PTSD and severe conduct disorder is a puzzle that requires some considerable sorting out.

The presence of extreme levels of cortisol (high or low) suggests a loss of synchrony or perhaps a blunting between the neurochemical signalling pathways within the brain. For example, experimental studies on conduct disordered children which induced frustration showed no increase in cortisol levels relative to age-matched controls who exhibited the predicted rise at the time of stress stimulus (van Goozen *et al.* 1998). Interestingly although cortisol levels remained flat during this emotionally charged challenge test, heart rate also remained flat although the conduct disordered children reported feeling out of control and angry (van Goozen *et al.* 2000). These findings showing dissociation between affective-cognitive response and physiological response following induced frustration suggest a potential loss of synchrony at the neurochemical level.

Repeating these studies using neuro-imaging techniques may be able to test if conduct-disordered subjects do indeed show a different pattern of neural response to controls. Interestingly lower heart rate in childhood is associated with higher risk for anti-social personality disorder in adult life (Raine *et al.* 1997) and behaviourally disordered individuals report fearlessness even when confronted with fearful stimuli (Raine *et al.* 1998; Blair *et al.* 2001). There are also reported reductions in the grey matter of the brain in adults diagnosed with psychopathic disorders (Raine *et al.* 2000). All these findings support a brain-based aetiology to explain responses to social adversity being different in behaviourally disordered individuals over the lifespan. Interestingly there are also changes in the serotonin system in severe psychopaths who show low serotonin function correlated with increased impulsivity compared with controls (Dolan *et al.* 2002).

What does this impaired serotonin and increased impulsivity response have to do with low or flat cortisol levels at times of stress? Cortisol is part of the chemical coding pathway that 'accesses' personally salient emotional related memories (episodic memories, Lupien and Lepage 2001). Low sensitivity to fearfulness may impair the mobilisation of a fear response through loss of retrieval of fear-related memories. Such memories may not even be 'kept in memory' by behaviour disordered individuals. This will blunt any signalling processes to cognitive centres in the cortex and serotonin vulnerable individuals will be at risk for disinhibited, impulsive non-socially adaptive behavioural responses following adverse experiences.

There may also be a developmental connection. The high rate of exposure to chronic adverse life events and difficulties from infancy over the childhood period may suppress or exacerbate the liability for a normal cortisol response to subsequent adversities. Extreme variations in either direction in the cortisol system may induce deleterious changes in monoamine systems in the cortex. The reasons for this may reside in the glucocorticoid rather than serotonin genes. As described earlier in this chapter the glucocorticoid receptor gene and the corticotrophin releasing hormone gene possess polymorphisms that influence the regulatory processes controlling the level of circulating cortisol (Rosmond *et al.* 2000a, 2000b, 2001; DeRijk *et al.* 2002). These polymorphisms may be functional and alter the response to circulating levels of cortisol at the level of the receptor. Thus the glucocorticoid receptor polymorphism may be one (of many) genes determining the liability for up or down regulating the signal from the limbic to the cortical systems following cortisol exposure. It does seem very possible that the level of circulating cortisol varying with experience and the sensitivity of tissue response determined by genetic variation in both cortisol and serotonin systems are working together to effect the most adaptive response to environmental demands.

Immunity

So far we have considered the relationships between the social environment and the endocrine system, but these are each related to our immune system (see Figure 4.2).

The immune system – like the CNS – must discriminate between self and non-self and protect the self from intrusions by non-self. It is responsible for protecting us from intrusions by bacteria, viruses and foreign proteins, as well as intrusions from within the self such as our own altered proteins and cancerous cells. Indeed, Blalock (1984) considers the immune system to be an internal sense organ that recognises non-cognitive stimuli such as bacteria, viruses and foreign proteins, and relays information to the neuro-endocrine system by hormones derived from lymphocytes.

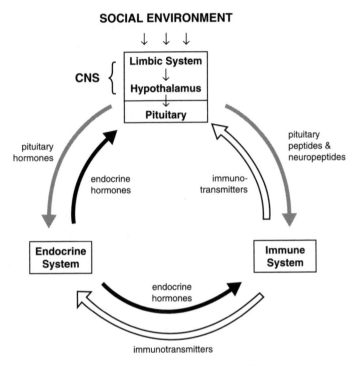

SOCIAL ENVIRONMENT

↓ ↓ ↓

CNS {
Limbic System
↓
Hypothalamus
↓
Pituitary
}

pituitary hormones

endocrine hormones

immuno-transmitters

pituitary peptides & neuropeptides

Endocrine System

Immune System

endocrine hormones

immunotransmitters

Figure 4.2 Relationship between social events and three bodily systems

Immune responses constitute another important link between social factors and mental disorders. These responses can be modified by hypnosis and by meditation (Black *et al.* 1963; Smith *et al.* 1985). In experimental animals stress and separation from parents in early life can both be shown to influence immune responsiveness in later life (Laudenslager *et al.* 1983).

Many studies of immune responses have been concerned with a white blood cell called a T-lymphocyte, which is largely concerned with immunity at a cellular level. These can be subdivided into helper cells (which amplify the immune response), suppressor cells (which down-regulate it), and 'natural killer cells' (NK cells) that are concerned with defences against tumours and viruses.

Immune changes in bereavement

One of the early demonstrations of a convincing relationship between an emotional state and immune function was Bartrop and others' (1977) demonstration that during bereavement the responses of lymphocytes to mitogens (substances that cause cells to divide) was significantly impaired when compared to a control group. Schleifer *et al.* (1983) confirmed this in a prospective study on the husbands of 15 women who were dying of advanced cancer.

Shekelle and his colleagues (1981) associated both depression and bereavement with increased prevalence of neoplastic and infectious disease, and increased mortality. Others have studied both bereaved women and those anticipating bereavement. While both groups showed reduced NK cell activity compared with normal controls, only the bereaved also showed increased levels of the stress hormone cortisol (Irwin *et al.* 1987). Other studies have shown reduced lympho-proliferative responses to mitogen stimulation only in those bereaved subjects with depressive symptoms (Linn *et al.* 1984).

Immune changes in depression

Over the past three decades there has been an increasing interest in investigating the potential role of abnormalities in the immune system of individuals with depressive disorders. The evidence here is extensive but complex, with many loose ends not understood. Irwin and his colleagues (1987) showed a strong negative correlation between severity of depressive symptoms and both NK and CD8+ cell counts. The same group (1990) showed that threatening life events produced a lowering of NK cells in both depressed subjects and normal controls. In a review of the field, Irwin (1999) describes three immune changes in depression: changes in major immune cell classes with an increase in total white blood cell counts and a relative increase in numbers of neutrophils, increases in at least one measure of immune activation, and a suppression of mitogen-induced lymphocyte proliferation and with a reduction of NK activity. However, he concludes that 'the clinical significance of changes in immune responses in depressed subjects remains an unanswered question'.

The depression in NK cells in depression is confirmed by some (Mizruchin *et al.* 1999, Schleifer *et al.* 1999), but only partially confirmed by others. Pettito *et al.* (2000) draw attention to different direction gender ratios on different studies; Miller *et al.* (1999) only finds it in older depressives; Kanba *et al.* (1998) only find it among severe depressives.

The role of interferons

Pro-inflammatory cytokines like interferon and interleukin-2 have effects on both tryptophan availability and serotonin synthesis. Interferons also bind to cell surface receptors and induce transcriptions of a variety of genes, the products of which probably mediate most interferon effects (Boehm *et al.* 1997). Maes *et al.* (1999) argue that this is the basis of depression partly mediated by immune mechanisms. The concept here is immune activation rather than immune suppression leading to excess release of cytokine products with deleterious effects on brain and mind.

Capuron and Miller (2004) show how the pro-inflammatory α-interferon (IFN α) can induce two distinct syndromes: a 'neurovegetative syndrome' of fatigue, heightened pain and disturbed sleep that starts early and a 'cognitive syndrome' of depression, anxiety and poor concentration that starts later. Only the latter responds to antidepressants. Levels of α-interferons are increased in cancer, but are also seen in the physically healthy depressed subjects. Their hypothesis is that their 'cognitive syndrome' is especially likely to develop in those with an increased vulnerability to depressive illness, and reduces serotonin levels.

Exogenous interferons are administered in the treatment of cancer and some viral diseases, which may itself induce depression (McDonald *et al.* 1987; Olsen 1992). Menkes and McDonald (2000) have argued that exogenous interferons cause depression and increased pain sensitivity *in susceptible individuals* by suppressing tryptophan availability and consequently serotonin synthesis. There is absolutely no doubt at all that exogenous interferons, administered in the treatment of systemic diseases, are a cause of depression, particularly the alpha interferons (Menkes and McDonald 2000).

Hickie and his colleagues (1999) in a twin study found that both genetic and environmental influences were responsible for the immune response to psychological distress. This study also examined determinants of chronic fatigue and found that while there were some shared genetic determinants of both, there were also independent genetic and environmental risk factors for fatigue.

In summary, while there are immune changes in many depressed patients, different studies have shown different subsets of the depressed population to be especially at risk of these changes. Depressed patients, as a group, have changes in their immune system roughly proportional to the severity of depression. Immune changes are also important in mediating the relationship between cancer and depression.

It is too soon to dismiss immune change as epiphenomena or arising through non related or even spurious processes. The study of the natural history of immunity (cytokines and other products in particular) in the natural history of emotional disorders must remain a significant priority for neuropsychiatric research.

Take-home messages

- The risk of common mental disorders (CMDs) depends on three factors: the extent to which an individual can remain functional during exposure to social adversity; the extent to which chemical signals are effective in alerting the brain to adversity; how responses are switched off once an adaptation has been made.
- Three areas of the brain are of particular importance in relation to CMDs: the limbic system, the pre-frontal and the orbito-frontal cortex.

- The neurochemical codes that are implicated in CMDs include peptides, neurotransmitters and hormones.
- Occupancy of steroid receptors in the hippocampus and the amygdala triggers a complex cascade of cellular events in the serotonin systems in the pre-frontal and orbito-frontal cortex, leading to cognitive controls and behavioural actions.
- Serotonin vulnerable individuals will react poorly to the corticoid driven affective signals arising from deeper in the brain. High cortisol will therefore not be adequately responded to and may lead to abnormal psychological processes and psychiatric disorders.
- The origins of abnormalities in the steroidal systems in the brain are both genetic and environmental. Variations in polymorphisms within the glucocorticoid receptor and the CRH receptor are associated with: changes in physiological levels of cortisol; cellular response cortisol; and perhaps with psychological processes associated with the risk for depression.
- Animal studies on monkeys have reported a substantial non-genetic effect of loss of maternal care through separation leading to a potential change in the chemical signalling processes between the limbic system and the frontal and pre-frontal cortex.
- The monkey offspring subjected to maternal separation that carry the 's' allele are more likely to show abnormal brain chemistry and be more fearful and less pro-social than their mother-reared counterparts with the same genetic make-up. This suggests an important G × E interaction.
- Premature infants have a greatly increased risk of depression in later life.
- Children subjected to physical or sexual abuse have abnormalities in their HPA systems – cortisol hypersecretion in some studies but also with cortisol hyposecretion in others.

Part III

The human life cycle relevant to common disorders

Chapter 5

Infancy

Infancy refers to the first two years of postnatal life at the end of which there is the emergence of language and knowledge that there is a self. Infancy has a attracted a disproportionate amount of interest throughout the twentieth century due to intense theorising about the importance of this the earliest period of life after birth for all subsequent social and emotional development over the lifespan. The first part of this chapter discusses those components of infant development that are candidates for inducing vulnerability for emotional and behavioural disorders within the childhood period.

Attachment

There is nothing particularly new about the idea that parental, instrumental and emotional management of the infant is a crucial process in the development of well-being for later life (Croft *et al.* 2001). By the late nineteenth and early twentieth century theories of child development had incorporated the basic assumptions that how mothers organised and delivered their child-rearing strategies had major effects on psychological characteristics that would endure perhaps throughout the rest of that individual's lifespan. This relational approach to individual development, and the assumption that these had enduring effects on human behaviour, was encapsulated by John Bowlby's seminal writings on the primary importance of the affectional bond between mother and infant (Bowlby 1981). Bowlby argued that there were survival advantages for vulnerable and defenceless human young to seek the protective proximity of responsive adults, especially when distressed alarmed or in danger. This theory proposes:

1 Particular adults function as a secure base for the infant.
2 Processes of evolutionary adaptation may account for emotional attachments of offspring to such responsive caretakers.
3 Emotion responsivity of caretaker motivates proximity seeking and contact behaviours between the pair bond.

4   Such a function establishes safety from danger, ensures warmth and nutrition and promotes sociability between pair bonds.
5   These processes transmit enhanced opportunity for growth and development not only of the individual but also of the species.
6   Infants are predisposed, through brain-based processes that arise in foetal life, to respond to social cues in the environment as part of this survival-adaptation process.
7   Failure to develop optimal pair bonding may develop from either the caregiver or the infant.

Attachment theory also predicts the growth of individual discrimination and emotional investment in the parent. Thus over the first year of life the infant's behavioural repertoire becomes increasingly sophisticated and complex in its relationship to parents.

Recent advances in evolutionary biology, cognitive neuroscience and social ecology have required a degree of reappraisal and reformulation of the nature of relational psychology and the world of the human infant. First, it is increasingly apparent that early human brain development equips infants at birth with more than an adaptive behavioural system. The extent to which these neural processes are used depends upon the demands made by the outside world. Thus the infant is an active agent in its own development, is capable of a range of responses to perceived variations in the social environment (not just to caregivers) and – importantly – acts as a partner in developing mother–infant relations.

Second, cognitive neuroscience is showing that mental processes in infancy are considerably more complex, varied and active than previously supposed. The form and content of infant behaviour in relation to caregiver increasingly shows levels of individual differences as the relationship between caregiver and the infant changes over time. Thus the developmental trajectories of child development are neither set in stone by genetic predispositions nor entirely predictable solely from maternal characteristics alone. Characterising in detail the infant components, their functional characteristics, their associated neural systems which underlie these functions and their sensitivity to the social world is a major future task.

Attachment and cognitive development

Attachment theory proposes that infants develop 'internal working models' of relationships that serve as a psychological blueprint for interpersonal functions with others in childhood and later life. An internal working model refers to a set of information processes that receive store, organise, comprehend and evaluate external signals in order to produce patterns of observable behaviours under different social contexts. Our current understanding of the development of this internal representation from early relationships is emerging, but remains incomplete. There is increasing evidence that there are marked individual differences in the responses of infants to variations in maternal care. For example, there are differential effects of early parent–child relationships on the development within the child of social competence, feeling sympathy with others and exerting regulatory controls on how to respond at times of interpersonal conflict (Hughes and Dunn 1998; Hughes *et al.* 1998). These variations in observed functions have physiological correlates but remain poorly understood (Johnson 1997; Nelson and Bloom 1997). Thus vulnerabilities for emotional and behavioural disorders in young children may indeed arise from deficits in early relationship building with their caretakers. Modern research has shown that these may have substantial effects on neural as well as mental development.

Dysfunctional attachment

Most research to date on normal populations has focused on describing the quality of the infant's attachment to mother via the use of the Strange Situation experiment described by Ainsworth and colleagues (Ainsworth and Bell 1970; Tracy and Ainsworth 1981). The procedure involves categorising the infant's response to being reunited with mother after a brief separation. Relationships between mothers and their developing infants have been described in two main ways: *secure*, where the child greets mother with pleasure smiles and gestures, and *insecure*, where there is an absence of either pleasure or proximity-seeking behaviour or even presence of negative phenomena including anger, ignoring, rejection or confusion and inconsistent behaviour. In most samples (which have generally been white, high-income families) some 65 per cent of infants are deemed securely attached and these infants also show emotionally meaningful attachments to other significant persons in their lives. By contrast, 35 per cent show one of the subcategories of being insecurely attached inferred not only as undesirable for social development but as a risk processes for emotional and behavioural disorders (O'Connor and Rutter 2000).

Secure attachment is known to be associated with subsequent co-operative, harmonious parent–child relations in the years to follow (van IJzendoorn *et al.* 1995). There is also evidence that securely attached children socialise more competently and are more popular with their peers (Roisman *et al.* 2002). These infants are also more likely to show the types of cognitive development associated with adaptation in more demanding social and educational worlds, including a positive self-concept, good semantic memory and high levels of attention and concentration. These positive outcomes are less apparent with increasing age being probably strongest in the first five years of life. This is because subsequent environmental influences alter the sensitivities of parent behaviours, individual changes in social cognition occur over time independent of interpersonal psychology and concurrent non-familial experiences, such as peer group exposure, modulate the influence of the past on the present.

By contrast insecure attachment is considered to reflect a deficit in parent–child relationships and as such increases the liability for a failure of normal social development in the offspring (Rutter and Sroufe 2000; Sroufe *et al.* 1999). This constitutes an adverse early social environment and its contribution to emotional and behavioural disorders has been a major target of research in child development in recent years. These children are vulnerable to expressing emotional and behavioural symptoms in family and peer group settings and appear to lack a range of necessary psychological components to facilitate close ties with others. For example, Hughes and colleagues showed that anti-social behaviour and displays of negative emotion as well as markedly lower rates of empathic/pro-social responses are significantly more frequent in 'hard to manage' pre-school children (Hughes *et al.* 2000).

These less than optimal patterns of the processing of emotional and cognitive material are likely to arise in children with insecure parent–infant attachments in many but not all cases. This serves to emphasise that other factors in the social environment (e.g. relations with significant others including father, siblings and grandparents) and within the child (e.g. neural and psychological responses to dysfunctional parenting) also have considerable importance. Thus whilst insecure attachment is a general indicator of emotional and behavioural symptoms, the precise associations with abnormal development over time are less predictable, as the developmental pathways of this early social adversity are moderated through subsequent experiences. If these remain persistently or even frequently negative there is an increase in anxious and behavioural disorders in middle childhood (Rutter and Sroufe 2000; Sroufe *et al.* 1999). Note that there is no clear-cut specificity between insecure attachment and the form of childhood mental disorder (clinical phenotype). In addition we are only just beginning to understand the effects of insecure attachment on the developing neuropsychological processes (the endophenotype) within the child. Currently we lack the necessary prospective studies to determine the potency of insecure attachment on the development of cognitive differences in behavioural regulation and social understanding. Thus the precise influence of a dysfunctional relationship with a caregiver on the development of memory, attention and concentration and skills development is unknown (Zimmermann 1999).

Recent neurobiological studies of maternal-offspring relations in non-humans, both rodent and monkey, have confirmed that separations from mother may result in dysfunctional neural systems in the limbic-cortical tracts known to be associated with the perception, organisation and appraisal of emotional and social stimuli (Heim and Nemeroff 1999). The extent to which these are permanent or reversible remains unclear (Caldji *et al.* 2000; Francis *et al.* 2002; Weaver *et al.* 2000). These studies begin to illuminate the putative negative effects of depriving experiences on mammalian brain development and the psychological processes that they subserve.

The evidence suggests that children with secure attachments are better placed to be resilient in the face of future adversities in the school age years through a complex set of unfolding normative developing events involving neural and mental proceses in the first two years of life. By contrast insecure attachment in the infant years may set up vulnerabilities within the child increasing the liability for emotional and behavioural difficulties through childhood and adolescence. What we now need are prospective studies of infants with different levels of secure and insecure attachments to determine how potent this process is for subsequent disorders of childhood. What clues we have suggest that being insecurely attached is a vulnerability for weak socio-emotional development into the school-age years (Murray and Cooper 2003; Murray et al. 1996, 2001b).

Disorders of attachment

From the psychiatric perspective disorders of attachment in infancy refer to disturbances between the infant and the primary caregiver and subsequent deficits in the ability to form social relationships. Thus there is a marked distinction between the broader clinical and narrower research definitions of attachment. The clinical framework for attachment disorders includes two subtypes (American Psychiatric Association 1994; WHO 1994).

- *inhibited*, characterised by 'excessively inhibited, hypervigilant or highly ambivalent and contradictory responses to others'. These infants may exhibit resistance to comforting and 'frozen watchfulness', a behavioural style where the infant is virtually immobile with a fixed stare at the caregiver.
- *disinhibited*, characterised by 'diffuse attachments manifest by indiscriminate sociability with marked inability to exhibit appropriate selective attachments'.

The proposed processes causing these arise as a consequence of abnormal care, a rather vague term covering a range of parenting deficits. The diagnosis is made on the basis of the presenting signs and symptoms, the infant's behaviour in the context of relationships with significant others and with strangers, and the developmental history. An explicit identification of a pathological parenting process at assessment is not a diagnostic requirement. Thus the clinical formulation is able to rely on the behaviour of the infant in a range of interpersonal contexts and not solely on mother–infant functions.

Whilst there is nearly a century of theoretical writings, half a century of experimental developmental research and a major priority given to improving parenting skills in the community at large, there is not much clinically based information on these conditions of infancy and the pre-school child. From the definitions above the prevalence rates in the population will include a wide range of young children who have been exposed to one or more forms of:

- maltreatment (physical and sexual), physical neglect and starvation
- emotional neglect and indifference, although adequately nourished
- negative emotional parenting where a critical and adverse communicative style occurs within a physically safe and protective environment
- an overprotective indulgent emotional environment where the child is not subject to constructive and necessary behavioural and emotional controls.

Attachment disorders may have pervasive negative effects on infant and child development in social, communicative, cognitive and behavioural terms. The social disturbance is encapsulated in the interpersonal deficits described above for the two subtypes, inhibited and disinhibited. Communication deficits are similar to those of children with specific language disabilities and range from poor articulation to severe echolalia (repeating the exact words spoken to the child, rather than responding to the content of what is said) but are less frequent and milder than those children who present with delayed speech (Richters and Volkmar 1994). In severe examples the deficits may even look like those seen in an autistic child. Language development frequently improves after social interventions to redress the environmental adversities, although such individuals often remain socially awkward. Non-language-based cognitive deficits have been well described in children subject to maltreatment and severe deprivation, but remarkable gains in general intellectual abilities have been shown following restoration of a positive socio-emotional environment (Rutter 1995; Rutter et al. 2001; Skuse et al. 1995; Zeanah et al. 2002).

Rutter and colleagues (2001) studied a cohort of Romanian infant adoptees who had suffered severe emotional and physical deprivation and concluded that restitution of cognitive skills was highly possible before 5 years of age with adequate environmental stimulation. The authors noted that duration rather than severity of deprivation seemed to have a more adverse effect on cognitive development. Furthermore these authors suggested that psychological deprivation during infancy was a bigger correlate of cognitive deficits than nutritional deprivation. This is consistent with non-organic failure to thrive data where children provided with positive parenting environments were found to have no cognitive deficits or educational disadvantages by the time they reached school age (Drewett et al. 1999).

From the behavioural perspective the most striking presentations of attachment disordered children are social withdrawal in the inhibited type and disorganised behaviours, low tolerance of frustration and poor affect regulation in the disinhibited type. High levels of distractability and attention problems have been reported in the latter, together with externalising problems as a consequence of severe deprivations. This suggests that disruptive behavioural as well as emotional problems are a clinical consequence for some such children (Rutter *et al.* 2001; Zeanah *et al.* 2002). Quasi-autistic features have also been described in some of the Romanian adoptees which improve slowly over time following restitution of an adequate environment (Rutter *et al.* 2001). These latter children differ markedly from idiopathic autism in that they have normal head circumference and no preponderance of males. These important studies emphasise the markedly diverse negative outcomes that can emerge from severe privation experiences in infancy.

Whilst attachment dysfunctions clearly arise from such experiences equally apparent is that we are not able to predict the form of disorder from the social adversity alone. This emphasises the role of the infant, other social processes and the duration of the pathogenic experience itself as potentially important modulators of the nature of the disorder. The effects on neural systems development in particular remain almost entirely obscure. It is highly encouraging however that reversal of the adverse environment has a critical positive effect on most forms of deprivation and can lead to relatively overall improvements in linguistic and cognitive performance in the offspring.

Unfortunately the evidence is far less secure regarding the outcome in socio-emotional abilities. Thus the social relatedness of these deprived children in childhood and later life remains unknown. The problems observed with social development may be more enduring, reinforced over time by high levels of indiscriminate friendliness to strangers, poor selective skills in peer group formation and perhaps a failure to both read and judge the intentions and emotions of others.

Much of what we know about attachment deficits has come from the study of special groups of infants and children. We know little about this fundamental group of infant developmental disorders in the community at large (Green and Goldwyn 2002). At the same time there is considerable expenditure by public sector services across most of the developed world, aimed at improving parenting skills and teaching adolescents in the 'arts' of child rearing. We appear to acknowledge the enormity of a mental health problem such that we develop social policy and assign resources to prevent, detect and treat putative effects of parenting failures whilst remaining relatively ignorant of the precise nature and consequences for child development, including who is most likely to benefit from current intervention options.

Maternal depression as a disruptor of attachment

Severe privation is complex and taking a number of different forms involving maltreatment and neglect. Maternal depression represents a risk to the child through privation experiences often occurring to offspring where nutrition and general instrumental care are within normal limits. Clinical depression may affect up to 9 per cent of young women of child-bearing age and as such constitutes a potentially large risk for maternal well-being in the child-rearing period (Murray and Cooper 2003). Considerable research throughout the 1980s consistently confirmed correlates between postnatal depression and a range of emotional and behavioural difficulties in infants and young children (Cox *et al.* 1987; Hammen *et al.* 1990; Puckering *et al.* 1995). There is no clear-cut clinical picture in the children who are commonly reported to show a rather wide range of both emotional and behavioural difficulties through-out infancy and the school-age years (Stevenson *et al.* 1985). This evidence that difficulties in the child remain after the cessation of maternal depression suggested a social origin for deficient internal working models emerging in middle childhood. For example, over the early weeks and months after birth distinctive patterns of interaction with familiar caretakers become well established, and the adult's role increasingly becomes one of supporting, or 'scaffolding', the infant's dealings with the wider environment. As well as promoting the infant's cognitive functioning, these parental interactions help to foster the development of infant affect and attention regulation, and estab-lish particular patterns of parent–infant attachment. Postnatal maternal depression alters the behaviours the infant expects from the mother through subtle acts of communication and response patterns that infants participate in. This reflects an unexpected and high level of demand for the infant. For example, the speech of depressed and well mothers during play with their infants at two months is no different between maternal groups on measures of complexity and syntax. However, the speech of depressed women expressed more negative affect, was less focused on infant experience and tended to show less acknowledgement of infant agency (Murray *et al.* 1993). In the first three months of the infant's life, even mothers who no longer meet diagnostic criteria for depression, but who have previously been depressed, may already be showing the signs associated with later aspects of insensitivity to the emotional signals of their infant.

Between 9 and 18 months, the children of the postnatally depressed mothers (boys and girls) were more likely than well mothers' children to fail object concept tasks. The boys of these women also had poorer scores than the other infants on a more general measure of cognitive functioning, the Mental Development Index of the Bayley Scales (Murray 1992; Murray *et al.* 1996). By 5 years of age however there was no significant difference between offspring of depressed and non-depressed mothers. This apparent restitution of cognitive performance implies that postnatal depression per se has not permanently impaired the cognitive abilities of their offspring. This finding has been broadly replicated in a number of other longitudinal studies (Kurstjens and Wolke 2001; Petterson and Albers 2001). The factors respon-sible for cognitive catch-up remain unclear. Maternal circumstances in the affected infants were not markedly different over the ensuing two and a half years so it may be that maturational processes within the infants promoted recovery in performance. It is important to note that cognitive catch-up is not the same as socio-emotional catch-up. As already noted with the studies of privation in orphans and other special groups, there is growing evidence that it is the capacity and efficiency of emotional sensitivity and social relatedness rather than cognitive abilities that remain vulnerable and/or overtly impaired. Furthermore, the more an infant with a postnatally depressed mother is exposed to an impoverished general social environment, the less likely the chances of cognitive restitution by the school-age years.

By the time children of both sexes of depressed mothers reach school entry around age 5 they have higher rates of aggression and hyperactivity (mainly, but not exclusively in boys) and higher rates of worry about self-efficacy and depressogenic cognitions, mainly but not exclusively in girls, especially under challenging circumstances. These children also show lower levels of creative thinking and higher levels of general worry about performance regardless of actual ability. These adverse child outcomes are more likely in offspring exposed to chronic ongoing maternal depressions who have developed insecure attachments resulting in disordered parenting. Thus the sex differences are one of emphasis in the form of the vulnerability rather than a differential level of resilience in female compared to male brains. These cognitive vulnerabilities show up at times of high interpersonal demand, and are indicative of those associated with major depressions from adolescence onwards. Here we see early evidence of what will later become a marked female preponderance in adolescent depression. Interestingly there are no such sex differences in children who become depressed. Characterising the developmental influences that give rise to these child onset cognitive vulnerabilities subsequently activated from adolescence onwards is a key issue for developmental psychiatry research.

An important observation from Murray and colleagues is that compared to controls, when 5-year-old offspring (males or females) of postnatally depressed women are placed in circumstances involving interpersonal challenge with another child that may involve potential failure, they show a marked tendency to make negative statements about themselves. They demonstrate 'depressogenic' cognitions of hopelessness, pessimism and low self-worth not observable unless they are challenged (Murray et al. 2001b). Furthermore these negative cognitions were consciously inaccessible (i.e. they remain latent) to the child and not recorded in self-report or parental measures of current self-percept. They were only measurable when the child was put into a demanding affectively charged environment. Thus cognitive vulnerabilities for later depression may arise in children exposed to depressed mothers but not be expressed in normal or neutral mood states associated with everyday circumstances. It is these mood congruent negative self-evaluations that appear to be most closely associated with psychopathologies in adolescence and adult life.

Early gender differences

Whilst there are clearly early social influences on psychological development in both sexes, there are also very clear-cut gender differences in function from birth. For example, Connellan and her colleagues (2001) studied 100 human babies during their first day of life. The experimenters showed these babies two objects, one a smiling face of a young woman, the other a mobile the same size and colour as the woman's face but with her features rearranged photographically so that it hardly resembled a human face at all. The experimenters were not told the gender of these babies. Girl infants looked for longer times at the human face, boys at the strange object. These behaviours were built in, as it were, and anticipated the greater female interest in human interactions that we will see in later development.

Lutchmaya and others (2002) studied testosterone levels in amniotic fluid of women undergoing amniocentesis, dividing them (irrespective of the gender of the child) into those with low and those with high testosterone. (Mothers have their own source of testosterone, from their adrenal glands.) Amniotic levels reflect levels circulating in the foetus. Thus correlations between foetal testosterone and infant function after birth can be interpreted as a hormone-behaviour relationship within the child. The toddlers were studied at 12 to 24 months: those with low amniotic testosterone levels now had good eye contact and larger vocabulary; while those with high testosterone had the reverse. Baron-Cohen (2003) reports that at 4 years old those exposed to high testosterone now had lower social skills and more restricted interests. Lower levels of testosterone (irrespective of sex of child) lead to superior communication skills, a higher level of language, more eye contact and social skills.

Studies of toddlers at play

Toddlers display a preference for same sex play, with girls interested in doll play and play involving intense social interactions with other girls, and boys preferring competitive play, with rough and tumble and protection of personal space. The preference for play with the same gender is something that children choose to do, without parental prompting.

The male superiority in throwing is seen in toddlers only 2 years old, so cannot be due to practice at school. Males may also be solitary, preferring to play with toy cars, aeroplanes and tractors or with constructional toys.

Girls on the other hand are engaged in co-operative play with teddy bears and dolls in prams. These differences can in turn be related to differences in cerebral laterality, themselves due to early stimulation of the developing brain with testosterone. These preferences in style and content of play are evident from an early age and will manifest themselves even in the face of parents anxious that their child does not acquire only those patterns of play that are 'gender appropriate'.

Of course, once childhood gets underway the 'gender role' thought appropriate by the parents will reinforce these differences between the sexes, but they clearly antedate anything that the parent does.

Empathising and systematising

Baron-Cohen (2002) writes of the general female superiority in 'empathising', by which he means the better ability of females to imagine what others are feeling, which he relates to their superior performance in language tasks and preference for intense socialising with other girls. In contrast the male is superior in 'systematising', by which he refers to the interest males show in how things work, in activities like computing and engineering, which in turn are related to their superior spatial skills. He emphasises that while these differences are consistently seen in large groups of males and females, that individuals in each gender can buck the trend. Thus effeminate boys may display few male behaviours, while female 'tomboys' may excel in them.

The sex-differentiated hard wiring may be indicated by foetal testosterone levels and indicate the way in which brain systems are differentially developing in utero between males and females. In foetal and early infant life testosterone has critical organisational effects on brain development. Testosterone is crucial in making the brain male-like, since without it there would only be females at birth. Precisely how this developmental neurobiology works remains unclear. The degree to which the brain is influenced by testosterone determines the extent to which it may function in male or female ways. This brain-based effect is independent from the effects on sex organ development: hence the individual differences within males and females regarding the degree of maleness (systematising in Baron-Cohen's terms) and femaleness (empathising, Baron-Cohen, 2002). Thus when early adversities are brought to bear on infants, the nature of the response is likely to show sex-differentiated patterns in part because of the neurochemically driven differentiation from female to male brain that occurs during foetal development.

Disordered parenting

Parental style

As children move through into the school-age years, the social and ecological influences both broaden and change through a widening of opportunity for social interaction and a recalibrating of child–parent relationships. From the psychopathological perspective parenting influences retain a central focus in the liability for emotional and behavioural disorders in the primary school age years although peer group influences also exert significant effects on normal and abnormal development.

Good parenting characteristics in the early to middle childhood years are about striking the right balance between instrumental and emotional care and exerting external controls on child behaviour. There is considerable evidence that sensitivity to a child's behaviours, negotiation at times of demand, firm rules within clear limit setting (so called 'authoritative parenting') are associated with adaptive development in offspring. Good parents have anticipatory skills, judge the environmental risks for their offspring, minimise uncertainty and unpredictability wherever possible whilst at the same time offering praise for successes whilst allowing failures in play and socialisation to occur.

From the psychiatric perspective disordered parenting of a depriving or overinvolving type carries considerable risks for a range of common emotional and behavioural symptoms and personal impairments in the child. The exact magnitude of the association between such parental deficits and psychiatric disorder is however not as large as it might seem. Thus a significant proportion of school-age children can present with emotional and behavioural difficulties from families where parenting is not compromised and conversely a proportion of parents with dysfunctional parenting styles do not have overtly disturbed children. Indeed as genetic contributions and gene–environment interactions have been progressively introduced into research designs it has become increasingly clear that some individuals contribute to the onset of their own adverse environments and that genetic effects may contribute to psychopathology indirectly through their influence on the individual's behaviour (Rudolph et al. 2000; Rutter et al. 1997).

It is increasingly apparent that the exact effect of risk carried by parental dysfunctions depends not only on the nature and characteristics of the phenomenon concerned but also the child's propensities to appraise and organise a response to that risk and the interplay that occurs as a consequence of these complex relational and individual skills. Rather surprisingly the developmental influences within children who have been exposed to parental discord on the liability of developing later mental disorders have never been studied. We have no clear-cut systematic descriptions of child competencies in the offspring of disordered parents compared with those in receipt of adequate parenting. In addition we do not know the relative effects of marital discord at different stages of child and adolescent development. Thus the differential liability arising from disordered parenting for emotional and behavioural disorders in 5 year olds compared with 10-year-old children is unclear. In addition we have little understanding of the sex influences so that, taking the same example, whether 5-year-old boys and girls are at the same level of risk when exposed to marital discord and whether any such sex differences remains or change in 10 year olds is unclear.

Overall however the findings from longitudinal investigations show us that highly discordant parenting style alone is unlikely to result in longstanding psychiatric disorder in either sex. Multiple psychosocial risks are needed in the main to be relatively enduring over time to exert large effects on the liability for common emotional and behavioural disorders in middle child-hood (Rudolph *et al.* 2000; Rutter *et al.* 1997; Rutter and Sroufe 2000). Thus the extent to which a rather complex variable such as disordered parenting may act as a vulnerability process for common emotional and behavioural difficulties is best examined by taking some specific examples.

Anti-social parents

Parental risks associated with anti-social behaviour in offspring of both sexes are large and include the effects of exposure to multiple parents, harsh or persistently critical parenting and parental psychiatric history. Parents with a history of anti-social behaviour themselves show a high rate of negative, insensitive and harsh parenting strategies in their approach to child rearing (Smith and Farrington, 2004). This maladaptation is of itself unlikely to be enough to result in conduct disorder in the offspring. Further environmental adversities are required in addition to a high genetic loading for anti-social behaviour. Rather than reasoning, negotiation and dialogue in response to challenging behaviour in their offspring there is a rapid use of negative strategies. Such parents do not show marked deficits in recognising deviant behaviour in their offspring but are unable to set limits, anticipate potentially high risk circumstances or act in non-aggressive ways following disruption. A coercive cycle of negative cues can build up in such families with children in such family environments reporting higher than expected levels of feelings of rejection by parents, increased perception of parents nagging, hostility and blame.

The observations that anti-social parents are insensitive to emotion cues emanating from their offspring suggest that some individuals may have a deficit in emotion recognition and/or response. Recent studies have confirmed that there are such deficits in anti-social children and adults which in some cases may be correlated with suboptimal neural functioning. These findings include a low recognition for sad affect and decreased sensitivity to visual stimuli that contain fear and loathing (Raine *et al.* 1998; Blair *et al.* 2001; Stevens, *et al.* 2001). There are no family studies of these abnormalities so it is not known if the use of punitive and negative strategies towards offspring associated with anti-social parenting are correlated with such individual profiles.

A second negative strand of anti-social and/or neglectful parenting stems from the consequences of poor supervision and low levels of involvement fostering the development of low moral values. Often in such households there is a tendency to condone abnormal, aggressive and violent behaviour that reflects the moral perceptions of parents themselves.

Marital discord

Dysfunctional marriage is characterised by episodes of quarrelling. However, this is a common phenomenon and as such is probably universal. Prolonged discord over days is however not normal and is associated with an increased risk of psychiatric disorder within offspring. This may be independent of the direct effects of disordered parenting. Sadly there is abundant evidence that chronic marital discord exerts prolonged negative effects on children (e.g. Davies and Cummings 1998). Such marriages are frequently associated with parental separations, violence to a spouse and drug and alcohol abuse. There is evidence that children copy the behavioural patterns of their parents and engage in conflict relationships with non-family members. Such children may show physiological changes of higher heart rates and blood pressure as well as greater levels of impulsivity (Lieberman and Van Horn 1998). High conflict marriages also alter parenting strategies. Mothers in such marriages are less empathic and more erratic in their parenting style and fathers more distant but also more hostile in their interactions with their offspring who show differing types of social withdrawal as a result (Harris *et al.* 1997).

Child maltreatment

Child maltreatment is the most overtly negative outcome of disordered parenting but there is no specific set of parental characteristics that predict the violent parent. Physical and sexual abuse can and does occur across social class, intelligence level, religious and ethnic background. Indeed it is a widespread, cross-cultural phenomenon, which in some parts of the world may even be condoned as part of a set of child-rearing practices. The majority of features described above contribute to the liability for physical assault on a child but there is a suggestion that abusive parents are significantly more likely to have been abused themselves during childhood and live in poor physical and social conditions (Harmer *et al.* 1999). There is general consensus that abusive acts arise through an interaction between acute immediate negative events in the presence of a poverty of emotional and physical support to the family but is more likely in those parents with longstanding personality difficulties and co-morbid psychopathologies including drug and alcohol abuse and chronic depression (Cicchetti and Carlson 1989). The most characteristic of personality factors are general emotional and cognitive immaturity in mothers who report a more external locus of control (others are more in charge of their lives than they are), higher aggression, suspicion and defensiveness.

The consequences of violence to children is one of the most pervasive and pressing social policy issues in developed societies. 'Initiatives' from governmental and non-governmental sources have proliferated in the last two decades in efforts to improve parenting and the family environment to prevent maltreatment and thereby lower the lifetime risk for psychiatric disorder, intergenerational transmission of risk and poor adult adjustment. It is too early to evaluate parenting programmes in high-risk populations. It has been estimated that anywhere between 3 and 10 million children in the United States are exposed to domestic violence per annum (Future of Children 1999). Approximately 30 to 60 per cent of the children exposed to domestic violence are liable to be maltreated (Edelson 1999). There is a strong association between maltreatment in childhood and the development of anti-social behaviour but not all children with such a history become deviant.

A recent study of a large sample of young males showed that a functional polymorphism in the gene encoding the neurotransmitter-metabolizing enzyme monoamine oxidase A (MAOA) was found to moderate the effect of maltreatment (Caspi *et al.* 2002). Maltreated children with the genotype conferring high levels of MAOA expression were less likely to develop anti-social problems (see Chapter 3). These findings may partly explain why not all victims of maltreatment grow up to victimise others, and they provide preliminary evidence that genotypes can moderate children's sensitivity to environmental insults. Violence between children in schools and on the streets also carries risks for the development of emotional and behavioural disorders in middle childhood and later (Schwab-Stone *et al.* 1995). For example, a nationwide study of 2-year-old twins shows that children in deprived neighbourhoods were at increased risk for emotional and behavioural problems over and above any genetic liability. Environmental factors shared by members of a family accounted for 20 per cent of the population variation in children's behaviour problems, and neighbourhood deprivation accounted for 5 per cent of this family-wide environmental effect (Caspi *et al.* 2000). This demonstrates the continuing effects of deprivation and poverty as critical modulators in the vulnerability process for behavioural and emotional difficulties in childhood.

Child temperament

The liability for violence and anti-social acts into adult life varies with the temperamental traits that emerge in early childhood. Thus children at 3 years of age with the behavioural characteristics of being under-controlled (includes children who are impulsive, restless and distractible) are more likely at 21 years to meet diagnostic criteria for anti-social personality disorder and to be involved in crime. In addition inhibited 3 year olds (includes children who are shy, fearful and easily upset) were more likely at 21 years to meet diagnostic criteria for depression (Caspi *et al.* 1996). Behavioural traits of poor control and inhibition continuously come up in childhood studies as modulators of the liability for behavioural and emotional psychopathology respectively (Caspi *et al.* 1995). But social factors continue to exert effects of some importance although the affective-cognitive mediating processes between temperament and environmental demands remain unclear.

What is needed now is to determine the psychological processes within the child that mediate the individual differences in response to varying levels and patterns of social adversities from infancy through to the end of the primary school years. There are five key questions:

1   What effects does insecure attachment exert on the liability for later anxious depression and cognitive distortions in 5-year-old and 10-year-old children exposed to neighbourhood deprivations compared to insecurely attached not so exposed?

2   Does the way that early temperamental traits are at present described relate clearly to the psychological processes involved?

3   Should we split up the notion of 'undercontrolled temperament' into components such as behavioural inhibition and decision making and determine their relative effects on the liability for behavioural dysfunctions?

4   Given that the latter components may be more closely mapped to neural systems than the former (see Chapter 4) this would seem a potentially useful advance in neuro-scientific research on anti-social behaviour.

5   How do genes exert effects on attachment processes and neural systems?

With advances in measurement and study design and a greater emphasis on prospective studies involving neurocognitive processes we will be able to delineate if there are restitutive effects arising in middle childhood through development to offset the risks from early adversities. The importance of genetic factors to this restitutive process has already been suggested from findings and inclusion of candidate genes from peptide, steroid monoamine systems and nerve growth factors, as variables in such studies will provide new insights into gene–environment effects on vulnerabilities for psychopathology.

Take-home messages

- Advances in attachment theory show that the infant is an active partner in mother–infant relationships and there are marked differences between individuals in their response to variations in maternal care.

- Compared to 'insecurely attached infants', 'securely attached' infants show more social competence in middle childhood with better semantic memory and higher levels of concentration.

- An 'insecurely attached' infant does not seek close contact with its caregiver and may show indifference or anger. This leads to poor social development with a tendency to more anti-social behaviour and displays of negative emotion. If insecure attachment is followed by persistent negative experiences this leads to anxious and behaviour disorders in middle childhood.

- Clinically, disorders of attachment are divided into an inhibited type where the child shows resistance to being comforted, hyper-vigilance and social withdrawal, and a disinhibited type marked by indiscriminate sociability and poor selective attachments. Provided better conditions are provided before the age of 5 years, considerable restitution can occur.
- Consistent differences between male and female infants can be observed from birth onwards and are related to levels of testoster-one during foetal life. Testosterone is the key organising hormone in foetal life whose actions change the brain from female to male. Later, there are consistent differences in the play behaviours of the pre-school toddler.
- Poor parenting, whether overinvolved or depriving, both carry increased risks of CMD later, but each can occur without the other.
- Parents of children with anti-social behaviour have an increased rate of insensitive, harsh parenting and tend not to set limits.
- Chronic marital discord, often associated with separations and vio-lence, exerts an effect on CMD in the children independent of poor parenting.
- An abnormality of the gene responsible for MAOA moderates the effects of maltreatment: with high levels of MAOA expression maltreatment is less likely to lead to ASB.
- Different infant temperaments relate to different disorders later: impulsive, restless and distractible to anti-social personality; and shy, tearful and easily upset to later depression.
- Exposure to testosterone masculinises the foetal brain and is associated with later typical 'male' behaviours.

Chapter 6

Childhood

The middle years of childhood span the age from school entry (approximately 5 years old) to approximately 11 years covering the primary school period through to early puberty. We have no clear understanding of the social and behavioural roles associated with the physiological changes of middle childhood. We do know that this middle childhood period is one of critical social development. There is a powerful striving for both educational performance and social progress with same-sex peers. At this phase of life the child is passing though a wide range of maturational processes which include learning principles that define moral terms of 'right' and wrong', moving from a self view dependent on the perceptions of others (primarily parents but other family members) to one based on competence (e.g. performance and success at tasks), developing and delineating 'best friends' from friends and acquaintances, empathising and perspective taking.

Contrary to late nineteenth and early twentieth century theory, there is considerable sexual development in both sexes over these years. First, there is considerable physical change, with the inception of psychosexual characteristics, particularly in girls. Second, there is an increase in sex talk, first within the same sex in childhood and early adolescence and second between sexes from early adolescence onwards. These two features set the physical and social context within which psychosexual development progresses.

The components of development in this age period that are closely associated with the emergence of vulnerability for common emotional and behavioural disorders are the social cognitive processes of self-worth, peer popularity and personal competence (Denham *et al.* 2003; Mayeux and Cillessen 2003; Carter *et al.* 2004). Deficits in other psychological processes, such as behavioural inhibition and decision making, which contribute to the executive cognition and action processes, also make important contributions to vulnerability but far less is known about these (Blair 2003; Riggs *et al.* 2003). As a result the developmental associations between executive skills and performance and social competence and sensitivity in this age range are almost entirely unknown.

Self-worth and friends

The origins of self-worth are found in family relationships through a continuing process of being admired by their parents who are attuned to their offsprings' feelings and aspiring to be like their parents without being unduly distracted by their faults and limitations. Parenting styles have been classified according to two dimensions, *responsiveness* (accurately assessing their child's needs) and *demandingness* (setting expectations). Four styles have been described (Baumrind 1996) that correlate with individual child outcomes:

- authoritative (high on both)
- uninvolved/neglectful (low on both)
- permissive (high responsiveness, low demands)
- authoritarian (low responsiveness, high demands).

Authoritative parenting is associated with the most positive outcomes both academically and socially but within some ethnic minorities in western culture an authoritarian style can also be correlated with a positive outcome demonstrating important cultural influences in early self-development. Permissive parenting is not associated with particularly good or bad outcomes, despite a trend in the latter of half of the twentieth century for 'liberal approaches' to parenting methods.

By middle childhood parents are becoming facilitators and coaches in their child's ongoing developmental process. Parenting styles do not in themselves appear to change so it is likely that authoritarian parenting is congruent with self-exploration. Family structures open up in this period of childhood with comings and goings of a wide variety of other same age children who are making social comparisons between family processes. These comparisons become interwoven into family communication patterns and modulate the child's understanding of values and rules. School and non-family based activities enrich the opportunity for social competence and self-development. Differential matching of personal skills to activity choice occurs and distinctive roles emerge that are not a direct consequence of parent action.

The development of friends is the most critical of these non-family based influences. Children take past experiences with them into the peer group arena which can have considerable effects on the success and failure with others in school and the local neighbourhood. One of the most important of these is the past and current experiences with siblings (Dunn 1988; Brody *et al.* 2003). In many non-industrialised communities siblings assume a major responsibility for caretaking but in developed societies siblings have little or no such responsibilities and spend a substantial proportion of their time in sib-pair activities. Older siblings offer younger siblings a rudimentary cognitive developmental framework and the style of sibling relationships can prove remarkably stable over time (Combrink-Graham and Fox 2002). Older siblings may teach skills and monitor behaviour and social relationships and assist in the development of social competence.

The development of social understanding is considerably enhanced by the presence of an older sibling (Dunn *et al.* 1999). Sibs form attachment bonds as described above for infants and parents, and these influence the rate of acquisition of empathy, social understanding and these sib–sib relationships modulate the degree of aggression, distress and conflict within the family (Dunn *et al.* 1998). Older sibs may also benefit through increased acquisition of perspective-taking abilities when they have an infant brother or sister. Sex-differentiated preferences can emerge through sib–sib relations and same-sex siblings show a tendency to get on with one another better than those of opposite sex (Dunn *et al.* 1998). In addition there are crucial differences between sibs within the same family indicating that genetic differences influence the development of sibling behaviour even when exposed to the same or similar parenting style (Dunn and Plomin 1991). This observation of considerable individual difference between offspring within the same family also suggests that there are non-shared processes as well as shared effects arising from the social environment (Plomin *et al.* 2001). At the social level one of the most differentiated unique or non-shared experiences is the peer group.

Best friends, friends and acquaintances

Between 5 and 8 years of age children's socialising with peers is relatively unsystematic, with limits being set by the social structures in which the child finds itself, rather than their own individual actions. Friendships are markedly fluid and dyadic connections within a larger peer group change over time (Cairns *et al.* 1995; Bukowski *et al.* 1996).

There appears to be a mutually reciprocal selection process so that young school-age children discover through experience who they wish to select in and out of their peer group to be their friends, in the main determined by the playmates' willingness to play the way the child wishes.

A friend is someone with whom there are shared tasks and consensus about what those tasks are to be. By approximately 8 years of age there has been a significant shift in a child's ability to compare and assess their own skills using both comparisons with other children and feedback from parents, teachers and sibs. The children begin to rank themselves against the gold standards of the peer group in a number of domains including scholarship, physical performance, popularity with peers and physical looks. Playmates and close friends are now selected through a desire to share the other's time, so that a more complex and internal psychology involving wishes, desires, beliefs and judgements has emerged.

Throughout the 5 to 11 years of this developmental period these rankings are adjusted and altered in relation to social experience and a summary 'report' of self is compiled that is dynamic, open and sensitive to current experience. This multimodal view of self-development is not complete until the end of this period when 'best friends' reflect a positively selected choice on the basis of consensual values and shared interests; 'friends' on the basis that there are other values and interests which are identifiable with and positive enough to deserve engagement; and 'acquaintances' with whom shared values and aspirations are small but where there are social rules or structures (same school, team, related to friend, lives in street, etc.) that result in greater contact than would be expected by chance and there is an absence of reasons not to engage in conversation, especially within the peer group (Hartup 1996).

A marked feature of friendship development is that it is primarily based on the affiliative ties generated between non-related individuals. This indicates a strong biological basis for friendship making and the drive to enrich social experience beyond the family and within an increasingly same-sex population. It has been suggested that the self percept that is constructed within this period of the lifespan is enduring and will continue throughout life to the extent that the effects of peers in middle childhood are more important than the effects of family for the development of a positive self-image (Harris 1998). There remains no definitive evidence to confirm or refute this notion of the primacy of middle childhood over infancy for the development of lifelong stable perception of oneself.

Sociometric studies of middle childhood have demonstrated that there are perhaps five groups of social relatedness: popular, average, rejected, neglected and controversial. *Rejected children* can be further subtyped into those who *undervalue themselves* and have low self-esteem even compared to teachers' ratings of their abilities, and those who have a positive view of themselves, but are seen by peers as both *defensive and aggressive* (Boivin and Begin 1989; Boivin and Hymel 1997).

Children identified by peers as aggressive tend to self-evaluate themselves as not significantly different from the peer group on any characteristic even though they have been identified and suffer from rejection of the peer group. Indeed a negative reputation increasingly separates the rejected group with increasing age. The origins of maladjustment are seen in the formation of the rejected child with the aggressive hostile subtype being most at risk. There is a sex bias here as the innate characteristics of being male increased the liability for maladjustment when faced with rejection. There is evidence for a proactive and a reactive aggressive type of child emerging early in childhood and remaining rather stable, at least over the first two decades of life (Poulin and Boivin 2000; Vaillancourt *et al.* 2003). The precise contributions of genetic and early environmental family and peer group processes to the development of these aggressive styles of interpersonal relating are a major area of research at this time. Early identification of aggressive children has implications for public health prevention of behavioural disorders (see Chapter 12).

The characteristics of within sex peer group behaviours are significantly different with girls markedly more verbal, focused on relationships, emotional cues, consensus and intimacy and boys on performance, competition and behavioural leadership. The exclusion for non-affiliative behaviours is observed in both sexes such that maladjustment can occur for either sex once affiliative ties with the peer group are impaired. Thus a key social vulnerability process in this age range is the affiliative relationship, which if absent or impaired may diminish the development of a necessary multidimensional 'sense of self' required to cope with negative life events. This process of self-development is broader than the more adult notion of a close confiding relationship, the absence of which is associated with the onset of major depression from adolescence through into late life. Indeed it may be that the ability to confide is dependent on the prior establishment in this age range of an adequate multidimensional sense of self, where social competence leading to the approval by peers in general and friends in particular is a major goal. There is now empirical support for a central role of social competence in perceiving and managing social adversities in this age range (Turner and Cole 1994; Cole *et al.* 1999). Emotional disorders with high levels of depressive symptoms are more likely in children with less effective social competence (Cole *et al.* 1997).

Less socially competent children of both sexes demonstrate a higher likelihood of perceiving the environment as potentially undesirable, are more likely to underestimate their competence as evaluated by teachers and show a stable liability for lowered self-competence over time. In this age range lower self-competence predicts higher depressive symptoms (Cole *et al.* 1997). This may be more likely for boys than girls who, as noted earlier, appear to be better placed to make use of affiliative ties at times of social demand. By contrast higher depressive symptoms predict change in self-competency scores more in girls than boys (Cole *et al.* 1997). This illustrates a potentially important sex difference in the primacy of affect and cognition for vulnerability in this age range, but also shows why there are few sex differences for emotional disorders in middle childhood as both symptoms and impairments will arise in males and females but via subtly different psychological routes. Interestingly depressive symptoms in boys appear to decline as they move through into early adolescence (Angold *et al.* 2002).

Vulnerability for maladjusted behaviour in this age range is correlated with peer group exclusions, which in turn depend in part on the quality of prior parenting experiences. Thus the liability for maladjustment is increased in middle childhood for children who experienced disordered parenting in the pre-school years. This is because such offspring take into their socialising experiences inhibited or disinhibited ways of relating that are impairing the selection and facilitation of affiliative ties within the peer group. This developmentally acquired vulnerability process indicates that those with insecure attachments from infancy may amplify the risk for later illness through the increasing negative developmental pathway of poor socialisation.

However there are also likely to be children exposed to disordered parenting processes whose affiliative ties in the school-age years will ameliorate earlier adverse infant experience. There is little prospective data on the transition from pre-school to school years that has examined the restitutive effects of the peer group on emotional and behavioural symptoms. As noted above, there is a drop in emotional symptom scores in late middle childhood for both sexes that may indicate such a process may indeed be important (Angold et al. 2002). Thus our understanding of the origins of social competence, which appears so critical for self-percept in this age range, remains imperfect. We may conclude that for children entering the school-age years the fostering of social competence is not only a worthwhile effort in itself, but may act as a protective process against subsequent risks for psychopathology. As yet we do not have the scientific information to determine if this is in fact true.

The development of social competence may proceed dimensionally, starting with refinement of basic perceptual and sensorimotor functions present from infancy and culminating with the physiological maturation of widespread neural networks that integrate complex processing demands from the environment leading to the capacity to organise a sense of self-percept and social competence. As yet we lack a coherent set of developmentally sensitive markers of maturation of the central nervous system. No such peripheral set of markers exists although studies using developmental 'proxies' such as age and pubertal development have demonstrated that entry into early puberty may be a more sensitive marker of cognitive maturation than age per se and is discussed in detail in the next chapter.

Potential physiological candidates of maturational change in middle childhood are becoming available. These include the hormone dehyroepiandrosterone (DHEA). This adrenal steroid hormone begins to circulate at around the age of 6 years with levels increasing substantially through the first two decades of life beginning to decline by the mid-twenties in both sexes (Kroboth et al. 1999). The functional and developmental significance of this hormone remains unclear, but it is increasingly recognised that it has important contributions in neuronal and vascular stability and protection, and variations in levels may influence the liability for psychopathology (Goodyer et al. 2001a). (For details of hormone and other chemical issues in vulnerability and resilience see Chapter 4.) Peripheral physiological markers that monitor heart rate and other subtle electrical markers of neural activity, such as evoked potentials from muscle contractions recorded with skin electrodes, may also provide clues to developmental maturity but have yet to be applied in a community-based developmentally sensitive study design.

Psychosocial risk for psychopathology

We have had nearly four decades of research in social and developmental psychology demonstrating the very clear effects of the social environment on risk for severe emotional and behavioural disorders (Rutter 1985b, 1994). A key sociological issue is that of growing up in an impoverished neighbour- hood which increases the vulnerability for difficult behaviour in particular (Caspi *et al.* 2000). Poverty is also a potentially undesirable factor in the liability for psychopathology but the processes are complex and race, ethnicity and neighbourhood culture may have considerable bearing on the general tendency for poverty to enhance the vulnerability to emotional and behavioural symptoms in children (Costello *et al.* 2001, 2003). Chronic adversities, including violence in the home, marital conflict, psychiatric dis- order in one or more parent, poor housing and low income all contribute to the overall vulnerability to later mental disorders. No single factor appears sufficient or necessary in itself, rather it is the cumulative nature of these ongoing difficulties that is correlated with disorder. Within this age range moderately acute to severely undesirable life events postulated to activate the 'onset' of disorder appear relatively less important than at other stages in the lifespan (Sandberg *et al.* 1998, 2001).

The majority of disorders in middle childhood do not have a classical onset period, rather they emerge through a temporal sequence of increasing dis- turbance within which the interplay between social adversities and impair- ment is interdependent rather than independent and sequential. Despite the modest role of acute events compared to chronic adverse difficulties in the emergence of severe emotional and behavioural disorders in this age range, there is an increased risk of such negative events in families with high levels of social adversity (Costello *et al.* 2002). Thus there is an accumulation of acute and chronic experiences over time to which the child is both exposed and may contribute to. It may be that one pathogenic aspect of the chron- ically unstable rearing environment in this age range is the repeated exposure to acute events that are, as it were, embedded in the consistently poor social environment. This might lead to some children being life-event prone because of a failure of the family environment to protect them from exposure to negative experiences (Goodyer *et al.* 1993).

Specific risks of middle childhood

There are a number of specific risk processes that have been studied which deserve mention in detail as they illustrate some of the key process issues in the development of psychopathology in this age range.

Child maltreatment

There is no universal definition of child maltreatment but most legal definitions encompass physical injury to the child that is inflicted or allowed to be inflicted by non-accidental means. Approximately 1200 to 1500 children are killed in the USA each year by their parents and a further 1.5 to 2.8 million are the subject of physical abuse (Emery and Laumann-Billings 2003). There are no clear-cut sex differences in the overall levels of maltreatment. In contrast sexual abuse, a subtype of maltreatment, is more common in girls and disabled children with an estimated prevalence reported retrospectively by adults 16.8 per cent and 7.9 per cent for adult women and men (Putnam 2003). Defining and characterising non-physical emotional abuse and neglect is much more problematic and precise estimates are not readily available (Hamarman *et al.* 2002). Child maltreatment has a wide range of consequences dependent on five broad classes of related events:

1   The nature of the abusive act.
2   Individual characteristics of the victim.
3   Nature of the relationship between the child and the abuser.
4   Response of others to the abuse.
5   Factors correlated with the abuse that exert their own effects on risk for psychiatric outcome.

The last set of events may be particularly important in understanding the liability for psychopathology that appears to arise directly from the abusive event itself. Thus correlated social risks such as poverty, parental psychiatric disorder, violent marriages and one-parent family status are all themselves risk factors for childhood emotional and behavioural problems and occur significantly more commonly in the families of maltreated children than in the general population at large (Emery and Laumann-Billings 2003). The most prevalent psychiatric outcomes are acute post-traumatic distress followed in a significant proportion of cases by chronic post-traumatic stress disorder. The likelihood of occurrence of acute distress syndromes with high levels of personal impairment are directly related to the degree of physical maltreatment. Emotion-based disorders, including reactive attachment and anxiety states, arise most commonly in children exposed to multiple negative events and chronic difficulties. The most frequent co-occurring chronic social difficulties are physical deprivation and low income (Sidebotham *et al.* 2002). The fact that there are high rates of co-occurring social adversities in the lives of maltreated children makes the precise contribution of physical (including sexual) abuse to the subsequent emergence of psychiatric disorder difficult to determine.

There is however good evidence to suggest that regardless of the correlated social risks maltreated children develop higher than expected levels of guilt and self-blame surrounding the abuse. This may be more prevalent in those exposed to recurrent serial abuse. The well-documented association between a history of child maltreatment and affective disorders in adults may be in part due to the development of such negative cognitive styles and be more common in sexually abused females (Stein *et al.* 2002; Putnam 2003). Studies of adults abused as children have shown no specificity between abuse type and form of psychiatric disorder. The most commonly reported symptom is depressed mood. Deliberate self-harm and substance and alcohol abuse are also important adult sequelae but appear more common in men with abusive histories (Mullen *et al.* 1993, 1994; Fleming *et al.* 1999). Eating disorders and depression are more frequent in women with such histories (Romans *et al.* 2001). In contrast chronic anxiety disorders appear no more common than in the general population at large.

Risks of maltreatment include negative temperamental characteristics in the child increasing their notoriety and unpredictability within the family. These include poor impulse control, high emotionality, low self-competencies. Family contexts are particularly important. High levels of marital conflict and low levels of empathy with children and spouse appear key in increasing the risk of maltreatment (Emery and Laumann-Billings 2003). Finally as already noted, neighbourhood ecological variables of poverty, absence of family services and lack of social cohesion are fundamentally important adverse social variables in promoting the liability for maltreatment.

Sexual abuse has some unique risk components not common or seen in physical or emotional maltreatment. First there are psychiatric syndromes in adults that increase the risk for abuse in children. There are those, mostly males, suffering from paedophilia – an irresistible urge to engage in sexual activity with children. Second, some adults, again mostly males, suffer with sadism focused on child victims. Such individuals may also engage in physical maltreatment of young people. Third, there are the apparently rare incestuous syndromes, mostly in adult females who develop a pathological desire to fully possess their children. The extent to which there is sexual interest in children in the minds of adults is not known. There are no clear-cut child predispositions. Thus negative temperament is not associated with an increase in sexual abuse as it appears to be for physical maltreatment and emotional neglect. The general impact of adverse social environments also appears less important. Overall sexual abuse appears more liable when children are exposed to adults who are predisposed to sexualised activity with children. Most victims probably only experience contact abuse as a single episode but there are no reliable data. Multiple abusive contacts are associated with a significantly higher lifetime risk for psychiatric disorder as noted above.

Divorce

One of the most widespread adversities for children is exposure to marital discord and divorce. Current estimates put the divorce rate in the western world at between 12 and 20 marriages per 1000 with nearly one half of adults of both sexes experiencing divorce over their lifetime. In addition cohabitation has increased threefold over the past three decades. The adverse impact of parental separation on children is significant. The last two decades of research have established however that the associations between divorce and later psychopathology are a consequence of five correlated risks not a direct effect of the divorce process (Hetherington *et al.* 1998):

- individual vulnerability and risk
- family composition
- stress, including socio-economic disadvantage
- parental distress
- disrupted family process.

All of these factors contribute to children's adjustment in divorced and remarried families. Thus understanding post-divorce behavioural outcomes requires delineating multiple trajectories of interacting risk and protective factors over time. Parental interpersonal aggression and violence prior to divorce is associated with emotional dysregulation in the offspring and impaired friendship building regardless of race, culture, social disadvantage, parenting style or adult psychiatric disorder (Davies and Windle 1997).

Depressive and conduct symptoms in offspring arise in the presence of marital conflict for offspring with and without a past history of behavioural difficulties. Girls may be more immediately vulnerable to marital discord prior to divorce than boys, but this is associated with a higher increase in conduct than depressive symptoms supporting experimental views that emotion dysregulation has overt behavioural consequences even for girls (Davies and Windle 2001). Girls show very high levels of emotional and behavioural disturbance within the first six months of divorce following marital conflict and many continue and require mental health intervention (Hetherington and Stanley-Hagan 1999; Davies and Windle 2001). This time-dependent, sex-differentiated effect on emotional and behavioural outcomes to chronic marital conflict and divorce deserves considerably more investigation.

Boys may however show sleeper or latent effects to marital conflict and divorce. During the period 1950 to 1999 there was a sharp male-dominated rising level of completed suicides in late adolescence and young adult life. This has been shown to be markedly associated with a history of marital conflict and divorce as well as low income (Gunnell *et al.* 2003). Females appear to be less vulnerable to such sleeper effects, perhaps because of a higher degree of adaptation over time to a permanent change in family circumstances.

Clearly it should not be assumed that diminishing divorce rates will improve mental health as there are substantial underlying risks due to the quality of the pre-existing parental relationship. Indeed marital conflict independent of divorce appears to be associated with an adverse long-term effect on offsprings' adult function with lower levels of life satisfaction and higher levels of psychological distress and alcoholism (McNeal and Amato 1998; Hetherington and Stanley-Hagan 1999). Nevertheless the divorce process itself is not easy in an adversarial legal system. It behoves all those involved to ensure that the best interests of the children are retained at all times. Sadly this is not always uppermost in the minds of the divorcing couple. The recently introduced processes of conciliation (assisting those intent on divorce to get through the process smoothly with as much harm reduction as possible) may go some way to minimise psychiatric risk to offspring.

Parental psychiatric disorder

Having a parent with a mental disorder is a significant risk to child and adolescent development. Children are made vulnerable through a combination of the genetic risks they may carry and the more unpredictable family environments that they may be exposed to. Children of adults with affective disorder show increased rates of depression throughout their first two decades of life, greater social difficulties and less effective work records in adult life (Beardslee *et al.* 1998). Parental alcoholism, schizophrenia and anti-social behaviour are all associated with impaired development in offspring and many of these problems may continue through into adulthood (Friedman and Chase-Lansdale 2003). The mechanisms through which risk processes are altered are likely to be somewhat different between adult disorders. For example, genetic influences will vary in part according to the extent to which the disorders are truly genetic and the degree to which that is transmitted. Overall however there is substantial evidence for similar adverse social effects across adult disorders resulting in negative psychosocial factors and most likely gene–environment interactions.

It is important to note however that there are substantial examples of resilient children and quite normative outcomes for many. In addition some children and families can learn resilient techniques that may lead to sustained reduction in risk processes arising from adult mental illness, particularly depression (Beardslee *et al.* 2003). Parents can be helped to build resilience in their children through encouraging their friendships, their success outside of the home, and their understanding of parental illness and of themselves. In addition, clinicians can facilitate the families own efforts to link psycho-educational material about the disorder in general to the family's own unique illness experience.

Violence and bullying

Perhaps a key chronic difficulty for middle childhood is exposure to violence including bullying and crime outside the home. Greater violence exposure in middle childhood is associated with higher prevalence of anti-social behaviour. High crime neighbourhoods have higher levels of childhood aggression. Overall however caution needs to be attributed to the impact of community violence and individual bullying on aggressive behavioural traits over the life course (Loeber and Hay 1997). The development of aggression as a normative behavioural characteristic shows that boys might show continuity from infancy through to adolescence but there are many desistors (Brame *et al.* 2001). Equally there is evidence for a discontinuity of aggression amongst girls over time from infancy through to adolescence and no evidence that children of either sex with low aggression develop high aggression in adolescence (Brame *et al.* 2001). Neither is there clear-cut evidence for a direct relation between childhood aggression and later offending, suggesting there are a number of developmental turning points which exert effects on intrinsic aggression even in those exposed to high levels of violence (Broidy *et al.* 2003; Nagin *et al.* 2003).

Again we see a complex picture on risk for psychopathology with regard to exposure to violence. There is little doubt that it is preferable not to be exposed to high levels of violence in your local neighbourhood. The final common pathway to such violence exposure resulting in offending and anti-social behaviour in those exposed is not clear-cut and depends on intrinsic risks for aggression which may decline over time and through developmental change. When there are effects they appear significantly greater for males compared to females from the school-age years onwards.

Poverty

Low-income families have significantly higher rates of poor health and greater risks for psychopathology in their offspring. Poverty is a frequent variable in multiple risk families and generally exerts direct effects of some magnitude on emotional and behavioural development, even when other chronic difficulties discussed above are taken into account. Indeed most of the social risks involving violence, the absence of amenities, higher crime, exposure to drugs and alcoholism, divorce and marital conflict are greater in low-income families. Few social or public policies in most societies have found ways to eradicate poverty in its entirety. Democracies do have a better track record than other political systems for ensuring that access to basic resources is more equitable and widespread. As yet we remain rather unsuccessful at preventing poverty and its attendant multiple risk effects on child development and psychopathology in a significant minority of families worldwide.

Resilience

By contrast to investigations of risk, studies on resilience have been less clear-cut than originally hoped for. Resilience refers to the ability of the individual to withstand the negative impact of adverse circumstances. Resilience components may be:

- present and measurable in individuals prior to exposure to risks
- increase in magnitude following risk exposure
- emerge at the time of risk occurrence.

There have been many attempts to detect social components that diminish or buffer the consequences of adversity. Frequently these were doing little more than measuring the positive pole of a social process. Thus a good parental marriage, low conflict in the nuclear family, high support to the child, absence of parental psychiatric disorder, positive friendships, all diminish the liability for psychopathology.

Resilience research, if it is to mean anything, should be able to detect processes that are independent of the known risk process and actively decrease the liability for disorder in the presence of known adversities. Resilience appears more likely to be an internal construct within the child and to include appraisal and perceptual components which view adverse circumstances as less negative, problem-solving abilities to diminish effects on the self, and planning skills to negotiate alternative social experiences and diminish future exposure. Recent studies have shown that resilience processes include higher levels of intelligence in the child and good parenting processes (i.e. authoritative as noted above) throughout the childhood years (Masten et al. 1999). Currently it appears that interpersonal resilience is not a special feature of childhood upbringing but a normative set of processes that are inherent in ordinary child rearing. Other resilient processes appear to be genetically mediated within the child with efficient emotion regulation and flexible cognitive competence being key aspects of an individual's resilience (Masten 2001).

Gender differences in middle childhood

Epidemiological studies of psychopathology in childhood have continuously noted sex differences in the prevalence of common behavioural disorders. Amongst children in the school-age years with behaviour disorder there are three boys to every one girl (Ford et al. 2003). There are also considerable gender differences in developmental processes that may influence the liability for psychopathology in this age range. For example, girls are on average more temperamentally emotional than boys and this difference is genetically mediated (Eley and Plomin 1997). There are also differences in how boys and girls relate to parents. These arise from bidirectional influences. That is to say that both the parent and child characteristics contribute to observable differences in how adults respond differentially to boys and girls. Thus gender differences are likely to arise from the interplay between nature and nurture rather than through any so-called independent effects of the individuals' biology or social systems within which they operate (Maccoby 2000).

The influence of parents

We have seen that there are important differences between boys and girls which do not depend on parental behaviour, as they antedate such behaviour.

But parents behave differently to male and female children from an early age. By choosing the child's name, deciding how to dress it and giving it gender-typical toys – dolls for girls, toy cars for boys – they emphasise the gender differences that are present at birth.

Mothers use more emotion words with girls compared with those they use with their sons, and are more likely to discuss positive emotions with them. They may invite their daughter to imagine how another child may have felt. Eleanor Maccoby has described the importance of gender-differentiated influences on parent–child exchanges throughout childhood (Maccoby 2002) and makes the important point that this may occur because parents sense that girls are more likely to understand emotion-focused communication. There are also risks in adult assumptions about what children may or may not know or what their behaviour is like. These may be less sex differentiated than previously supposed. For example, even in positive role-playing tasks where praise for success is given if children of either sex are personally criticised (could do this better, more efficiently even though you did well), they are just as likely to have negative helpless emotions as those who did badly on the task and received criticism (Kamins and Dweck 1999).

There are however clear sex-stereotyped adult responses to child behaviours. For example, Baron-Cohen (2003) describes an experiment in which fathers were videotaped in a waiting room with their one-year-old children. Sons were reprimanded twice as often as daughters. Also, boys are more likely to be admired for not crying and told that they are tough ('boys don't cry'), to be admired for their physical achievements and encouraged to do even more. Teachers are also more likely to reprimand boys than girls and may assume different levels of competence depending on gender (Dweck *et al.* 1978).

The precise role of sex differences in developmental abilities and social behaviour in sex-differentiated disorders in middle childhood remains far from clear. Currently there is no evidence that there are sex-specific mechanisms for emotional and behavioural disorders. Thus emotional or behavioural disorders arising in boys and girls do so through the same broad underlying causal processes. The difference in prevalence appears to come about because in the case of behavioural disorders in middle childhood more boys than girls are likely to succumb to the risk processes in the social environment and possess the internal vulnerabilities that predispose the individual to psychopathology.

Dominance hierarchies

As children's friendships develop through middle childhood there is an increasing interest in closer same-sex friendships and there are individuals who appear as leaders and others as followers. Children of both sexes establish dominance hierarchies when they meet one another, but they go about it in very different ways. In a mixed-sex nursery school, boys are likely to be at the top of these hierarchies, as they are pushier than girls and back down less often. Dominance seems to matter more to boys and they spend more time monitoring and maintaining it. They try not to appear weak, so that they do not lose their position. They use quite direct methods, abusing their opponent, and even trying to involve other boys in putting their opponent down by ridicule and teasing. This is consonant with their greater interest in competitive games, and rough play. In their use of language boys interrupt or contradict other boys, refuse to comply with authority, top one another's stories, or call the other boy names.

Girls on the other hand use more subtle tactics and their dominance hierarchies are by no means as stable as those of boys. They may threaten to withdraw their friendship, or put an opponent down by making catty remarks – but without acquiring the reputation of being a bully. They appear more concerned about the loss of intimacy and friendship. They spend more time discussing who is best friends with whom, and communicating with their intimates and encouraging close relationships. In their use of language girls are more likely to agree with other girls, pause to allow the other girl to speak, or acknowledge what another girl has said (Hartup 1996; Maccoby 1998).

Male gender-typical behaviours are likely to be based on common interests, whether stamp collecting, computing or sport. These activities are often themselves seen as competitive. The games they play are based on rules and reflect the importance of group membership to them. Even with a lone partner a game will end in one boy winning and the other losing.

When girls need the approval of other girls to feel successful it is their appearance, their valued possessions (e.g. dolls) or their personal skills (e.g. ability to dance or sing) that seem most important. The content of their play is more imaginative. They may attribute feelings to their dolls, try calming them down or petting them. Their play often involves co-operation with other girls, each playing different parts – mother and father, teacher and pupil, and so on. Games played with another girl do not typically result in winners and losers, but may be involved with social and family relationships and imagining what someone else is feeling. Thus it appears that girls have developed a more mature mental state understanding than boys in the pre-school and therefore by the early middle childhood years (Hughes and Dunn 1998).

The significance of these sex differences in styles of play and mental state abilities for the liability for psychopathology is not entirely clear. They may become important when things go wrong. It seems highly likely that being at the bottom or low down in the dominance hierarchy for either sex is highly undesirable and likely to increase the risk for emotional and behavioural difficulties. Increases in solitariness, rejection and separation from the group clearly indicate social risk processes for both sexes. Externalising behaviours involving aggression, violence to people and property are more likely in these circumstances in those who carry intrinsic risks for psychopathology reflected in poor performance skills. These will include lower general intelligence, a less flexible cognitive style and a greater difficulty in putting themselves in other people's shoes. These deficits may be more common in young males.

In contrast internalising difficulties involving self-blame and devaluation are more likely in those who carry intrinsic risks for psychopathology reflecting increased social sensitivity. These include self-devaluation of personal skills, a belief that others see them in the same negative light (less worthy, more trouble) and a marked tendency to dwell on these perceived personal shortcomings (ruminative style of thinking). These deficits are more common in girls.

Thus the sex differences in the form of the common emotional and behavioural disorders in middle childhood are not a direct consequence of either sex-differentiated social, emotional or cognitive style but arise through the patterning of all three components. The origins of these features can be seen in pre-schoolers (Hughes *et al.* 1998, 2000) and it is highly likely that these individual differences in ability are taken into the middle childhood years.

Finally there is the question of sex differences in the liability for psychopathology in middle childhood. There is very little understanding indeed of the processes that underpin sex-differentiated risk and resilience to emotional and behavioural difficulties. In the 5- to 10-year-old population the most striking sex difference is in the emergence of conduct disorders which are between three and ten times more likely in boys compared to girls (Hill and Maughan 2001). These conditions do not arise *de novo* but occur in children in the main with pre-existing histories of poor behavioural regulation in the pre-school years. The long-term course is poor and the delinquent and criminal populations of adolescence and adult life derive substantially (but not exclusively) from this population (Loeber and Farrington 2000; Loeber *et al.* 2000).

The origins of the sex differences in childhood onset conduct disorder are not clear. Compared to adolescent onset both males and the far fewer females are likely to show neuropsychological impairments, negative temperaments with high irritability and low tolerance to frustration, and general intelligence in the low normal range (Moffitt and Caspi 2001). The sex differences appear to arise in how these internal traits are differentially expressed between the sexes. Thus under conditions of demand when children are challenged and task failure is highly likely, boys with high behavioural symptoms are more likely to disrupt proceedings than girls with the same levels of parent-reported externalised difficulties (Hughes *et al.* 2002). This important finding suggests that there remain factors other than temperamental and neuropsychological that determine the liability for vulnerable children to disrupt social environments under demanding circumstances. and these are likely to be sex differentiated.

Furthermore it appears that a history of childhood onset conduct disorder is very likely to lead either to anti-social disorders or other mental disorders in adult life (Kim-Cohen *et al.* 2003). This has led to these early onset conduct disorders being described as *life course persistent* (Hughes *et al.* 2002). These are different from those with an onset in adolescence where the sex ratio is 1.5:1 males to females and the neuropsychological profile is relatively normal. This points strongly to different causal processes for these two groups. The latter are discussed in some detail in Chapter 7.

The lifecourse persistent group of conduct disorders appear highly genetic in their origins and social vulnerabilities may be additive to the overall vulnerability for males or females. A study of twins has shown that the most genetic components are aggressive tendencies which show continuity throughout the first two decades of life (Eley *et al.* 2003). Non-aggressive aspects of conduct disorders also show genetic influence but the shared family environment is highly contributory. Severe social privations such as child maltreatment and poverty are exerting effects of importance in conduct disorders more on the non-social components such as lying, stealing and poor socialisation. As yet we do not know the precise role of social adversities in determining the potency of genetically mediated neural vulnerabilities to onset and persistence of these conditions. Again however there are likely to be individual differences in vulnerability driven in part by genetic as well as environmental variations. For example, Caspi and colleagues (2002) have shown that maltreated children with a genotype conferring high levels of MAOA expression were less likely to develop anti-social problems. Again there is a powerful G × E interaction, with childhood maltreatment more likely to lead to anti-social behaviour if there is low expression of MAOA in the offspring. The combined effect leads to a greater incidence of conduct disorders and 'disposition towards violence' in adult life.

The gender differences in early onset lifecourse persistent conduct disorder are intriguing and a considerable amount of research has been undertaken to identify if there are sex-differentiated mechanisms that increase the liability for boys in the early school years to present with this severe behavioural condition.

It is crucial to distinguish between these disorders and children with moderate to severe behavioural difficulties who do not meet criteria for conduct disorder. Such children present with defiance, stubbornness and oppositional behaviours to family and friends and are often observably emotional at these times. Tears, anger and sadness frequently accompany these presentations. When highly disruptive to themselves and others they are likely to be a significant cause for concern. This latter group is large and makes up the majority of referrals to mental health services. These emotional-behavioural syndromes have a much better outcome with no significant risk for delinquency and criminality in adult life. Although they appear somewhat more common in boys they are poorly understood, probably consisting of a heterogeneous set of conditions that frequently do not meet current criteria for a 'childhood mental disorder'. What we do know is that vulnerabilities in the childhood years exert significant long-term effects on the liability for anti-social problems in adult life (Caspi *et al.* 2002). This in itself is power-ful argument for continuing substantial investigation into vulnerabilities and restitutive factors involved in modulating human development and psy-chopathology in the childhood years.

Take-home messages

- Concepts of self-worth, peer popularity and social competence develop during childhood and have important later consequences for common mental disorders. Of these, the development of friends is the most important non-family activity.
- Those who do not develop friendships may have difficulties hand-ling negative life events in later life.
- Children rejected by their peers either undervalue themselves, or are seen as defensive and aggressive by others.
- Gender differences have three antecedents: differential behaviours by the parents; the fact that boys like to ascend dominance hier-archies and use less subtle techniques than girls to do so; and because boys tend to externalise their problems and disrupt social environ-ments, while girls internalise them and withdraw from social environments.
- There is a lifecourse persistent form of conduct disorder but many children with behavioural disorders have a good prognosis and do not become anti-social adults.
- Abused and neglected children are more likely to develop anti-social behaviour, but many do not do so. A G × E interaction may be important here.
- Children with early onset lifecourse anti-social behaviour are more likely to have soft CNS signs, undercontrolled temperaments and hyperactivity and poor performance on intelligence tests. These disorders are more common among boys.
- Boys and girls with early onset conduct disorder both show abnormal neuropsychological traits but under demanding and challenging circumstances boys show disruptive behaviours and girls less so.

Chapter 7

Adolescence

Adolescence is a lengthy transitional state of development through which children mature into adults capable of reproduction. The process is distinctive in its length lasting more than ten years and with variable rates of change within and between individuals. Thus physiological and psychological processes do not evolve at the same pace or with the same efficiency. This marked variation of development is overtly visible with clear-cut differences in physical growth and secondary sexual characteristics. These variations occur throughout the species and relatively independent of socio-cultural influences. The exception is where environmental adversities influence basic nutrition. There is abundant evidence that height, weight and therefore physical and sexual development are positively correlated with nutritional status in both sexes. Attainment of adequate height and weight in the first two decades of life is associated with a generally higher level of adult well-being. In contrast to childhood, there is a remarkable paucity of information regarding the developmental timing and emergence of psychological features of maturation over the adolescent period.

As well as variations in rates of overall development, adolescence is associated with the emergence of substantial sex differences in physical and psychological functions. Both males and females continue to show signs of growth and change throughout the adolescent (teenage) period lasting from 13 to 19 years. Using age parameters for research, clinical and policy development purposes is at first sight convenient shorthand that can be understood throughout the world. Unfortunately developmental science is increasingly demonstrating how unreliable age is as an index of maturational attainment. For example, the central nervous system matures throughout the first three decades of life (Giedd *et al.* 1996; Sowell *et al.* 2000; Spear 2000), a considerably longer period of time than the reproductive system. Menarche and the production of spermatozoa ('spermarche') are complete by the end of the second decade in all societies. In contrast myelination of the brain, which occurs from back to front, is not fully complete until the middle to end of the third decade (Sowell *et al.* 2000). Thus it is not surprising to observe mental functioning in 'normal adolescents' only loosely correlated with observed physical development.

Within the adolescent time period there is a significant emergence of the majority of the major mental illnesses seen over the next five decades of the adult lifespan. In addition there are both continuities and discontinuities between childhood onset and adult disorders that become apparent in the second decade of life. The reasons for this decade being the period of risk for the onset of major mental illness and a period of change for childhood disorders remain unclear.

The nature and nurture of adolescence

Social adolescence

Adolescence is a complex maturational process with genetic predispositions for a set of physiological processes whose outcomes are themselves highly sensitive to and shaped by a wide pattern of environmental factors. Because of the uneven nature of physical development and the low level of correlation with psychological development, adolescence is a period of marked fluctuations in observable behaviours. Throughout the twentieth century there was a secular trend towards earlier puberty, combined with an increasing cultural awareness of sexuality. Many adolescents are sexually attuned even if they remain inactive. Paradoxically with this marked alteration in psychosexual development societal rules have attempted to extend the length of education and restrict the employment opportunities within this age range. For example, in the United States in 1900 a rural economy prevailed with 80 to 90 per cent of adolescents working and perhaps no more than 10 per cent attending high schools compared with the current attendance of 95 per cent (Arnett 2000). This potential mismatch between 'adult type' maturation and 'child type' education is mirrored in the legislative processes of many western countries where 'ageist' contradictions are apparent. These are purported to reflect the need to balance emerging individual autonomy with the need for protection of the innocent and the naive. No one would dispute that this is an important balance and one that requires complex and sensitive legislation, yet there are many clear-cut examples where a 'balance of effects' has not been achieved. For example, there is no country that has managed to harmonise the legal age at which it is 'right' to: leave full-time education, drive a motor car, get married, join the armed forces, smoke cigarettes, drink alcohol, or consent to sexual relations. Legislation is based exclusively on age for all of these serious issues but is seldom the same.

Puberty

The most apparent component of adolescent development is the onset of puberty which refers to the morphological and physiological changes that mark the transition from childhood to adulthood (from the Latin *pubertas* meaning age of manhood). Puberty onset is marked by the pulsatile release of gonadotrophin-releasing hormone, producing increased pituitary release of follicle-stimulating hormone and luteinising hormone that in turn drive the production of gonadal hormones, primarily testosterone in boys and oestrogen in girls.

With the release of these hormones there is a concomitant increase of growth hormone stimulating the pubertal growth spurt. The most physically apparent aspects of adolescence relate to the hormonally mediated changes in physical development. These include the onset of primary and secondary sexual characteristics, marked growth in physical stature, muscle mass and strength and increased sebaceous gland activity. The activation mechanisms for the onset of puberty are unclear but it is apparent that physical size and general nutrition reflect important unique environmental processes. The human developmental success of food rich societies is seen in the lowering of the onsets of menarche into middle childhood and the muscle growth in both sexes by late childhood before the teenage years in diverse cultures. In the industrialised world the pubertal process takes about five years with the median onset for girls being around 9 and 11 years and for boys 11 and 13 years. A critical body/weight ratio and fat/muscle ratio appears to be a necessary precondition for menarche which may be delayed in those who minimise these parameters. This can occur in certain intense sports (e.g. athletics, swimming, dance) and may reflect the presence of an exercise-dependent pathology (Bamber *et al.* 2003).

There has been a steady secular decrease in the age of menarche since the industrial revolution at approximately 2.3 months per decade. Currently the average age of menarche in developed societies is 12.8 years in white girls and 12.1 in Afro-American girls (Herman-Giddens 1997). In developing countries the age of onset of menarche is around 17 years, similar to that in pre-industrial Europe. The onset of spermarche amongst boys is not known. Indeed very little is known about male development throughout the second decade of life. It appears that boys remain intensely private at this time which raises some difficulties for ascertaining a wide range of developmental and psychiatric phenomena and has a bearing on current interpretations of sex differences for psychopathology. Sex hormones also have important effects on brain growth and function at puberty (Romeo 2003). These influences are likely to have functional consequences on behaviour but there is as yet little evidence for a direct association between rising sex hormone levels in the adolescent years, brain development and specific types of behavioural change over the reproductive years (Spear 2000).

Sex hormones and psychological development

Systematic longitudinal studies of the effects of sex hormones on emotions, thoughts and behaviours during the adolescent period have been few and far between. There is therefore a paucity of data preventing any firm conclusions regarding the causal nature of hormones on psychiatric disorder (Buchanan *et al.* 1992). The effect of the timing of physical development on the risk for psychopathology in this age range has been an area of considerable investigation although direct measurement of hormone levels has been undertaken in only a few of these studies (Paikoff *et al.* 1991; Graber *et al.* 1997; Ge *et al.* 2003; Kaltiala-Heino *et al.*, 2003). These findings suggest that for boys early maturing is advantageous with increases in popularity, self-esteem and intellectual abilities but does confer a slight increased risk for delinquent behaviours, perhaps because of friendship networks that involve older (but same sized and developed) peers (Steinberg and Morris 2001). For girls the picture is more complex. Early maturing females have more adjustment difficulties, are somewhat at increased risk for anxiety, depression and eating disorders, and engage in more risk behaviours including sexual intercourse. There is however a complex and poorly understood interaction for females between sex hormones and social context.

Thus the extent to which maturation (hormonal and physical) exerts effects in females is significantly influenced by social class, pubertal status of peers, cultural norms and prepubertal behavioural adjustment (Steinberg and Morris 2001). Again there are virtually no studies of boys so we cannot rule out that similar hormone-social context interactions are equally as important. Recent longitudinal investigations of early adolescents aged 11 through to 13 years strongly suggest a sex-differentiated effect of timing of pubertal maturation on the liability for emotional difficulties (Ge *et al.* 2003). For girls early maturation at 11 years is associated with distress at both 11 and 13 years. For boys the effects are apparent at 11 years but not at 13 years. This suggests genetic and/or environmental modulation in early adolescence on the risk engendered for early maturation in males only. Rate of pace of puberty may also exert effects on emotional well-being. Thus the speed at which adolescents change physically in relation to their peer group may influence their emotional and cognitive characteristics. There may also be hormone effects on the underlying vulnerabilities for emotional and behavioural disorders in this age range. For example, increases in testosterone are associated with greater dominance behaviour amongst behaviourally disordered boys (Rowe *et al.* 2004) but greater depressive symptoms in girls (Angold *et al.* 1999). The implication that the same hormone is associated with different behavioural effects in adolescent males and females respectively is intriguing and deserves further study.

The adolescent brain

Hormones and the brain

Advances in the affective and cognitive developmental neurosciences have suggested that the impact of puberty–behaviour relationships is highly likely to depend on the effects of hormones on brain function over time. Changes at adolescence in brain size and function have been known for decades but the size and magnitude of these changes is much greater than considered hitherto (Spear 2000). Whilst there are quantitative increases in brain size throughout the teenage years for both sexes, the greater extent of these changes occurs in the mid and the forebrain regions involving the mesolimbic, cortical and pre-frontal cortical tracts (Giedd *et al.* 1996; Sowell *et al.* 2000; Spear 2000). Thus adolescent neural development is focused in the main on the major neural systems involved in mental development and in particular with the critical interplay between emotion recognition and responsiveness, executive control and external behaviours. It is this large increase in neural configuration and function and its concomitant effects on psychological processes that mediates the emergence of major mental illnesses. The evidence is clear in indicating that the emergence of psychiatric disorders between 10 and 30 years of age is through the interplay of genes, pre-adolescent experiences and the events of puberty including brain development.

Programmed brain cell removal

A second marked neurobiological event is the loss of the overall number of cortical synapses in the brain that occurs through this developmental period. It has been estimated that up to 3000 synapses per second (out of many millions) may be lost over the adolescent period. The loss of up to half of the cortical synaptic connections present before puberty is believed to affect preferentially excitatory synapses and is accompanied by a decline in brain glucose metabolism, oxygen metabolism and blood flow. It is now clear that this effect of a programmed cell death (known as apoptosis) is critical for normal brain development (Kuan *et al.* 2000). Thus there are subtle changes in brain structure through and into adolescence and beyond (Casey 1999; Giedd *et al.* 1999; Sowell *et al.* 2000). The psychological consequences of this synaptic remodelling and myelination pattern are especially prominent in functions associated with the pre-frontal cortex. These include the cognitive inhibitory and control processes required for efficient executive functions and adaptive behaviours at times of demand (Roberts *et al.* 2000). Some sex differences have been reported with the male brain being overall 10 per cent larger than the female and most structures displaying this volume difference. These substantive changes in brain development clearly have significant implications for mental and behavioural functions but as yet our understanding of the precise influences on emotional and cognitive development during the adolescent years remains unclear.

Physiology of adolescence

Overall it is apparent that there is a widening of a range of cognitions with increased intellectual skills such as reasoning, problem solving, reflection and abstraction; more sophisticated social skills with improved understanding of the motives and intentions of others and a greater awareness of expectations and societal rules; and a more efficient set of executive processing abilities including inhibiting unwanted behaviours and more efficient attentional and memory skills. We have virtually no understanding as to how these general domains of cognitive function relate to each other over time nor if there are sequential processes of importance. Furthermore the influence of physiology and brain development on the rate, pace and connections between these mental functions is entirely unknown. For example, with the onset of puberty come clear-cut changes in eating and sleeping patterns. As any parent of a teenager knows, adolescence is accompanied by a tendency to fall asleep later and wake up later. On average 10 to 12-year-old children sleep approximately 9.3 hours a night and awake spontaneously. In contrast, the mean length of sleep for high school students is 7.5 hours with as many as 20 per cent sleeping less than 6 hours. Adolescents in general suffer from daytime drowsiness which may impair cognitive functions, whereas children do not (King 2002). Whilst there is a natural tendency amongst adults to blame teenage daytime behaviour for these sleep alterations, part of these are a consequence of normative biological change associated with physical maturation.

Cognitive changes

Adolescence is marked psychologically by a change in thinking processes characterised by the attainment of the ability to construct contrary to fact propositions, a growth in hypothetic deductive reasoning and problem solving and understanding the propositions of logic and probability (King 2002). The passions are often more intense with interests often taken on with a substantial level of enthusiasm, interest and energy. There is a growing thinking complexity associated with an increased speed of information processing. Perspective taking and considering the views of others is accompanied by a decline in childhood egocentrism. Notions of rights, social order, moral values all expand and idealism frequently develops with regard to social values and principles.

The rapid development of such a complex set of processing often leads to difficulties in assimilation. Both emotion and cognitive processing outstrip the capacity to comprehend and make sense of all these new inputs and for some adolescents this can lead to behavioural styles that are maladaptive in the long term. These can include the rigid embracing of ideologies (political, religious, pseudo-philosophy, nihilism) or the rejection of their social context turning to high risk behaviours as a 'lifestyle choice'. For the vast majority however this period is marked by intensity, change, impulsivity, social engagement and high intellectual achievement that is more often than not a joy to watch and leads many adults to wistful reminiscences of their own youth.

Psychiatric implications of adolescence

The maturational period of adolescence appears actively to moderate the liability for psychiatric disorders in at least four ways:

1   Normal maturational processes (physiological, psychological and social) can act to resolve processes that caused childhood disorders, leading to recovery. A substantial number of separation disorders, social phobias and mixed emotion/behaviour disorders can resolve in this manner. This is termed normative restitution.
2   Maturational processes modify the form of disorder, but causal processes and the risk for psychiatric illness continue. For example, anxiety disorders in childhood often pre-date depressive disorders in adolescence and psychoses are more common in adolescents with a history of childhood neuro-developmental disorders. This is termed *heterotypic continuity* implying a change of clinical signs and symptoms but a persistent risk for psychopathology not resolved by adolescent changes.
3   Maturational processes have no effect on the form or risk for childhood disorder which continues through the adolescent years with the same characteristics as during childhood. Some individuals with obsessive compulsive disorder or Tourette's syndrome are examples, as are autism and Asperger's syndrome. This is termed homotypic continuity.
4   Disorder is made more difficult through a widening of risks due to internal biological changes or because environmental opportunities for deviancy are increased. For example, autistic states may be made worse in adolescence with the onset of epilepsy. Behaviour disorders may develop a wider range of anti-social activity due to neighbourhood opportunity for stealing and vandalism. This can be considered as heterotypic expansion.

Adolescents with a history of childhood psychiatric disorder also have an increased risk for further psychiatric disorders during adolescence and young adult life (Arseneault *et al.* 2003; Kim-Cohen *et al.* 2003). Equally there are many adults who develop psychopathology with no history of childhood mental illness.

Adolescent influences on childhood emotional and behavioural disorders

As noted in Chapter 5, early onset *emotion and behavioural disorders* are invariably associated with parenting difficulties and marital disagreements about child rearing. The origins of these disorders are therefore found in the family environment and many undergo restitution with family guidance assisted by normal child development. In most circumstances the children do not posses 'intrinsic' deficits and continuity of behavioural difficulties is therefore unlikely. Recovery is associated with the restitution of the family environment allowing the child to return to a normal developmental trajectory. Adolescence appears to convey no particular effects good or bad for these forms of behavioural disorder. There is however a proportion of children who move into adolescence with persistent behavioural disorder. These tend to occur when there are chronic dysfunctions in family structure and/or function. These maladjusted adolescents make-up a substantial component of teenage psychiatric morbidity in the community and are invariably correlated with one or more of three family-focused difficulties: parental separation and divorce, parental psychiatric disorder and economic hardship. Acute negative family events such as sudden bereavement may also exert significant understandable effects on well-being but seldom in the absence of another form of social difficulty. An exception is when in rare circumstances children are exposed to multiple bereavements over the childhood years when the risk for emotional and behavioural disorders appears to be substantially increased (Goodyer and Altham 1991).

Overall mild to moderate behavioural disorders that persist through into adolescence do so because of chronic unremitting family adversities and are likely to be referred to clinical services (Verhulst and van der Ende 1997). Such children on average have somewhat lower general level of cognitive abilities than the population at large (Goodman 1995) suggesting that they may be somewhat less well equipped personally to deal with environmental hazards. These youngsters are at risk for adolescent difficulties due to the combination of less personal ability, poor family-based behavioural controls and a widening of environmental opportunities for deviancy. Maturational restitution may occur in those with somewhat better cognate functions and parents who develop or improve their abilities to parent adolescents compared to children. Whilst considerable attention has been paid to parenting styles for infants and young children, little is known about parenting styles and functions from middle childhood through the adolescent family life cycle phase.

In contrast to the restitution by adolescence of *oppositional defiant disorders* arising in early and middle childhood severe persisting behavioural syndromes are associated with a poor prognosis. Continuity into adolescence is invariably associated with a persistence of anti-social activity and a widening of deviant forms of behaviour. Criminality, alcohol and substance misuse are frequent. The cost to society is high with extensive psychiatric resources devoted throughout the first two decades of life often involving social services over the long term and in many cases, special needs education facilities. A striking feature of severe early onset conduct disorder is the relative lack of moderating effects of maturation on the natural history of the condition. Despite the neuro-cognitive changes through adolescence, a majority of these cases show the same core clinical features into adult life (Moffitt and Caspi 2001; Moffitt *et al.* 2002). This has led researchers to investigate the possibility that adaptive maturational changes in the brain do not occur to the same degree in such individuals. There is now good evidence for the brain structures and functions in adults with severe psychopathic traits and anti-social behaviours in childhood indeed to be abnormal (Bassarath 2001; Raine *et al.* 2000). This indicates that early onset disorders of this nature have suffered disruptions to brain development in early life or in utero through as yet unidentified genetic and/or environmental factors. This is an unfortunate and unusual example of neuro-developmental resistance to maturational change in the adolescent years.

Children of either gender who manifest persistent anti-social behaviour (ASB) into adolescence are more likely to form friendships with others who have criminal records or attitudes that encourage. They are more likely to form sexual relationships with partners who are poor readers with little education and who abuse them physically. These factors make it more likely that both partners will be involved in illegal behaviour in adulthood. They are also more likely to reproduce at an early age, with an anti-social mate (Moffitt and Caspi 2001; Moffitt *et al.* 2002).

Adolescent onset behaviour disorders

A second group of adolescents engaging in delinquency and violent behaviour arises from those with minor or no childhood difficulties (Moffitt and Caspi 2001). There is significantly less liability for these adolescent onset behaviour disorders to run in families. Onset of anti-social behaviour is closely associated with membership of a changing and often deviant peer group but is not associated with marked intrinsic psychological difficulties in emotion processing or cognitive performance (Moffitt *et al.* 2002). These young people are not markedly underperforming educationally and their anti-social acts may be less solitary than similar acts in childhood onset cases. The latter suggests a powerful effect of affiliative ties with a deviant peer group that drives the increase in anti-social activity. Rather than a disinterest in the views of others as appears to be common in childhood onset conduct disorder, adolescent onset may be occurring in part because of the desire to be the same as the peer group and be respected by them and share the same values. It is of interest that adolescent onset disorders also show an almost equal sex ratio (1.5 males:1 female) with a natural history that is developmentally sensitive as the majority, but not all, 'recover' through their twenties. Thus maturational changes in the second decade of life do exert effects on the risk for persistence in these adolescent onset cases.

One crucial aspect of maturation is the development of a confiding relationship with a non-deviant other. This romantic tie may well ameliorate the impact of the more deviant adolescent peer group. Thus difficult adolescents can move out of their deviant peer group through the development of non-deviant close personal affiliative ties with the same or opposite sex. Approximately one in four of these adolescent onset conduct disorders have not desisted by their twenties. These youngsters may have high levels of aggression present throughout childhood but constrained by parenting and school factors. Studies of aggression suggest that an aggressive behavioural style does not increase significantly in adolescent onset behavioural disorders beyond that present in childhood (Broidy et al. 2003; Nagin et al. 2003). This appears to be particularly true for boys. High aggressive male children are likely to remain high aggressive adolescents although it is not clear if this trait desists in adult life. There is no evidence that low aggressive children become high aggressive adolescents or adults. Thus the emergence of adolescent onset behavioural disorders is unlikely to be due to developmentally mediated increases in aggressive tendencies in youth.

The social environment is key in moderating the effects of an aggressive style present in the childhood years (Loeber and Hay 1997). If highly aggressive children were protected by strong parenting in the first decade of life adolescent maturation may paradoxically act as a socially releasing risk process on this longstanding vulnerability. Such adolescents as they widen their social group are no longer protected by external family controls on behaviour and socialisation or on school culture to moderate aggressive playground behaviour. It appears likely that the majority of persistent adolescent onset cases are male and that females make-up the majority of those with sporadic deviancy that recovers by young adult life.

As with child onset forms, the role of acute threatening life events (regardless of their psychological characteristics) seems somewhat less important than the ongoing negative influence of the deviant peer group. For the majority of behavioural disorders in childhood and some anxious emotional disorders, acutely threatening life events do not exert a marked causal effect on onset once more longstanding difficulties have been taken into account (Sandberg et al. 2001). Perhaps not surprisingly, the physical and social quality of the local neighbourhood is a significant predictor for adolescent deviant behaviour, as is the close proximity to a peer group with criminal records and the availability and opportunity for serious drug misuse (Caspi et al. 2000). Improving the social ecology of schools, neighbourhoods and housing, diminishing the availability of illegal drugs and preventing crime are the key issues for producing a discernible downturn in the prevalence of adolescent deviant behaviour. This is because it will diminish the social risk elements that interact with predisposing factors such as high aggressive style and negative undercontrolled temperaments (Caspi *et al.* 1995, 1996) that predisposed individuals to poor resilience in the face of social adversity.

These laudable goals do seem very difficult to achieve, especially in the most affluent and democratic societies where individual choice and personal freedom currently have clear-cut priority over collective goals and social management of behaviour.

By contrast to a positive social policy for adolescent onset cases, there is little evidence that childhood onset deviants with a high degree of callousness, impulsivity, low empathy and poor motivation for personal change could benefit from voluntary social programmes. For these individuals there is a need for policies that can reduce the risk of harm to others and diminish the liability for their exposure to provoking factors such as drug misuse.

Recent longitudinal data has reported a novel correlate with a gene expressed in all tissues including the brain that codes for a key enzyme, monoamine oxidase, involved in the breakdown of key amines (serotonin, noradrenaline and dopamine) involved in psychological processing of social events (see Chapter 4 on neurochemistry for details of amines in the brain). The findings show that a genotype conferring high levels of MAOA expression resulting in rapid change of amines in the brain and who were the victims of maltreatment in childhood were less likely to develop anti-social problems than those with low MAOA levels and similar histories (Caspi *et al.* 2002). These findings may partly explain why not all victims of maltreatment grow up to victimise others. They also provide epidemiological evidence that genotypes can moderate children's sensitivity to environmental insults and thereby contribute to risk.

Adolescent onset emotional disorders

Adolescent onset emotional disorders consist of two forms:

1   *Anxiety disorders*: characterised by core features of fearfulness over objects or people, general worry about social image or performance and physiological symptoms invariably consisting of increased heart rate, sweating and feelings of faintness in association with fear and worry.
2   *Depressive disorders*: characterised by negative moods of unpleasantness (dysphoria), irritability and/or absence of pleasure (anhedonia), critical and devaluative thoughts about the self, impaired concentration and attention and physical symptoms of tiredness, lethargy.

The most common emotional disorders that emerge during the adolescent years are the depressive conditions (Angold and Costello 2001). Over the whole of the first two decades of life anxiety disorders are however much more common than depression. This is because depressions are rare before the teenage years and the overall prevalence of anxiety disorders remains broadly unchanged although the form changes with development (Klein and Pine 2003).

As children progress through adolescence rates of separation anxiety disorders decline but social anxiety disorders rise. Longitudinal study of phobic states from early to late adolescence has shown that clinical phobias (simple, social and clear-cut agoraphobia) are markedly persistent from early to late adolescence but mild subclinical states tend to improve (Tocharoen *et al.* 2000). Whilst in the child fear and worry promote avoidance of the stimulus and proximity-seeking behaviour to the main caregiver, by adolescence the same emotions engender social avoidance from both the stimulus and caregiver. The changes during adolescence in peer group structure and functions (increasing socialisation, friendship selection, competition and conflict with same and opposite sex) exert new demands on social behaviour. Thus adolescent emergent anxiety disorders become an expression of trying to avoid the onset of highly discomforting physiological feelings provoked by cognitive appraisal of social demands on the self. The latter generate thoughts of social difficulty and the impact of embarrassment. In achievement situations (exams, sports and work performance) the adolescent worry is associated with a fear of failure. This may be a distortion of the likely outcome based on an internal set of high standards regardless of the individual's ability or standing. Alternatively it may reflect a realistic appraisal of competencies and abilities in relation to expectations of others (teachers, peer group or parents).

The precise pre-existing vulnerabilities that we might use to delineate the subset of adolescents who are going to fail to cope with these new developmentally mediated social demands are not clear-cut. Those with childhood psychiatric histories or families with high levels of emotional disorders are considerably more at risk (Boer and Lindhout 2001). Children with shy temperaments, insecure relations with their parents and a high level of wariness to other children in the pre-school years are markedly vulnerable to these conditions in later life although the form may vary (Caspi *et al.* 1996). There is also evidence that there is a strong genetic influence on the predisposition for these anxiety states partly explaining the familial aggregation (Thapar and McGuffin 1997).

Their childhood clinical characteristics are remodelled in the teenage years as the normative effects of maturation increase the demands for more complex social behaviours and decrease the drive to stay close to parent figures. (This should not be confused with normative contact with parents which is variable but continuous throughout life and remains marked in most societies, developed and developing.) Thus instead of shaping their behaviours through new and difficult but normal social interactions these adolescents increase their worries and anxieties. Exactly how these early vulnerabilities lead to severe social anxiety disorders following adolescent maturation remains unclear. What is apparent is that for some children with a prior history of childhood anxiety disorders adolescent maturational change can act as a destabilising rather than a restitutive process on overall mental health.

Social causation not mediated by maturation

By contrast to the impact of maturation severe social adversities in the teenage years have the ability to destabilise adolescents with no prior psychopathology or biological risk process (although these may also be present). Family breakdown through divorce or leaving the home because of intolerable family relationships is a major source of risk for subsequent social decline and mental illness. The event of an adolescent leaving the family home is seldom, if ever, due to a single acute negative experience with a parent. In almost all circumstances it is a cumulative set of chronic ongoing adversities that directly impact on the offspring. A longstanding history of poor or no confiding relations with a parent, a history of physical maltreatment, sexual abuse and emotional neglect, is common and invariably originates early in childhood rather than the adolescent years (see Chapter 6 for a discussion of maltreatment events as risk processes for psychopathology). The role of acute life events is less clear but emotional and behavioural syndromes are extremely common in this group. For example, chronic unremitting low mood and negative thoughts about themselves the world and the future are unsurprising in runaway adolescents. Exposure to deviant experiences is common and the peer group developments liable to be with criminal and anti-social elements. Sexual exploitation and low educational attainment are frequent as is a high suicide rate, especially within institutions for young offenders and prisons.

It is likely that some of these chronic emotional deprived and neglected adolescents who develop emotional syndromes are genetically vulnerable via indirect effects on general emotional and cognitive development. Perhaps through the known genetic predispositions (Kendler *et al.* 1992c) they may be generally socially less competent than their peers. Thus intrinsically poor social skills and ineffective decision making may be dominated by an overwhelming desire to retain friends at any cost, an intense style of relating to others, preparedness to be exploited in order to retain intimate relationships and social approval and an overly sensitive perception of what others think of them. These facets of social cognition and behaviour are markedly different to those with a low emotional sensitivity, high callousness and disinterest in emotional relations seen in adolescents with a history of early onset conduct disorders in children. The key mental health policy issues are overwhelmingly social and require collective efforts to improve family relations, ensure the safety and protection of runaways and engage them in well-being programmes to prevent the aforementioned risks from overtaking their vulnerable lives.

Emergence of depressive disorders in adolescence

The depressive disorders show a marked increase in prevalence between the ages of 13 and 16 years which continues to rise through the adolescent period into young adult life with a 2:1 ratio in favour of females (Angold and Costello 2001). The precise processes that result in an increase in depressions in the adolescent period remain unclear. There are two broad sets of vulnerabilities involved. First, genetic predispositions and early environmental adversities in infancy and early childhood (distal processes) increase the overall liability for emotional and behavioural disorders in general. We remain ignorant of the specific genes or early environments that are involved or how they operate. Second, adolescent development involving physical and psychological maturation (proximal processes) and the role of adverse factors in the non-familial environment (peers, friends, school experiences) result in the emergence of the specific clinical phenotype. By and large most of our understanding of depressions in general in this age range arises from the study of major unipolar depression, a relatively severe depressive disorder.

Distal processes

There is substantial evidence that genetic factors are important in the overall liability for developing depression in adolescence but not children (Thapar and McGuffin 1997; Rice *et al.* 2002). This developmental distinction in genetic vulnerability is one of the important clues that points to a causal difference between depressions with the same clinical signs and symptoms occurring at different periods in the life cycle (homotypic but discontinuous – same clinical features for different causal reasons). All depressions in childhood are uncommon (around 0.5 per cent in the child community at large) and occur equally in both males and females. In contrast all depressions by 16 years of age are more frequent. Major unipolar depression is around 3 per cent in the adolescent community at large and more moderate and minor forms about a further 9 per cent (Angold and Costello 2001; Cooper and Goodyer 1993). There are twice as many females as males in general although this sex difference is less amongst severe cases. Twin studies have shown that anxiety and depression may share the same genes but arise because of exposure to different types of adverse environments (Kendler *et al.* 1992c). Thus the period of adolescence contains the distinctive processes that result in major depression emerging in those with the underlying distal vulnerabilities for emotional disorders.

We have already noted that major social adversities involving family breakdown, maltreatment and a history of psychiatric disorder increase the general liability for psychopathology across childhood and adolescence. A specific environmental process that increases adolescent onset depression has yet to be specified. Maternal postnatal depression (PND) has been studied closely as a 'candidate' depressogenic environment in infant life. Certainly the offspring of PND appear more vulnerable for emotional and behavioural disorders in middle childhood but as yet we do not know if there is a differential increase in the liability for depressions in the adolescent years (Murray and Sines 1996; Murray et al. 1996). Child sexual abuse has also been proposed as a 'candidate adversity' for subsequent major depression but there is no evidence to support a direct and specific link between abuse experiences in childhood and depression in adolescence. There is no doubt that maltreatment experiences are associated with subsequent depression but they appear to operate in association with other early environmental adversities such as poor marriage, neglect and disinterest in offspring, parental psychiatric history and family dysfunctions (Bifulco et al. 1991, 2002).

Clues that there are important gene–environment interactions for depressions in the postpubertal years are beginning to emerge. For example, a functional polymorphism in the promoter region of the serotonin transporter (5HTT) gene was found to moderate the influence of stressful life events on depression (Caspi et al. 2003). There are two copies of this allele a long (l) and a short (s). Thus the serotonin transporter promoter will vary between individuals who may have inherited the s/s, s/l or l/l forms from their parents. Overall individuals possessing an s allele (s/s or s/l) are twice as likely to develop depression when exposed to a recent stressful life event compared with those homozygous for the l form (Caspi et al. 2003). This epidemiological study thus provides evidence of a gene-by-environment interaction, in which an individual's response to environmental insults is moderated by his or her genetic make-up.

Proximal processes

In teenagers of both sexes recent life events or difficulties are important but only in about 50 per cent of new onset cases (Goodyer et al. 2000a, 2000b). Nearly all onsets (>95 per cent) occur in adolescents with two or more longstanding psychosocial adversities involving family breakdown, marital disharmony, previous multiple losses of important others, parental psychiatric disorder and personal disappointments mostly from within their peer group. Half of these develop depression with no further recent negative experiences. These disorders appear to emerge relatively slowly over weeks and months in high risk teenagers of either sex. It seems likely that very proximal undesirable and disappointing events are important in adolescent depression, especially in first episodes (Lewinsohn et al. 1999; Monroe et al. 1999). Clearly however they are neither necessary nor sufficient in all such cases whereas ongoing chronic social environments and/or a family history of affective psychopathology are invariably present. Bringing together distal and proximal risk processes in new investigations will help unravel which adolescents are vulnerable to develop depressive disorders. Proximal processes are discussed in greater details in Chapter 9, 'Destabilisation'.

Reasons for the gender differences

Adolescent females are not exposed to more acute life events before first episode onsets but compared to boys they do report more adversity in their lives (Goodyer *et al.* 2000a). This suggests that the way females perceive their environments and interpret them in relation to their own well-being and competence may be the key distinctive process. Females of the species are more empathic, seek closer ties with same sex friends (affiliative need) and report higher levels of attributing social environmental difficulties to their own shortcomings. These increase in adolescence and have led to theorising that as puberty proceeds sex hormones differentially heighten affiliative need in girls which interact with adolescent transition difficulties (e.g. peer groups or dyadic intimate relations) to create a depressogenic diathesis as at-risk females go through puberty. In the presence of personally disappointing events arising from a breakdown in relationships females are therefore more prone to depressogenic reactions (Cyranowski *et al.* 2000). There is evidence that the rise in sex hormones may mediate the rise in affective disorders in females (Angold *et al.* 1999). It is not known if this is also true for males so we cannot currently confirm that there is a sex hormone differentiated risk for females over males. Given that more than 50 per cent of depressive disorders in adolescence arise via slow onset processes over adolescence, at variable points in the developing pubertal process and in both sexes at high psychosocial risk, the theory seems to lack sufficient universal application to first episode depressions as a whole. A key issue in attempting to determine sex differentiated mechanisms is to establish the extent to which there are unique sex-specific vulnerability processes at the distal genetic and perhaps early environmental processes as well as in proximal psychosocial and developmental processes occurring in adolescence.

Overall it seems likely that adolescence, more so than childhood, is not only associated with a greater propensity for the development of negative or critical views of the self but also the first developmental period when such negative cognitions become incorporated in a sustained manner into mental processes presumably in episodic memory. Psychosocial adversities are crucially implicated in the development of a negative style of thinking about the self. Well adolescents at high risk for psychopathology report significantly lower self-esteem and greater depressogenic thoughts than low risk adolescents in both sexes (Goodyer *et al.* 2000a). It may take a level of clinical impairment to amplify negative self-devaluation to a more concrete and self-evident style of thinking (Lewinsohn *et al.* 1999). Individual responses to social demands therefore depend on the extent to which they are appraised as salient and threatening to the self. Adolescence may be the first time when individuals start to markedly organise and evaluate their self-competencies and their ability to cope with life experiences using internal yardsticks of 'success' rather than relying on the positive and negative views of others. Those yardsticks come from earlier experiences but their personal evaluation begins as an adolescent task. Adolescent females are intrinsically more biased to negative self-devaluations than males and to higher levels of cortisol (Goodyer *et al.* 2000a, 2000b). The increased levels of depression in females over males may be due in part to these sex-differentiated psycho-endocrine characteristics. But this is not a sex-differentiated mechanism as such because males with these features are just as likely to develop depressions, there are just fewer of them.

Take-home messages

- Early physical maturation is advantageous for boys, with higher peer popularity, self-esteem and intellectual abilities but an increased risk for deviant behaviour.
- Early maturation in girls produces more adjustment difficulties, an increased risk for anxiety, depression and more risk behaviours (including sexual intercourse).
- The emergence of psychiatric disorders between 10 and 30 years of age is through the interplay of genes, pre-adolescent experiences and the events of puberty including ongoing brain development.
- Adolescence affects childhood mental disorders in four ways: they may resolve; they may continue but be modified in form; they may be unaffected by the changes of adolescence; or they may be intensified.
- Behavioural disorders that persist through into adolescence do so because of chronic unremitting family adversities and low levels of empathy and emotion sensitivity in the child. The majority of such cases are males.
- Delinquency and violent behaviour may arise during adolescence in those with minor or no childhood difficulties. The risks for both sexes are in the teenage social network, particularly with membership of a deviant peer group.
- The most common emotional disorders that emerge during the adolescent years are the depressions. The causes are multifactorial and depend on the relations between genetics and early adverse childhood experiences, influencing the development of self-evaluation in the prepubertal years and the unique events of puberty and their effects on psychosocial and physiological process during adolescence. It is much more common among girls, in part related to increases in adolescent sex hormones.

- The reasons for the gender differences lie in the greater female tendency to internalise, combined with the needs for peer support at a time of bodily change due to hormonal upheavals. Recently postpubertal girls who experience breakdown in close relationships may be at especial risk for onsets of depression.

Chapter 8

Adult life and old age

Adult life

While many of the determinants of vulnerability and resilience are fixed in early life, events during adult life can serve to consolidate resilience, or to increase vulnerability. Prominent among the factors increasing vulnerability are chronic social deficits and this includes not only disadvantageous aspects of an individual's current life situation, but also poverty and characteristics of a person's marriage and employment. By the time adulthood is reached, abnormalities of personality will be evident if they are going to appear, and these in turn have a role in determining the sort of stressful life events that an individual is likely to experience. In this chapter we will first take these factors in turn as they apply during adult life, before going on to consider the part that personality plays in determining life events. The important role of life events in releasing some episodes of illness will be considered in the next chapter, on destabilisation. This chapter will conclude with special features of old age, in contrast to factors that are important in earlier adult life.

The transitions of early adult life

The Dutch Nemesis study (Overbeek *et al.* 2003) followed young adults between the ages of 18 and 35 in a three-wave longitudinal survey extending over 4 years. The purpose of doing this was to examine the extent to which normal transitions (getting married or cohabiting, becoming a parent) had different rates of onset than atypical states (staying single and not cohabiting, break-up of cohabitation and divorce) and to find if they were associated with rates of onset of mental disorders. They found that in their longitudinal study (predicting onsets between T1 and T3 from stability of relationships between T1 and T3) while anxiety disorders had no such relationships, mood disorders were related to both the atypical states. The onset of mood disorders was found to be related to previous relationship difficulties and to be followed by higher rates of not becoming a parent, of divorce or break-up of relationships.

Drug and alcohol problems were associated with higher rates of onset in all groups studied, except those living together in a stable dyadic relationship (marriage or cohabitation). In a prospective study (predicting onsets between T2 and T3 from stability of relationships between T1 and T2) there were no associations for anxiety or depression, but there were increased rates of onset of drug and alcohol problems among those that stayed with a partner (without marrying or cohabiting), those that entered cohabitation or marriage, and those who broke up with their partner.

Chronic social difficulties

Brown and Harris (1978) studied working-class London women using their 'life events and difficulties schedule' (LEDS), and showed that chronic difficulties and social disadvantage were associated with onsets of depression. Many others, using other measures, have confirmed this robust finding. Ormel and Wohlfarth (1991) distinguished between chronic difficulties that were independent of the individual, and those that were at least partly dependent upon the individual. They argue that independent chronic difficulties interact with neuroticism, so that those with high scores on neuroticism are especially likely to experience distress if they also have such chronic difficulties – and that such difficulties are somewhat more important than changes in the individual's life situation.

Other aspects of social adjustment are of course associated with chronic social difficulties: thus overcrowding is associated with high distress scores (Gabe and Williams 1987), and that living in poor housing is also associated with depression (Birtchnell et al. 1988).

Poverty

There are strong associations between poverty and psychological distress. This is particularly evident in places where there are great discrepancies in personal income. However, 'poverty' is a somewhat crude and relative variable and it is likely that its effects are mediated by adverse social conditions, low self-esteem and, in many parts of the world, by malnutrition.

Gender differences

In almost all cultures, female rates for common disorders exceed male rates, and we have already seen some of the factors in earlier life that make such differences more likely. In adult life, unmarried mothers have very high rates and mothers of several small children have much higher rates than nulliparous or single-child families. After age 65, the female preponderance becomes less marked, although it can still be discerned.

Marriage

It is consistently found in community surveys that for men being married or cohabiting is less stressful than being single, or being separated, divorced or widowed. For women, being single or cohabiting is associated with a higher prevalence of common mental disorders than being married, and that in turn more advantageous than being separated or divorced. Gove (1972) argued that marriage appears to protect men only against depression, as he asserted that the gender ratio is greatest for depression among the married. Recent data by no means confirm this. We can see from Table 8.1 that women are much more depressed than men until they get married, but more anxious than men when separated or widowed. Men are anxious until they marry and much more depressed on separation and widowhood.

Unmarried mothers are at particular risk of depression. Brown and Moran (1997) showed that they were twice as likely as married mothers to become depressed and were also more often in financial hardship and at work. Onset of depression was more likely when the women had poor self-esteem and low social support. Nazroo and others (1997) showed that wives are at greater risk of depression following a stressful life event than their husbands. This greater risk is due to their respective gender roles. Wives found events involving children, housing or reproductive problems more salient, while husbands found events involving work and financial provision more salient. The wives were more likely to become depressed following their events, and more likely than their husbands to report self-blame. These findings are similar to those of Kendler and others (2001), who showed that while the rates at which the two sexes experienced life events were similar, that females are more likely to experience housing problems, loss of confidant, crises and interpersonal difficulties, while men are more likely to experience problems at work, job loss, robbery and legal problems.

Employment

The effects of unemployment depend on many other variables. Although in general employment confers psychological benefits – in pooled data it always does – there are exceptions to this rule. We saw above that a single mother having to care for her child desperately needs an income from employment, but it imposes an additional psychological burden upon her. Unemployment among young males is much more stressful if the individual feels marginalised and his peer group is mainly at work; much less if there is an unemployed subcommunity with which he can share leisure activities.

Table 8.1 Gender ratios (F:M) and one-month period prevalence rates/1000 for depressive episode, generalised anxiety and mild mixed anxiety depression by marital status (data from Meltzer et al. 1995)

	Single	Cohabiting	Married	Separated	Divorced	Widowed
Depressive episode	**2.1** 33/16	**2.7** 30/11	1.2 17/14	**0.5** 56/111	1.2 46/37	**0.5** 38/70
Generalised anxiety	**0.7** 18/27	**2.6** 39/15	1.2 17/14	1.2 32/27	1.2 41/36	**6.2** 75/12
Mild mixed anxiety depression	1.9 102/54	2.1 133/64	1.6 86/51	1.0 121/117	**2.6** 161/62	1.0 97/95
All common disorders (incl. panic, phobias, OCD)	1.6 201/123	**2.1 240/115**	1.5 170/116	0.85 263/309	**1.7 304/178**	1.34 268/200

Effects of personality in determining stressful life events

While some stressful life events are quite independent of our personality, it is evident that many others are not. To quite a large extent, each of us constructs his or her own environment. This tendency is largely determined by aspects of personality. This is itself a product of additive genes, with a fairly small contribution from shared family environment and the rest by an individual's unique environment. Bouchard has used twin studies to throw light on the determination of the 'big five' personality dimensions (openness, neuroticism or harm avoidance; novelty seeking, extraversion and reward dependence), and finds that genetic factors are responsible for just over half the variance in each dimension, with shared family environment about 10 per cent of openness and neuroticism, and the rest unique environment and measurement error. Heady and Waring (1989) showed that favourable life events were predicted by extraversion and openness, unfavourable events by neuroticism and openness, while neuroticism predicted adverse finances and poor job adjustment.

It has been known for some time that neuroticism plays a major role in determining adverse life events. Fergusson and Horwood (1987) showed that about a third of the variance in stressful life events is determined by two factors – neuroticism and chronic social disadvantage. In this study the latter was a composite rating, comprising low educational level, ethnic minority status, low socio-economic status and being a single-parent family. In 1992 Poulton and Andrews also found that neuroticism was their best predictor of stressful life events in a large non-clinical population.

Daley and others (1988) showed that it was not the case that the greater the personality abnormality, the greater the likelihood that subsequent stress would release depression, but they found support for a 'mediation model' whereby women with higher levels of initial personality disturbance in clusters A and B generated excessive amounts of episodic stress and interpersonal chronic stress in the next two years, which in turn increased vulnerability for depressive symptoms.

Saudino and her colleagues (1997) analysed data from the Swedish Adoption/twin study, and found that not only undesirable events but also controllable and desirable events had significant genetic variance among the female twins, but as one would have expected uncontrollable events had no genetic variance for either sex. Previous studies were extended, by the demonstration that all the genetic variance on these events is mediated by personality.

Turning to substance abuse, Wills and others (1994) showed that substance use was particularly common in young males with high novelty seeking, low harm avoidance and low reward dependence. Thus we can see that aspects of personality are of great importance in helping to determine the frequency by which stressful events are experienced in adult life, and the kind of disorder that may be developed. To the extent that personality is partly determined by our genetic make-up, we see another pathway by which genes exert an effect in later life.

Kinds of stressful life events

In addition to distinguishing between life events that are partly under one's own control (dependent events) and those which are quite external to the individual, early work distinguished between events involving loss and those involving danger (Brown and Harris 1978). The former are more likely to be implicated in depression, the latter in anxiety. More recent work (Brown et al. 1995) has refined this typology and drawn attention to humiliation and entrapment as important aspects of situations that are particularly depressogenic. Humiliation is defined as an event rendering a person devalued in relation to himself or others, while entrapment is defined as a marked difficulty that has lasted for longer than six months and is likely to persist. Examples of humiliation would be being deserted or deceived by one's partner, while examples of entrapment are numerous: one can be trapped in an abusive relationship, a dismal job, an unhappy marriage or an unsatisfactory house. In addition to these, new episodes of physical illness are also potentially highly depressogenic, particularly those associated with marked disability or of serious prognosis. These events tend to be neglected in community surveys as new episodes are of low frequency in the general population, but they are well recognised by liaison psychiatrists. The important theme of the role played by physical disease in precipitating depression, and indeed the role of depression in possibly precipitating relapse in a chronic physical disease, will be fully dealt with in the next chapter.

Old age

While younger adults lose their partners through separation and divorce, older people lose close confidants and friends through death, and thus often have a steadily reducing social circle. Financial problems are often much worse in old age and encroaching illness brings with it loss of capacities and increasing disability. Cerebro-vascular and dementing diseases also are associated with depression. For all these reasons, there are special features to depression in old age.

Prevalence, gender ratio and effect of increasing age

Community surveys in the UK, USA, Canada and Australia agree that the overall prevalence of depression among the elderly is less than in earlier adult life, with figures of about 1 per cent being reported (figures quoted in Prince et al. 1999). However, these figures undoubtedly underestimate the prevalence, as numerous old people are excluded: notably the bereaved, those with physi-cal illness and those with cognitive impairment. These are important exclu-sions. Estimates made with specially adapted scales give considerably higher estimates. Osborn and others (2003) report a prevalence rates of 7.7 per cent using the Geriatric depression scale in a large sample of the UK population aged over 75. Prince and colleagues (1997) report a rate for 'pervasive depres-sion' of 17 per cent using the Short-Care depression scale in a London bor-ough. Recently a further scale has been developed for use across Europe, but now the rate falls to between 2 and 3.6 per cent in 14 European centres. The OPCS survey of the UK only included subjects up to the age 65, and the overall prevalence of depressive episode and 'mixed anxiety depression' was 9.8 per cent, with an undoubted fall between ages of 50 and 65. A more recent repeat survey (Office of National Statistics 2000) included people up to the age of 75, but also confirmed that the rate for depression is falling. It appears that if depression is narrowly defined with several important exclusions that the rate falls, but if one studies depressive symptomatology without such exclusions then the rate tends to increase.

Osborn and others (2003) show that the overall rate is fairly constant between the ages 65 and 85, but definitely rises after that, while Prince et al. (1999) show a weak effect of increases with advancing age in Europe. In this paper, the structure of the 12 items comprising the Euro-dep scale are decomposed into an affective suffering component and a low motivation component: it is the latter that is responsible for the small increase with age, probably due to cerebro-vascular disease. Scores on the affective suffering component are generally higher among women, and the divorced, separated and widowed generally (but not always) have higher scores as well.

In a companion paper Prince et al. (1999) show that among the married the female excess for depression persists into old age, while females who have never married have less depression.

Importance of associated handicap, loneliness and poor social support

Prince and others (1998) show that handicap – defined as the disadvantage for an individual resulting from ill health – is very strongly associated with depression in the elderly, with 25 per cent of the most handicapped being a massive 24 times more likely to be depressed than the least handicapped. These figures take all causes of handicap into account.

Osborn et al. (2003) show that the highest odds ratio for depression (3.5) is among those without anyone to confide in. Prince et al. (1997) show that the odds ratio for depression among the lonely is 12.4. If social support deficits are considered, with four such deficits the odds ratio rises to 4.0, and with five or more deficits it rises to almost 18. These findings confirm Murphy's (1982) observations on the social causation of depression among the elderly. Osborn *et al.* (2003) studied risk factors other than loneliness and found that living in sheltered/residential accommodation, experiencing stressful life events, smoking and suffering from two or more physical illnesses were all associated with raised rates. However, gender, living alone and alcohol had no such associations.

Variations in life events by age and their association with common mental disorders

The kinds of life event that depress the elderly are by no means the same as those that are common in earlier adult life. While interpersonal conflicts at home or at work, becoming humiliated, separation from one's partner and becoming entrapped are all commonly reported in earlier life, among the elderly common stressful events are bereavement, financial crises and theft (odds ratios of 5.9, 4.9 and 2.5 respectively reported by Prince *et al.* 1997). However, the effects of bereavement are usually not longlasting, but theft and money problems are associated with an increased risk over the next two years.

The National Psychiatric Morbidity Survey, carried out by the Office of National Statistics in 2000, included a probability sample of 8500 adults who were asked questions not only about common mental disorders, but also about stressful life events and what action was taken on account of them. Some problems like illness or death of a close relative show no clear effect with age, while many others become progressively less common as people become older. This list is a long one, including marital problems and divorce, interpersonal conflict and violence, redundancy and unemployment, and problems with finances and the police.

However, some problems become more common with increasing age. These are illness, injury and assault and death of a partner or close relative. Old people are more likely than younger ones to seek professional help for these problems. Old people experiencing the first three of these events who sought professional help were significantly more likely to suffer from a common mental disorder (odds ratio 2.5, CL 1.7–3.7).

Childhood traumas – sexual abuse, running away from home, being expelled from school or being bullied – are reported progressively less frequently as age proceeds, the rate falling steadily from 32.6 per cent of respondents aged 15 to 24, to 10 per cent in those over 65. This may well represent the effects of failing memory or active forgetting.

When life events were collected into three groups – representing health problems in self or close relative, death and bereavement of partner or close relative and interpersonal conflicts – common mental disorders had significantly high odds ratios for all three groups (2.65, 1.43 and 2.9, all with confidence limits well above unity), but were also high for those who had experienced childhood trauma 2.9 (CLs 2.54–3.31).

Table 8.2 shows the frequency of individual events, the prevalence of

Table 8.2 Associations between life events and common mental disorders (odds ratios) by gender and age, showing population attributable fractions

| | Frequency of life event (%) | Prevalence of CMD (%) | | Strength of association (odds ratio, 95% CI) | Population attributable fraction (%) (for CMD) |
		If life event absent	If life event present		
Health of self	1.1	14.7	42.9	4.4 (3.1–6.0)	3.6
Health of relative	2.9	15.0	24.1	1.8 (1.3–2.5)	2.3
Death of first degree relative	2.9	14.9	26.4	2.0 (1.5–2.8)	2.8
Death of other friend/relative	8.5	15.1	17.4	1.2 (0.9–3.8)	1.7
Relationship breakdown	2.0	14.9	32.0	2.7 (1.9–3.8)	3.3
Interpersonal problem	3.1	14.7	33.9	3.0 (2.2–4.0)	5.8
Childhood trauma					
Bullying	18.1	12.9	26.1	2.4 (2.1–2.8)	20.2
Sexual abuse	3.4	13.9	53.2	7.0 (5.5–8.9)	16.9
Expulsion from school	1.7	14.9	36.6	3.3 (2.2–4.9)	3.8
Running away from home	5.2	13.9	39.8	4.1 (3.2–5.2)	13.9

common mental disorders without a recent life event and following one, and the population attributable fraction for each event and for four kinds of childhood trauma. It can be seen that in all cases except death of a close relative, a recent life event causes a greatly increased prevalence of disorder. and that the population attributable fraction is highest for interpersonal problems for the six groups of life events reported. However, those who have experienced childhood trauma are especially likely to develop common disorders following life events, and the population attributable fractions are highest in these people. Being bullied or sexually abused emerge as being especially likely to produce vulnerability to common mental disorders. However, those remembering such events are consistently more likely to be suffering from CMDs, the odds ratios being about 3.0 in all age groups.

Ormel and his colleagues (2001), in a Dutch case-control study of 83 elderly depressives, found that the commonest stressful life events were loss of capacities, loss of close ties and having few social contacts. Oldehinkel and her colleagues (2003) make an important point about these life events in the elderly – in contrast to those is earlier life, they tend to be uncontrollable. She also shows that they are unrelated to personality.

Nonetheless, neuroticism retains its importance in later life. Indeed, Ormel *et al.* (2001) showed that if neuroticism scores are low, and in the absence of chronic difficulties, older people are able to tolerate stressful life events without developing depression. With high neuroticism scores, another group of elderly depressives with many chronic difficulties become depressed in the absence of life events. However, stressful life events, if present, increase the likelihood of depression developing.

In the case-control study mentioned earlier, Ormel *et al.* (2001) showed that although stressful life events when they were present increased the odds of an onset of depression (OR = 22) to a greater extent than chronic difficulties (OR = 3), the latter were in fact more common: the two factors accounted for 21 per cent and 45 per cent of onsets respectively. They also found that whereas people without a previous episode of depression were very much more likely to develop depression in the presence of a severe life event, that the likelihood was less in the presence of such a previous episode. Mild life events were unlikely to precipitate a new episode of depression.

Take-home messages

- Both depressive illnesses and drug problems, but not anxiety disorders, are associated with 'abnormal transitions' in early adult life (remaining single and not cohabiting, breaking up a cohabitation with a partner, and divorce).
- Chronic social difficulties are associated with higher rates of onset of common mental disorders.

- Marriage confers an advantage for women over being single or cohabiting, and cohabiting and marriage an advantage for men over being single. Unmarried mothers have very high rates. Married men have lower rates of alcohol dependence than cohabiting men, and these in turn have lower rates than single men.
- Being separated or divorced is a disaster for both sexes, but being separated or widowed is a relatively much greater disaster for men.
- Adult personality affects both rate and type of stressful life events.
- Some personality types are at special risk of drug and alcohol disorders.
- Illness, injury and trauma and death of a relative become more common as age progresses, and are associated with an increased odds of CMDs.
- Childhood traumas are remembered by fewer people as age progresses, but among those remembering them there is a consistently higher rate of disorders throughout the life cycle.

Part IV

The model proposed

Chapter 9

Destabilisation

The emergence and release of common mental disorders

Holistic theoretical frameworks

Throughout this book we have focused on the interplay between predispositions to common mental disorders occurring at different levels of biology. There are clearly causal patterns of genetic and environmental vulnerabilities that lead to the common syndromes of anxiety, depression and behavioural disorders. The broad framework is that there are individual differences in *distal factors* (genetic make-up and early social adversities in the first few years of life) that result in individual physiological and more *proximal factors*: psychological differences at the level of the brain and mind which are responsible for processing information from the outside world. The distal factors result in individual physiological and psychological differences at the level of the brain and mind which are responsible for processing information from the outside world. A vulnerable person is one whose distal processing set is biased towards increasing psychiatric risk. The 'distal set' may be the early determinants for two closely interrelated behavioural phenomena: how a person (a) develops their own environments; (b) sets up the processes that respond to environmental demands. A vulnerable person may be more likely to put themselves into risk environments or respond maladaptively to environments that they are exposed to. These vulnerabilities may combine with more here and now or proximal adverse environments that result in onsets of common mental disorders.

This two-stage framework has been prominent in two fields: social psychiatry exemplified best by the early studies of Paykel (1974) and then by the classical work of Brown and Harris (1978, see below); cognitive psychopathology exemplified by the early studies of Beck (1967) and Abramson *et al.* (1978), subsequently by Alloy and colleagues (1999, 2000) and the detailed human experimental and theoretical work of Teasdale and Barnard (1993).

It is striking how both sets of researchers coming from markedly different traditions and measuring quite distinct processes assume that distal processes set up individual differences and proximal processes activate the onset of emotional disorder.

In contrast physiological researchers have tended to focus more narrowly on immediate response elements to stressful circumstances. Mental disorders have invariably been of secondary concern. The main hypotheses have been concerned with delineating how individuals react chemically to stress. Here distal influences on reactivity have only recently come to influence these experimental approaches. Experimental stress research is now substantially concerned with examining the genetic and early environmental influences that may bias how individuals deal with acute and chronic stressful circumstances. As yet however there are no clear-cut holistic theories of physiological reactivity taking into account both distal and proximal biology to explain common mental disorders. It is of interest that this approach has made somewhat more headway in explaining the proximal emergence of behavioural disorders than the social-cognitive approach and will be discussed briefly.

Most recently of all has been the addition of a developmental approach to these theoretical models and their resultant research outputs. The works of Rutter and Sroufe have perhaps been the most prominent in arguing for a much better understanding of the developmental trajectories of individuals to explain why some children despite substantial childhood adversities do not develop adult mental illness and that adult disorders are not always preceded by early environmental insults (Rutter 2000; Rutter 2002). In addition lifespan developmental theories focus on the importance of how widening developmental opportunities (including biological events such as puberty and social events such as peer groups and work-related experiences) are powerful agents in diminishing the negative effects of early adversity and forming the basis for a restitution to an adaptive developmental pathway. The key issue here is the clear argument that a distal-proximal framework is not the correct theoretical approach to investigating the origins of common mental disorders. In the Rutter–Sroufe model whether one takes a social, psychological or physiological approach, the key assumption is that there are both continuity and discontinuity within and between experiences and behaviours that are mediated by the lifespan development of the individual.

Are these theories and their accompanying research inquiries mutually exclusive, making one more likely than the other? The answer is an unequivocal no. In many ways these represent increasing levels of sophistication and understanding of the process of human biology as they are applied to mental illness. For example, both social and cognitive models acknowledge the importance of each other's processing. Social psychiatry has long incorporated the notions of low self-esteem and personality variables in theory and research. Cognitive models have always assumed the social environment is the origin of self and the promoter of individual differences in self-evaluation. Physiological models have concluded that significant reactivity and behavioural change are achieved when acute stimuli are of social value and meaning to the individual. Finally the developmental model does not argue for the removal of social, cognitive or physiological change but wants them placed in a lifespan perspective. Perhaps the key distinction with this latter view is that it rejects the idea that the events of early childhood determine all subsequent risks for mental disorders in an immutable way: later events can and do modify the risk.

Processes and mechanisms

Determining the precise processes and mechanisms that lead to different forms of psychopathology across the lifespan is a major task for the twenty-first century. No model has achieved more than the most preliminary description of the final common pathways between the environment and mental disorder. Researchers have only recently begun to share research techniques of inquiry with each other and as a consequence we remain almost totally ignorant of how bad environments (distal or proximal) actually bring about psychopathology. For example, the psychological mechanism that leads to a change from a positive to a negative view of the self has been extensively studied experimentally and described in some detail (Tavares et al. 2003; Teasdale and Barnard 1993), but it is entirely unclear if these undesirable psychological changes are related to particular types of negative social experiences, their specific timing over the lifespan or due exclusively to distal processes in the genome or earlier environments. Similarly there is extensive work on the two-stage model of distal-proximal social processes making it clear that there are continuities and discontinuities between experiences occurring at different points in time. It remains entirely unclear however exactly how proximal processes actually bring about the change from non-clinical to clinical states of mind. We will now provide a description of the main activation and destabilisation processes mentioned above.

Activation refers to the formation and bringing into consciousness of abnormal psychological processes that are required to evoke psychiatric disorder: for example, persistently thinking 'This is all my fault I am no good, I am a bad person' following the failure of a personal intimate relationship. *Destabilisation* refers to the behavioural consequences of these: for example, withdrawing from all friends and workmates.

This theoretical framework assumes therefore that not all activations will result in destabilisation but the latter cannot occur without the former. Thus adverse social experiences may activate within a person the above-mentioned set of thoughts that they are no good, responsible for bad things and not nice to know. But if that person continues to function at work, engages in social activity and retains their daily routines, they are not destabilised. In contrast, individuals for whom the activation of this negative cognitive set leads to work and social failure and impairments in daily routines, they have become overtly behaviourally destabilised.

Many people may think ill of themselves but retain sufficient performance skills to remain functional. Those most at risk for destabilising in the presence

of negative thoughts about the self are those who persistently dwell or ruminate on their perceived failures (Noten-Hoeksema 2000). This may reflect a
deficit in the performance aspects of thinking. Thus we may not be able to
stop ourselves thinking negative personal events are our fault (and it may be
true in some circumstances) but we retain a psychological ability to think of
other things and distract ourselves away from dwelling on the recent negative
experiences. For some however distraction and accompanying abilities to
stop dwelling on negative thoughts appear very difficult. These ruminating
processes appear to be the most proximal activating agent for depression
(Spasojevic and Alloy 2001).

Further we should distinguish between transient and persistent destabilisation. The former may be a normative and expected short-term response to
events such as exam failure, loss of job or marital breakdown. The latter is
distinguished by the maintenance of personal impairment and a failure to
return to previously healthy function beyond a period of time when readapta-
tion (i.e. evoking homeostatic or allostatic mechanisms) should have occurred.
This introduces a temporal component to the notion of destabilisation that is
associated with the onset of psychopathology. These issues have long been
recognised in behavioural science and in psychiatric nosology. A brief look at
current classification systems for mental and behavioural disorders (American
Psychiatric Association 1994; WHO 1994) shows that a categorical diagnosis
for common disorders involves the presence of particular set of signs, symptoms and/or behaviours, occurring over operationally defined periods of time
that have resulted in personal impairment.

We will now consider examples of activation/destabilisation models from
social and psychological research in detail. Brief references will then be made to
the potential influence of a developmental framework on behaviour disorders.

Life events and difficulties as antecedents of onsets of depression and anxiety

The work of George Brown and Tirril Harris

Brown is a medical sociologist who employs 'grounded theory'. This model
gives a high priority to the importance of individual's experience in causal
processes. Brown and Harris (1978) developed a social inquiry method which
focused on the interplay between observation, data collection and analysis.
The remarkable advance was to incorporate extensive information derived
from the semi-structured social interview and impose hypothesis-driven concepts at the level of measurement to obtain a universally applicable quantitative estimate of positive and negative experience. In effect they took individual
and highly detailed autobiographical recalls of life events and chronic difficulties and had independent investigators gauge the potential impact of
these 'experiences' on that individual against a yardstick of what the 'ordinary'

man or woman would have felt. In this way they sought to combine highly individual information as the data set with a highly general psychological process within that information that could apply to all of us. After many trials and reformulations they settled for a set of mutually exclusive classifications based on two latent psychological constructs of loss and threat. These they discovered applied best to relatively acute and recent life events and difficulties. This has resulted in a gradually evolving theory concerning the phenomenon to be explained. In his hands, the approach has been remarkably fertile. Although his early researches in depression were largely concerned with urban, working-class women, his many students have broadened the scope of observation so that it now includes a wide range of very diverse human populations. One of the results of these comparative surveys has been to show that rates of depression vary directly with rates of irregular or disruptive events in different populations, which serves as a warning against exclusively relying on genetic differences to explain different rates. A general account of his work on life events, including his views on more distal vulnerabilities to anxiety and depression, will be given here, as the two are inseparable in understanding the development of his work.

Brown and Harris were the first to show conclusively that loss events that were likely to exert their effects for longer than a few days or weeks were undoubtedly more common in four months before onset of an episode of unipolar depression during adult life: 68 per cent of community onset cases had one or more, versus only 25 per cent of normal controls. The term loss was used in a way that is not straightforward. It covered a range of events that included the permanent loss of a cherished person, the death of a loved one and even the loss of an 'idea' such as the belief in a close friend which turned out to be false. They avoided the conflation with simple stress by only using events whose negative effects would be considerably longer than that of a response to stress.

While this undoubtedly establishes severe loss events as precipitants of depressive episodes, we may make two further observations: 32 per cent of onsets of depression do not have a severe loss event. The fairly high rate of loss events in the general population is not followed by an onset of depression for a substantial proportion of those so exposed. In other words, loss events are neither sufficient nor necessary to precipitate episodes.

In order to deal with this lack of specificity, Brown and Harris incorporated both a distal and a second proximal hypothesis. They termed these vulnerability factors to distinguish them from the acute life events they termed provoking agents. The theory was that vulnerability factors could not of themselves 'cause' an onset of depression but when present they acted as the necessary template for provoking agents to give rise to an onset of depression. Brown and Harris showed their belief in the early diathesis and two-stage theory by nominating childhood adversity as a major period for the formation of vulnerability factors.

They conjectured that one distal factor – loss of mother before 11 – and three more proximal factors – lack of an intimate confiding relationship, having three or more children under 15, and not having a job – would collectively index this underlying vulnerability to depression. These major difficulties occurred in 65 per cent of onsets, but only 20 per cent of non-cases. If severe provoking events and difficulties were combined, the incidence of depressive episodes becomes 89 per cent versus 35 per cent in those with neither vulnerability factors nor provoking agents. Further analysis of their data revealed that in those women with intimate confiding relationships in their current relationships (and only one was needed which in many cases was their own mother rather than current partner or spouse) even in the presence of vulnerability and provoking factors the incidence of depression was less. This clearly indicated a current confiding relationship as moderating the impact of adversities. They termed this a protective factor.

The evidence also suggested that having three or more children at home, being currently unemployed and suffering early maternal loss may be more than vulnerability factors – they may be sufficient to 'cause' depression without further highly proximal negative events. Indeed the number of depressive episodes that have only an acute event as a social precipitant is around 11 per cent. Given the prevalence of these disorders in the community this remains a substantial number of cases for public health concern. Equally however it demonstrates that more longstanding processes may themselves be sufficient in some instances to result in major depression.

From the start, Brown has insisted on the importance of the personal meaning that an event has for the individual being considered. These ideas had been made explicit in the idea of a 'matching' life event that had particular salience for the person studied, either because the event matches a preceding difficulty, or a prior commitment (Brown et al. 1989). Over the years, this model has become steadily more elaborate, as new measures of vulnerability factors are devised and new concepts of life events evolve (Brown et al. 1987).

Thus, in 1993 they showed that parental indifference, sexual and physical abuse during childhood raise the risk of both anxiety disorders and depression in later life, but that anxiety disorders and depression have rather different antecedents – both during childhood and immediately preceding onset (Brown and Harris 1993). The importance of childhood sexual and physical abuse and parental neglect has been confirmed by others using case-control designs (Mullen et al. 1994; Swanston et al. 1997). Mullen and his colleagues' study showed that the effects of childhood adversity went well beyond anxiety and depressive disorders, to include sexual difficulties and interpersonal problems. Swanston et al.'s study not only also confirmed the relationship with depression and anxiety, but showed relationships with other adolescent behaviour disorders – notably binge eating and episodes of self-harm. However, there is an important limitation to these case-control studies, since the sexually abused children were disadvantaged in many other ways as well:

for example, neglected, subject to parental separations, paternal alcoholism and violence, and so on. The sexual abuse is one disadvantage among many others and it does not make sense to attribute all the harm documented in the case-control studies to this single cause.

In 1994 Brown and his colleagues showed that episodes of depression lasting more than a year, in both community and mental health samples, were predicted by childhood adversity followed by current adult interpersonal difficulties. The latter were more common among the mental health sample of patients, perhaps partly explaining the higher rate of chronicity: only current social support appeared to reduce the risk. The following year, Brown and his colleagues distinguished between humiliation and entrapment experiences – as described in the previous chapter. Next, in 1998 Bifulco and her colleagues identified 'teenage depression' as a variable that follows childhood adversity, and which itself increased the rate of onset of episodes of adult depression following severe life events. Indeed the findings from this study suggested that the onset of teenage depression entirely accounted for the association between a history of child abuse and the onset of adult depression. This was one of the first empirical hints that there were developmental effects on the two-stage model, in this case the intercurrent onset of depression in the pubertal years.

In 2000, Harris presented a complete account of the contribution she and George Brown had made in the previous 25 years. At each step in the causal pathway, the vulnerability factors have become more elaborate (Harris 2000: 19). Parental neglect or abuse was hypothesised as producing a state of helplessness and low self-esteem, with feelings of insecure attachment. These factors in turn were proposed as making teenage pregnancy more likely. Should this occur poor adult support becomes more likely, as well as poor material conditions and a higher expectancy of life events, both economic and interpersonal. She makes the point that while their studies have shown that the rates of severe life events and the risk of onsets are similar in both sons and daughters, that the type of disorder is different – being anxiety and depression for the daughters and conduct disorder for the sons.

Types of life event and onsets of depression and anxiety

Finlay-Jones and Brown (1981) argued that episodes of loss were more common before onsets of depression, while episodes of threat commonly preceded anxiety. They pointed out that many stressful events contain elements of both – and when this occurred the individual was more likely to be both depressed and anxious. However, the relationship was not a perfect one and there were many exceptions. The segregation of events and illnesses has been observed by others, Cook and Hole (1983) confirmed it (Table 9.1)

Many others have shown this association (e.g. Torgerson 1985) and more

Table 9.1 Association between loss and danger, and anxiety and depression (Cook and Hole 1983)

	Loss	Danger
Anxiety	5	72
Depression	58	37

recently Breslau and others (1991) have documented the association between traumatic events and post-traumatic stress disorder. In the National Co-morbidity study it has been shown on a large population that onsets of phobic illnesses are preceded by threat: agoraphobia occurring after combat in wars, life-threatening accidents and threat to life from fire and flood, and social phobias in women after sexual assaults by relatives (Magee 1999).

Brown and Harris (1993) put forward a hypothesis that it was a combination of early childhood experience and the kind of life events that was important: depression in women was predicted by early childhood adversity followed by loss events in adult life, in the context of poor current social support. Anxiety disorders on their own have childhood adversity and may be preceded by events which are threatening or dangerous; while a mixture of the two ('co-morbid anxiety and depression') occurs where childhood adversity is followed by adult adversity (loss of close ties, death of child, marital violence or adult sexual abuse), and may be preceded by life events which involve both danger and loss. Again a striking feature of this two-stage model (derived in the main from selected aspects of psychoanalytic and attachment theories of human development and psychopathology) is the absence of how early experiences operated in relation to later adversities. Further refinements, even at the social level, clearly required greater specification of the nature of experience at different time points and how they may or not relate to each other. Does child maltreatment increase the liability for adolescent peer group failures? Does the latter exert marked effects on the types of individuals young adults associate with? What exactly are the chaining of vulnerability events in the pathway between the child and adult periods of life? We return to these issues in the developmental section of this chapter.

Patients in primary care and children in the first two decades of life typically have combinations of anxious and depressive symptoms, so there is an element of artificiality in these distinctions. Both major international diagnostic systems now only diagnose 'generalised anxiety' if it has been present for six months, yet 'major depression' need only last two weeks: so the distinction between the two often reflects chronicity of symptoms, rather than pattern of symptoms. The main symptomatic distinction between anxiety and depression is the presence of depressed, sad or irritable mood in the latter. Brown's work used the Present State Examination, which only required symptoms to have been present for one month in order to diagnose anxiety states. He allowed a three-way classification of each set of symptoms into non-case, borderline case and case. This allowed him to see what users of dichotomous systems cannot: namely that borderline anxious symptoms are a vulnerability factor for episodes of case anxiety or case depression. Users of dimensional models will not be surprised by these findings. In addition the psychiatric assessments did not include even estimates of lifetime psychiatric disorders. Whilst there is considerable justifiable concern over the ability of respondents to recall distinct episodes of mental illness in years gone by, it is difficult to exclude a heterotypic continuity of effects through psychopathology for some adults with chronic anxious or depressive conditions.

Gilbert and his colleagues (2003) have extended Brown's views with a detailed study of arrested defensive behaviours in 50 patients with depression under treatment from the mental health services. Most (88 per cent) expressed strong themes of entrapment in their account of life events and difficulties – as would have been predicted by Brown – but most had not escaped from the situation that entrapped them, so that 82 per cent of these had suppressed their anger as a result, usually before the onset of depression. External circumstances and other people were usually blamed for the entrapment.

Determinants of life events

In the previous chapter we saw how personality affects the experience of stressful life events, accounting for the otherwise perplexing demonstrations that life events not only run in families but have an important genetic component. Thus Billig and his colleagues (1996) incriminate non-independent, non-family life as the only kind having a genetic component ($h^2 = 49$ per cent), which they attribute to a personality dimension called 'constraint'. Farmer and her colleagues (2000) come to a somewhat different conclusion, attributing the familial aspects of life events entirely to shared (within family) experiences. However, the two investigators were using different measures and different genetic designs.

Fergusson and Horwood (1987), in a longitudinal community survey in New Zealand, showed that 30 per cent of variance of stressful life events was due to common vulnerability factor, which itself had two components – neuroticism and social disadvantage. The latter was a composite rating, comprising low educational level, ethnic minority status, low socio-economic status and single-parent family. Van Os and Jones (1999), in an English longitudinal study, extend this finding by demonstrating that high childhood neuroticism, as well as higher cognitive ability, both predict more life events later. They also show that maternal neuroticism, as well as childhood neuroticism, predict greater sensitivity to life events. They speculate that sensitivity to life events is transmitted from parents to children by altered stress sensitivity.

In a community study of adolescents Patton and his colleagues (2003) show that pre-existing anxious or depressive symptoms increase the risk of negative life events threefold in females and sevenfold in males, and that life events predict the onset of depression independently of such previous symptoms. Those with multiple life events experience a greatly increased risk. Personal threat and loss were associated with depression in females but not in males. In contrast Goodyer and colleagues (2000b) showed in a study of adolescents at high risk for psychopathology that the most important class of 'loss events' to be associated with the onset of depression were personal disappointments involving a failure of previously held expectations in an interpersonal relationship (within family or between friends) and this was true for both sexes (Goodyer *et al.* 2000b). Loss through bereavement is uncommon in this age range. Greater than 90 per cent of depressed cases had experienced at least two psychosocial difficulties and acute proximal 'provoking' life events were only present in 50 per cent of onsets.

Kendler and colleagues composed a comprehensive developmental pathway model based on their Virginia twin study sample which confirms the broad distal-proximal diathesis illustrated by Brown and Harris, but with a number of differing pathways implicating shared genetic risk for emotional disorders in general but distinctive distal and proximal environmental pathways leading differentially to anxiety and depression in adult life (Kendler *et al.* 2002). The dilemma for developmental theory building from studies based on adults is that there is no real developmental data. As yet there is no measure in adult life that reflects with sufficient validity persistent vulnerabilities measured in childhood or adolescence and shown to correlate with adult onset anxiety and depression. These may exist in psychological and/or physiological models of destabilisation.

Effects of an episode of depression on future events and illnesses

Once an episode of depression has occurred, individuals experience negative life events at an increased rate. Cui and Vaillant (1997) followed a group of normal college men for about 36 years from the age of 26, and showed that depressed individuals had a higher density of dependent negative life events after their first episode of depression – a dependent event being one where the man's own behaviour could have played a role in causing the event.

Ghaziuddin and others (1990) compared a small group of first episode cases with another group experiencing a recurrent episode. While the vast majority – 91 per cent in this study – of first episodes had experienced life events prior to onset, only a half of the recurrent episodes had been so preceded. Further, while over two life events had been experienced by the first onsets, only 0.8 were experienced by the recurrent episodes. These findings fit with what has become known as 'kindling', whereby a smaller external stress can provoke an episode once the process has occurred once. The 'kindled' state, where depressive episodes occur with little provocation, may occur by two pathways: many previous episodes (perhaps due to multiple social adversity); and high genetic risk – in the latter case, the number of previous episodes has only a small contribution to the effect of life events on provoking depression (Kendler *et al.* 2001).

Brown and Harris did not differentiate between first episode and recurrent depressions in their studies to any marked degree. Thus it is difficult to know if their model varies with the number of depressive episodes. Although Bifulco and colleagues (1998) demonstrated an independent and additive effect of adolescent depression to adult depression, it is unclear to what extent the social models may vary for adult depressive episodes with and without adolescent psychiatric histories. It is unclear if a childhood history of mental disorder, particularly anxiety states, may be implicated in an increased liability for subsequent chronic social difficulties and life events in later life. Finally the matching model implicating the 'double hit' notion of events of the same personal meaning occurring first in childhood and again in adults increasing the liability for depression in adult life appears to be present for some but not all patients attending outpatient services but not at all specific to depression. These issues and others are discussed further in the psychological and developmental theories below.

Cognitive theories of activation and destabilisation

Social theories provide the key environmental frameworks in delineating what predisposes individuals to certain common psychiatric disorders. Individual differences in response to social adversities have been a constant feature of almost all studies. Some individuals exposed to high levels of psychosocial adversities both current and in the past do not develop psychopathology. Equally there are individuals who appear easily activated and destabilised in the presence of relatively minor everyday hassles. These differences may be explained by genetic predispositions to social adversities as we discussed in previous chapters. Over the past century however a proximal set of theories has been developed based on the premise that the key pathological mechanisms are largely psychological and arise from the abnormal cognitive appraisal of life events and difficulties.

Hopelessness, helplessness and self-devaluation

A key theory formulated over the past four decades is the 'hopelessness theory' of depression. In this model depressions are brought about because of a stable set of cognitive features within the individual consisting of dysfunctional attitudes and attributional style towards oneself and others. Vulnerable individuals will activate this cognitive style to appraise negative experiences as their fault, that others blame them, and there is no alternative explanation but one's own failings.

Another influential series of studies has been based on Beck's theory of maladaptive self-schemas (Beck 1967). This theory suggests that a cognitively vulnerable individual is one with a negative view of the self, world and others that remains latent and not available to consciousness until activated, primarily through a personally relevant negative life event.

Over the last two decades a large body of empirical evidence has amassed linking such negative cognitions or attributions with depression. Reviews of a substantial literature have found that in the main the evidence suggests equivocal evidence for a causal process with many studies failing to distinguish if negative cognitions precede the onset of disorder (Segal and Ingram 1994). What was required were theory guided prospective studies preferably on high-risk community based populations (Just *et al.* 2001).

The Oregon Adolescent Depression Project was the first large-scale prospective study that showed cognitive vulnerabilities are associated with the subsequent onset of depression but especially in those with a previous episode (Lewinsohn *et al.* 1994, 2001; Monroe *et al.* 1999). Dysphoric mood and dysfunctional thinking were also strong predictors of recurrent and major life stresses of first onset depressive episodes (Lewinsohn *et al.* 1999). Thus negative life events may themselves be brought about in already cognitively vulnerable individuals. The Cognitive Vulnerability to Depression Project is a large high-risk study of currently well students (mean age 19), selected as at high or low risk on the basis of psychological features and compared for incidence of depression over a follow-up period (Alloy *et al.* 2000). Findings showed that depressogenic cognitive styles conferred specific risk for first onset depression, regardless of the number of preceding negative life events. That is there are specific patterns of thoughts and feelings that are powerful predictors of the onset of depression which are not accounted for by the amount of current social difficulties.

Negative self-schemas and self-devaluation in dysphoric mood

Teasdale proposed a modified form of the cognitive vulnerability theory which he termed the differential activation hypothesis (Teasdale and Barnard 1993). He proposed that individuals vulnerable to depression differ from those less vulnerable in patterns of negative thinking that are activated by mildly depressed mood even when no differences are observed in euthymic mood (Teasdale and Dent 1987). Evidence to support this proposition has emerged from studies which ask respondents to indicate whether certain globally negative words describe them 'as a person', after a mood induction procedure (Teasdale and Dent 1987; Kelvin *et al.* 1999). A comprehensive review concluded that a mood priming procedure prior to cognitive assessment does reveal depressogenic cognitions in individuals theoretically at risk, though not currently depressed (Segal and Ingram 1994). Thus cognitive vulnerabilities do exist in well subjects with no history but the mechanism which makes them active and potentially destabilising is negative mood.

Ruminative style

It has been proposed that the style of a person's response to low mood will influence their liability for subsequent depression. Nolen-Hoeksema's 'response style' theory of depression postulated that a ruminative style in response to low mood is both causal and maintaining in depressive episodes (Nolen-Hoeksema 2000). Subsequent cross-sectional, prospective and experimental studies showed that ruminative style was associated with prolonged low mood, increased symptoms and onset of clinical depression in young adults (Nolen-Hoeksema 2000). Spasojevic and Alloy (2001) found that rumination mediated the predictive relationship between a range of cognitive risk factors and prospective episodes of depressive disorder in college students. A more ruminative style prior to the onset of depressive illness is also associated with persistent depression at two years (Goodyer 2003). Furthermore, inducing rumination experimentally differentially increases depressed mood in both depressed and well individuals (Park *et al.* 2004). The current evidence supports an activation and destabilising model.

Rumination is the most proximal mechanism through which other cognitive vulnerability factors cause depression. Individuals who have a high ruminating style are most likely to destabilise if they possess a self-devaluative mode of thinking and have had a dysphoric response to an adverse event. This is because distorted pathological cognitions about the self and others come to occupy the conscious mind and cannot be shifted. A vicious cycle of affective-cognitive processing is activated which destabilises behavioural functions. This psychological process is shown in Figure 9.1.

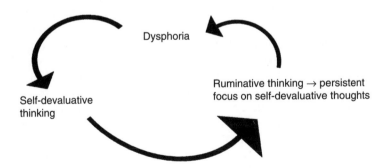

Figure 9.1 The depressogenic affective cognitive cycle

Executive processing dysfunctions

The evidence that it is rumination that destabilises behaviour has led most recently to a consideration of what psychological processing elements are impaired in such a preservative style of thinking. To date there has not been a systematic investigation of the cognitive characteristics of rumination per se. Rather there has been increasing interest in characterising in more detail than hitherto the neuro-cognitive impairments of depression themselves that may then be most associated with the social processing elements and ruminative style prior to the onset of disorder. This has led to a much greater understanding of the cognitive abnormalities involved in depression including memory, attention, motor ability and control functions. Neuro-psychologists have made use of the notion of mood activated cognitive difficulties, but instead of focusing on self-percept they have demonstrated deficits in key executive control areas including:

- decision making with an increase in impulsive decisions, poor choice selection and indecisiveness increasing in mood activated states
- demonstrating that recalling negative material about the self indicates an affectively biased attentional system as well as memory
- loss of inhibition to affectively charged material suggesting that when individuals appraise stimuli which possess a negative affective tone they are more likely to fail to inhibit their responses (Roiser *et al.* 2003; Tavares *et al.* 2003).

Ruminative style is a generic measure of control processes and it is therefore very possible that deficits in decision making, behavioural inhibition and/or attentional switching (i.e. ability to move from ruminating to a distracting stimulus) represent cognitive components of rumination.

Mental coherence to social adversity

Future research needs to bring together in the same investigations the life events models of social psychiatry and the cognitive models of abnormal psychology. The two methods of assessment – systematic social inquiry and experimental manipulation of mood and thoughts – have not been undertaken in prospective designs for any of the common mental disorders. We do not know if socially vulnerable individuals with recently negative life events and with no history of psychopathology also possess cognitive vulnerabilities in self-devaluative, ruminative or executive control processes. This needs to be undertaken. Thus we can only speculate on the possible mechanisms that arise when an individual is exposed to a highly negative experience.

We suggest that when any of us is exposed to an undesirable life event or difficulty a complex series of psychological functions may be brought into play in order to effect an adaptive response. Four interconnected psychological steps are hypothesised that are likely to occur rapidly and automatically:

1   Processing the immediate emotion response.
2   Evaluating the salience of the experience through appraisal and matching with recalled past experiences.
3   Organising a mental strategy for responding to this mnemonic process through parallel activation of (at least) decision making and behavioural inhibition.
4   Synchronising the operation of the aforesaid mental functions to reduce the risk of negative effects on the self.

We also consider that this proposed model for processing social experience operates most effectively when the mind is emotionally 'hot'. This makes efficient emotion processing a key first step of the overall mental response to social adversity.

Thus the level of psychiatric risk following exposure to undesirable life events and difficulties at any stage in the lifespan may be related to one or more of three intermediate cognitive processes:

- over-sensitive response to the associated emotional tone of the experience which may activate cognitive vulnerabilities
- weak control functions allowing for a disorganised behavioural response leading to destabilisation
- failure of overall mental integration such that sensitive and control processes even if potentially effective lack synchrony.

Prospective studies need to determine the concurrence and coherence of the aforesaid mental functions in both 'cold' and 'hot' cognitive states. This is likely to require the incorporation of challenge or demand paradigms in study designs and relating these to the nature of both recent and past social adversities. This methodological issue is clinically as well as theoretically relevant as choice of treatment may depend not only on the clinical features and social environment but also on the characteristics of sensitive and performance mental functions (i.e. the detailed characteristics of the abnormal psychological processes).

Development and destabilisation

Finally we should mention the developmental lifespan perspective to activation and destabilisation. Whilst this model is relatively new, it has been influential in challenging the notion that there are psychologically quiescent periods between distal and proximal vulnerabilities. It has also been most illustrative in the area of behavioural syndromes. This is in marked contrast to the social and cognitive models described in detail above which have focused almost exclusively on emotional syndromes.

A key feature of this model is that it has been developed by researchers concerned in the first instance to determine the environmental precipitants of mental disorders during childhood. In this respect it is not surprising that they should challenge a rather static two-stage model of early and later vulnerabilities. Developmentalists undertake forward rather than backward looking studies and are sceptical of the validity of retrospective approaches in collating and measuring childhood experiences in general and episodes of psychopathology in particular. Indeed the evidence from studies who have followed children into adult life is that when, as adults, they are asked to recall specific experiences they had as children they are highly selective even when prompted for particular events and episodes of illness. Perhaps the key concern in the social-cognitive models derived from studies of adults to date is the absence of the knowledge regarding the concurrent impact of child experiences on the child. Very clear clues that this might be a serious issue for building a model of activation and destabilisation comes from the work of Brown and Harris. Thus in the study where women were asked to recall both child maltreatment experiences and adolescent depression, the findings indicated that the major contribution to the subsequent onset of adult episodes of depression was derived from the teenage depression and not from the reported sexual abuse itself (Bifulco *et al.* 1998). This was one of the first studies to suggest that psychopathology within the first two decades of life was itself a critically important predictor of adult mental disorder. Moreover this finding indicated that the developmental pathway to adult depression may depend not on the exposure to a putatively vulnerable experience but critically to the response mounted at that time.

Theoretically therefore the lifespan approach argues that there are continuous 'proximal vulnerabilities–response characteristics', and it is the dynamic manner within which these interrelate over time that determines whether an individual's trajectory moves more or less towards a destabilising process. It also gives more weight to the notion of a slow formation of disorders and through multiple ongoing processes than a notion of two or more adverse hits occurring at different points in time leading to an onset–offset model of disorder. Rather than the notion of a matching pair of events being important for the sudden onset of disorder the developmental lifespan approach would predict that such an individual will have likely been exposed to multiple similar events of variable intensity over time. For example, Rueter and colleagues (1999) investigated the interdependence between persistent parental disagreements and psychiatric symptoms in 13-year-old adolescents over a period of four years and re-interviewed the subjects for emotional disorders between 19 and 20 years of age. The direct predictors of disorder between 19 and 20 were higher self-report depression scores at 13 years and rising depression scores over the next three years, the two being intercorrelated. It is of interest that parental disagreements at each year point did not directly predict onsets but were crucial moderators of the change in depression scores over time. Rises in parental disagreements correlated with increases in self-reported depressive symptoms. Thus chronic parental disagreements appear to be slow but relentless producers of depressive symptoms leading to subsequent later clinical disorder. Whether highly specific proximal life events involving peers would have altered the nature of these relationships is not clear, as these were not independently measured.

It may also be that social inquiry methods under-recorded important private events such as intra-familial physical and sexual abuse, that are particularly likely to be correlated with psychopathology. Such experiences could be embedded in the broader non-specific category of family discord. Nevertheless, these longitudinal observations suggest an evolving psychosocial process over mid-adolescence exerting significant effects on onset of anxiety and depressive disorders by late adolescence. The findings support a developmental trajectory for depression best predicted by rising depressive symptom levels over time themselves rising in some adolescents via the effects of continuing family difficulties throughout.

In children with behavioural and/or anxiety disorders a similar picture has been noted but from cross-sectional data using retrospective social inquiries conducted with mothers. Sandberg *et al.* (2001) showed that acute personally threatening life events in the year before 'onset' exerted virtually no effect at all on the liability for behavioural or emotional disorders in the school-age years once chronic longstanding family and marital difficulties and events that were a consequence of the child's own behaviour are taken into account. Finally Goodyer and colleagues (2000b) showed that 95 per cent of first episode depression in adolescents occurred in those with two or more longstanding but mainly proximal risk processes, but only a half of these were exposed to a further personally disappointing life event in the 12 months prior to onset. It seems that for adolescent first episode depressions a slow and a fast onset process can occur. Slow emerging illness is probably an example of Rueter's developmental rise into clinical caseness and fast onset illness may reflect that a two-stage model indeed exists in some cases with an acute event correlating closely with disorder. Determining the distinguishing features between slow and fast onsets within a developmental framework has yet to be undertaken.

From the cognitive perspective the models proposed for depression in adults appears developmentally applicable to children above 8 years of age. Thus there is no unique developmental cognitive theory to account for activation and destabilisation of emotional disorders in younger people.

For behaviour disorders we remain almost totally ignorant of the internal activation and destabilisation processes. As noted in Chapters 5 and 6, the neuropsychological antecedents and correlates of childhood onset life course persistent conduct disorder are markedly different from adolescent onsets described in Chapter 7. Thus a developmental perspective is required to examine the social and psychological processes that lead to the destabilisation of young people at risk for conduct disorder through chronic adversities.

Life events, depression and onsets of physical illness

Onsets of physical illness may also act as precipitants of episodes of affective illnesses. One can speculate that they are more likely to do so in vulnerable individuals, but it has not been demonstrated. Life events, when present, appear to increase the likelihood of onsets of depression. However, they are by no means generally followed by episodes of either affective illness or physical disease. In the control groups in the various studies to be reported in this section severe and distressing life events occur in between a fifth and a third of the individuals studied.

Onsets of physical illness as provoking agents

Onsets of serious physical illness are relatively rare in community samples, but liaison psychiatrists working in general hospitals see them all the time. If we discount the rare examples of mood disorder being a direct consequence of the physical disease process (for example, depression in Cushing's disease; anxiety in thyrotoxicosis) or being the direct result of a medical treatment (medication with, for example, phenobarbitone), then we are left with three distinct mechanisms whereby mood disorders can be so precipitated.

Some new physical symptoms are so alarming that anxiety is easily understandable – a breast lump or a heart attack in a previously healthy person, for example. A second way is because multiple pains are also associated with depression. In a large series of patients attending a primary care clinic, Dworkin and his colleagues (1990) showed that in a consecutive series of patients in primary care, the presence of a single pain did not increase the relative risk of depression, but patients with two independent pains had double the risk, while those with three or more had over five times the risk. The third way in which physical illness can increase the risk of depression is because of any handicap (defined as the disadvantage for an individual resulting from ill health). Thus a previously healthy man who finds himself paralysed after a spinal accident may become depressed because of the limitations his paralysis imposes on his activities and the loss of previous abilities.

Indeed, Prince and others (1998) estimated that in the elderly the population attributable fraction of disability or handicap as a predictor of onset was 0.69. Ormel and colleagues (1997) come to a substantially similar conclusion among the elderly in Holland. They find that distress is a function of disability, rather than the type of chronic medical condition the patients had. They make the additional point that once depression has developed, it makes all measures of well-being and functioning worse, both in those with and those without chronic medical conditions. Berg and others (2001) make the additional point that among the elderly, cerebro-vascular disease makes an additional contribution.

Patients with cancer have more than one explanation to their increased likelihood of depressive illness, and that causality may work in both directions. Thus, the reduction in NK cells that is associated with cancer may allow a neoplastic process to start. Once established, the fact that they have a life-threatening illness, the many somatic symptoms they may be experiencing, the fact that their own body will be producing endogenous interferons in response to the cancer as well as any treatment with exogenous interferons, may all contribute to depression.

Life events leading to episodes of physical illness

Life events not only commonly antedate episodes of depression, but are also more common before onsets of some physical diseases. Such relationships are reported before myocardial infarction by Neilsen *et al.* (1989), and before episodes of multiple sclerosis by Grant *et al.* (1989). Schwartz and others (1999) report a vicious circle between stressful events and episodes of disease, with a slightly increased risk of disease progression when rate of reported stressful events was higher (OR = 1.13) and an increased risk of reported stressful events when rate of disease progression was higher (OR = 2.13). Depression is not a necessary intervening variable in this relationship.

Life events leading to depression, leading to unexplained physical symptoms

There are numerous examples of this relationship, which accounts for many consultations in primary care (Goldberg and Bridges 1988). Creed (1989) reported on a series of patients whose severe abdominal pain had resulted in surgeons performing an appendicectomy, but the appendix had turned out to be normal. He found that such pains were more commonly preceded by severe life events than in patients with abnormal appendices, and that an affective disorder was often present. These patients also reported more persistent post-operative pain than those with abnormal appendices, consistent with the effects of the depression.

Life events leading to subclinical anxiety or depression, leading to unexplained physical symptoms

Harris (1989) reports an excess of loss and danger events or provoking agents among patients with menorrhagia, which have led to a state of borderline anxiety. However, as many as 40 per cent of such patients have not experienced such events. These events appear to have a longer time relationship to the disorder than is commonly seen in depression, as they occur at some time in the year preceding the onset of the menorrhagia.

Craig (1989) reported a series of patients with abdominal pain for which no cause had been found seen in a gastro-enterology clinic and found that – in contrast to those for whom a physical cause for the pain was discovered – about two-thirds had a severe event or major difficulty, most often a threatening event focused on the subject. They were also more likely to have experienced goal frustration.

In this study about one-third of those for whom no cause was found for their pain were psychiatric cases, and 56 per cent were either cases or border-line cases: this to be compared with only 17 per cent in the control group. However, almost a half of the 'organic' cases of abdominal pain were also found to be either borderline or actual cases.

Take-home messages

- Vulnerability is determined by distal factors – genetic, intrauterine, infancy, childhood and adolescence – but these are not on their own sufficient to release them.
- Mental disorders are released by proximal factors. Activation refers to the formation and bringing into consciousness of abnormal psychological processes that are required to evoke psychiatric disorder, and destabilisation refers to the behavioural consequences which may follow such activation.
- Developmental theories insist that vulnerabilities may be modified by later experiences – increased further by negative experiences, or decreased by favourable experiences.
- Stressful life events occur with greater than expected frequency before onsets of common disorders, with loss events more common before onsets of depression and danger events before anxious onsets.
- Personality – itself partially under genetic control – determines the types of life event experienced in life, as people create their own environments.
- Once an episode of depression has occurred, a smaller stressor can precipitate a future episode.
- Cognitive appraisal of stressful events is crucially important in determining later onsets of CMD.
- The ruminative style of an individual is associated with the tendency to experience chronic depression.
- Episodes of CMD can also be precipitated by new onsets of severe physical illness.

- Depressed patients, as a group, have changes in their immune system roughly proportional to the severity of depression. Immune changes are also important in mediating the relationship between cancer and depression.

Chapter 10

Restitution

Many health professionals appear to believe that once an illness starts, it will only stop if the person receives an intervention – either a psychological intervention or a psychotropic drug. This is far from being the case. Most common mood disorders resolve spontaneously, and interventions (if successful) merely shorten their course. Other disorders such as obsessional states not secondary to a mood disorder or dependence on alcohol or drugs are far less likely to resolve spontaneously. Finally, there is no evidence that anti-social personality ever resolves spontaneously.

Spontaneous resolution

Many mood disorders are of mild severity and will resolve spontaneously either without lasting long enough, or having quite enough symptoms to satisfy the (arbitrary) diagnostic thresholds of the ICD-10 or DSM-4 classifications. For example, a screening questionnaire like the GHQ asks merely about 'recent' symptoms, without asking how long they have been present. If a second stage case finding interview is carried out immediately or even within one week, validity coefficients are gratifyingly high, but if there is a delay of one month they fall dramatically (Goldberg and Williams 1988).

Surveys that have swept the same population repeatedly confirm this. Brodaty and Andrews (1983) administered the GHQ four times over six months. Although 211 people had high scores on first administration, this figure fell steadily until by six months only 40 per cent of these scores remained high. In 1976 Johnstone and Goldberg assigned patients with unexpectedly high scores to two groups, one where the high score was discussed by the GP, and the other where the score was withheld from the GP. The behaviour of this last group, who received no intervention for their distress, is of particular interest in this context. There was a steady improvement with time, so that by one year after the initial consultation their status was no different from the detected group.

Similar findings emerge with other measures. With the Present State Examination in the community (Brown and Harris 1978; Tennant *et al.* 1981), although with clear initial criteria for defining a case, spontaneous remission becomes much less frequent. The mean duration of episode of depression has been assessed as 12 weeks (Kendler *et al.* 1997, female twins in Virginia, USA), 16 weeks (Kessler *et al.* 2003, both sexes, National Co-morbidity study, USA) and 26 weeks (Angst and Preisig 1995, both sexes Switzerland). In all these surveys, only a minority of the depressions will have received treatment. Thus, the spontaneous remission rate in the community is very high.

The greater the initial severity, the less likely is the disorder to remit quickly (Pevalin and Goldberg 2003). Inevitably, there are more mild disorders in the community than at higher levels of the model, as not only clinical severity increases, but social deviance increases. For this reason the research findings will be set out separately at the various levels of the model.

Depression in community samples

Some of the factors that are important in releasing episodes of illness are also responsible for prolonging the duration of the illness, but others are only related to duration. The former group can be divided into vulnerability factors, and those related to destabilisation – or the release of illness. Vulnerability factors that both increase the probability of illness onset and prolong the illness once it has started include 'neuroticism' and lack of social support, while releasing factors include severe life events and losing one's job. Factors that prolong illness without having a known relationship with onset include care of a sick relative and low social class, while factors that speed recovery up include getting married, and getting a new job. Pevalin and Goldberg (2003) report on data from the British Household Survey, in which 10,000 people were annually surveyed on eight occasions, administering the GHQ as a measure of emotional distress, and various measures of social and other risk factors. They provided data on factors that are associated with both onset and offset of distress. In addition to confirming many of the social factors known to be responsible for delayed recovery were associated one's health-limiting daily activities, having to care for a sick relative and advancing age. As might have been expected, the longer the period of distress, the less one's chances of recovery. Only starting to cohabit, getting married or starting a new job were associated with a faster recovery.

Some indication of the atypical nature of depressives who seek treatment may be discerned by Kendler and colleagues' statement that only 2 per cent of the depressions among his female twins did not recover within one year. In those seeking medical treatment, between one-quarter and one-third were 'treatment resistant'. They show that for all depressions taken together genetic factors and stressful life events (SLEs) predict recovery, but if the data are divided between depressions of shorter and longer duration, a different picture emerges. In short depressions severe SLEs, mastery, family protectiveness, neuroticism and separation are important. For long durations severe SLEs and frequency of contact with relatives are important. Since 'neuroticism' has been found to predict slower recovery in many other studies, it may perhaps be responsible for the genetic factor that emerges in the pooled data.

Brown and Harris (1986) argued that support during a life crisis from a close confidant ('core crisis support') was important in predicting recovery in working-class women. Brown's group (1988, 1992, 1994) have subsequently argued that 'fresh start' and neutralising events commonly precede recovery. An example of the former would be passing an important examination or a new baby, while the latter would be finding a new job after losing one's previous job. Most studies find that a reduction in chronic difficulties also often precedes recovery. Brown and Moran (1994) studied community depressions over three years and found that chronic depression related to childhood adversity, family violence and sexual abuse, as well as to current interpersonal difficulties. A lack of positive events was also important, but less so than in depressions of shorter duration. In the 1992 paper it was argued that fresh start events, which signal hope, would precede recovery from depression, while anchoring and neutralising events, signalling safety, were more common before recovery from anxious symptoms. Harris and her colleagues (1999) have shown the value of 'befriending' for depressed women who lack a close confidant.

Miller and Surtees (1995) studied women who had experienced one of three life crises: bereavement, their partner having a first coronary artery thrombosis, and being admitted to a woman's refuge. In addition to symptom measures, they administered Tyrer and Alexander's (1979) personality schedule. Most women reported receiving much social support from relatives and friends, so this did not emerge as a factor determining outcome. However, subjects who were unexpectedly 'let down' or criticised by friends or family tended to show higher symptom levels, and this was especially true of subjects low on 'impulsivity'. There was evidence that subjects high on 'nervousness' remained symptomatic longer following the adverse experience. The aggressiveness factor showed a curvilinear trend, with those scoring high and low on the scale showing higher symptom levels than those with intermediate scores.

Depression in primary care samples

Coryell and colleagues (1994) followed up 114 patients with untreated depression for 6 months: the mean duration of episode was 6 months, with 50 per cent remission in 25 weeks. More recently Posternak and Miller (2001) studied 221 patients assigned to waiting lists in 19 treatment trials of specific interventions, and found that 20 per cent improved between 4 and 8 weeks, and 50 per cent improved in 6 months. They estimate that 60 per cent of placebo responders and 30 per cent of responders to antidepressants may experience spontaneous resolution of symptoms if untreated. However, it should be noted that people with severe depression are most unlikely to be assigned to waiting lists, so the data is inevitably biased towards milder disorders. These figures are much less sanguine than those for random samples, indicating that some of those whose depressions remit spontaneously in the community do not seek an intervention.

Much of the early work on recovery was carried out in primary care settings, and showed social support to be important, congruent with Brown's findings on core crisis support. Leenstra and her colleagues (1995) were unable to confirm Brown's findings about the specific nature of different kinds of life event in the relief of anxiety versus depression in Dutch general practice, but they did confirm that reduction in chronic difficulties was the single most important factor in producing recovery, and that there is indeed an excess of positive life changes (PLCs, a term that includes all the various kinds of positive life event) before recovery. However, they stress that 39 per cent of the recovered group had *not* had a PLC, and 81 per cent of the non-recovered group had had one. Thus PLCs are neither necessary nor sufficient to produce recovery. Oldehinkel and others (2000) found that positive life change reduced time of remission in women, but not in men. The effects of positive life change in hastening remission were particularly marked in those with high neuroticism. Other factors that hastened remission were fewer pre-morbid difficulties, higher self-esteem and coping styles that favoured tension reduction. Neeleman and others (2003) found that positive life change increases remission rates almost threefold. Lower neuroticism is linked to shorter episode duration, and this is unrelated to positive life change. Remission rates are higher in those with larger social networks and who seek more help.

Ronalds and her colleagues (1997) confirmed that difficulty reduction was an important determinant of outcome, but argued that the severity of the initial illness at the time the patient was first seen was also very important. High educational level also predicted improvement.

Earlier work had underlined the importance of physical illness in failure to remit and emotionally disturbed childhoods in delaying restitution (Cooper 1964); the presence of physical illness and unresolvable social and financial problems (Kedward 1969). Mann *et al.* (1981) pointed out the importance of initial severity as a prognostic factor.

Depression seen by the mental illness service

Several studies deal with depressed outpatients seen by psychiatrists. Brown's group (1994) applied the same measures of childhood adversity and current interpersonal difficulties as they had in their community sample (1994), and found that these same factors predicted episodes taking a course of more than 12 months' duration. The patients were at higher risk than the community

166 The model proposed

series (75 per cent vs 34 per cent) and this explains their much greater rate of chronicity. There was also some evidence that social support reduced risk. This study attempted a rough classification of the four DSM-4 personality disorders, and reported that those with such disorders were not at greater risk of a chronic course.

Others have used questionnaire measures of personality and have not replicated this finding. Surtees and Wainwright (1998) followed patients presenting to hospital with depression for 12 years. They found that the lack of self-confidence scale of Foulds and Bedford's personality deviance scales and neuroticism from the Eysenck Personality Inventory both predicted aspects of the future illness. Low self-confidence measures similar to 'negative evaluation of the self' (NES in Brown's work) strongly predicted recurrence in the first year, while both these and loss events predicted eventual outcome. This study did not find that severity, as measured by the initial score on the Hamilton scale, had prognostic importance but all the illnesses were fairly severe. Ezquiaga and colleagues (1998) studied 90 patients with depression treated in mental health centres and found that the presence of personality disorders assessed by NES, having suffered a previous episode, some overall severity of the illness and the presence of social support were the variables most associated with incomplete remission.

Earlier studies (Huxley and Goldberg 1975; Sims 1975; Huxley et al. 1979) identified poor parental relations, unhappy childhood, pathological and immature personalities, presence of somatic problems, frequent change of job and a poor marital relationship.

Patients admitted to inpatient units with depression are more likely to have severe depressive features of 'melancholia' than ambulant patients, as well as more severe illnesses and more deviant personalities. Duggan and others (1990) report an 18-year follow-up of 89 patients admitted to hospital with severe depression and confirm that high neuroticism and high scores on an obsessional inventory were both associated with poor long-term outcome. As might be expected, high scores on psychotic features of depression were also related to a worse outcome. Andrews and others (1990) report broadly similar findings from Australia. Diagnosis was less important than personality deviation, which accounted for 20 per cent of the variation in outcome.

Summary

Recovery from common mental disorders seems largely dependent upon events taking place outside the doctor or therapist's office. The factors that determine speed of recovery are remarkably similar in the various settings. It is the frequency of risk factors and the mean severity of illness, the remediability of social problems and the history of previous illnesses that differ between the various settings. Effective therapies are those that shorten the duration that the illness would otherwise take, rather than make the difference between continued illness and complete recovery.

Take-home messages

- Most common mental disorders will remit given enough time. The effect of treatment, when effective, is to shorten the duration of episode.
- The more severe the disorder, the longer it is likely to last.
- One community study showed that delayed recovery was associated with one's health-limiting daily activities, having to care for a sick relative and advancing age.
- Close support from a person in whom one can confide, events signalling a 'fresh start' and reduction in chronic difficulties are all associated with recovery.
- Lower neuroticism is linked to shorter episode duration, and this is unrelated to positive life change.
- Remission rates are higher in those with larger social networks and who seek more help

---

Chapter 11

Synthesis

Vulnerability, destabilisation and restitution

In this chapter we will gather together the threads of our various arguments under three headings – depression and anxiety, anti-social behaviour and gender differences – and summarise what we have learned about the determinants of vulnerability as they relate to the three commonest mental disorders: anxiety disorders, depressive disorders and anti-social behaviour. We will state what is known about factors that favour depression, and those that favour anxiety, and summarise knowledge about gender differences. Those wishing to have references to the studies cited will find them in earlier chapters.

When this has been done, we will state in our final chapter what is known about factors that promote resilience, and consider what might be done to prevent many mental disorders by increasing resilience.

Vulnerability to depression and anxiety

Vulnerability is defined as a process that increases the liability for mental disorder but of itself is insufficient to cause disorder. A vulnerability process is likely to contain one or more factors each likely to carry a small effect such that on their own their association with the subsequent onset of mental illness is small. For example, we saw in Chapter 3 that the genetic factors contributing to vulnerability are shared between depression and anxiety. What the precise genes are remains unclear but it is apparent that it is not one gene or even one particular set of genes. Thus many genes that code for neuro-developmental processes (i.e. how the brain is built) and those involved peptide formation (i.e. chemicals that are key in moderating behavioural signals and responses) may contribute differentially to the risk for mental illnesses. The combination of genes within and between neural systems responsible for psychological development, response to stress and mainten-ance of homeostasis may have one or more deficiencies that can lead to genetic vulnerability. Similar principles apply to cognitions and social environments. For example, single adverse environments, even very severe ones such as personal assault, carry modest long-term (beyond the days and few weeks after the acute impact) risk to well-being. Most victims of maltreatment who suffer long-term sequelae have been exposed to multiple events of that type and indeed others. Deficits in emotion (e.g. overly sensitive, or blunted ability to read others' emotion, or to respond to emotion signals), social cognition (e.g. a distortion in perspective taking that others have about oneself), and executive functions (e.g. preservative thinking style dwelling on negative themes due to failures of attention), all represent potential components of an internal vulnerability process.

So vulnerability processes are complex phenomena likely to involve patterns of factors within a given domain (genes, mood and thought patterns, social environments) and between these domains. When researchers report a 'vulnerability factor' they are therefore likely to be detecting only one part of a highly complex process altering the individual's liability for common mental disorder. Similarly when clinicians formulate a working hypothesis that this episode of depression was 'caused by' a breakdown in current relationships they are only identifying one aspect of a potential chain of events and happenings both outwith and within the person.

A final point to note is how little specificity we have found in vulnerability processes to date. It seems that inherited or early developmental predispositions are not intrinsically setting up particular forms of mental illness. Having said this no studies have yet been in a position to calculate the liability for say depressions versus anxiety or behavioural disorders because we do not know the precise 'vulnerability map' for given disorders. Indeed we have seen from Chapter 2 that individuals may be 'co-morbid' for both disorders. This may be concurrent (different clinical phenotypes at the same time) or sequential co-morbidity (i.e. different clinical phenotypes at different times in their life). We have shown that vulnerability 'factors' recognised to date are often common to both disorders. This suggests that it is only when both genetic and environmental factors are considered together that we will begin to detect underlying divergence between the processes that result in different emotional disorders.

Genetics

A substantial contribution – somewhere around 40 per cent – of the determinants and symptoms of both *anxiety and depression* are genetic, but it seems likely that these are multiple recessive genes that determine a common vulnerability to both sets of symptoms. The location of these genes is still a matter of conjecture, but recent studies have isolated numerous locations on different chromosomes. Even when such work is more advanced, it will be necessary to understand precisely which ones are involved, and which proteins each gene controls. Our best guess is that these genes are mainly controlling emotional traits emerging through childhood, such as fearfulness and shyness, rather than being specific for more complex states such as anxiety and depression. Genes are also clearly important in other basic emotions such as aggression and in executive emotional processes such as approach–withdrawal and behavioural inhibition. It may be that the expression of these genes for these basic emotional processes are developmentally sensitive. For example, the initial sensitivity of the HPA axis is set genetically, although this sensitivity can be adjusted upwards or downwards by subsequent experiences.

It does not seem at all likely that specific genes are controlling specific disorders. There is evidence that there are some other genes responsible for vulnerability to disorders related to fear like *panic and phobias*; but the overlap with genes responsible for anxiety and depression is substantial. 'G×E interactions' are important for depression: loss events exert only a small relationship to depression unless a particular abnormality on the 5HTT transporter gene is present. We have argued that many such genes will be determining the 'upstream' controlling processes at the resilient end of the dimension – the tendency to resist disorders in later life at times of special stress.

At present we have no means of directly assessing the strength of such genes for complex behavioural traits. The personality dimension of *neuroticism* (loosely equivalent to harm avoidance or negative emotionality in other systems) is a composite that is highly influenced by these genes, but also by early environmental factors. Similarly in children the temperamental trait of emotionality (easily reacting to minor stimuli in the environment with fearfulness, tears and inhibition but also quick to settle following exposure) is genetically determined. Other genes control both hormones and immune responses, and thus determine brain sex and the foetal development of primary sexual characteristics, as well as the secondary sexual characteristics that will develop at puberty. Within the brain it is also increasingly apparent that genes for behaviour may be turned on and off by non-genomic factors. For example, it is now clear that steroid receptors act as transcription factors turning on genes for subsequent complex behavioural tasks. The gene for coding the formation of the peptide oxytocin is activated when the sex hormone oestrogen binds to its beta-receptor subunit. This is a highly specific effect indicating a key specific steroid-gene process in the control of the level of approach and avoidance behaviours towards another individual. This is not a sex-specific mechanism however, as this happens in the brains of females and males. What we do not know in this highly neurobiological example of behavioural control is whether there are different set points in the male and female brain and whether in the male brain other androgens influence this operation.

Another G×E interaction is seen with animal studies on monkeys subjected to maternal separation, which show that those offspring who carry the 's' allele of the 5HTT gene are more likely to show abnormal brain chemistry and be more fearful and less pro-social than their mother-reared counterparts with the same genetic make-up.

Much of the later vulnerability over the lifespan will be determined by a combination of genes predisposing a child to the formation of anxious traits and others partly controlling the development of complex personality characteristics. These behavioural aspects are formed gradually over development. The vulnerabilities within the person, such as high fearfulness for emotional disorders or low empathy for behavioural syndromes, may be increased still further by experiences which occur after birth, or may be reduced by favourable experiences. The extent to which positive experiences diminish genetic risk is a key component for resilience research in the future.

Infancy

The most important early environmental contribution to later anxiety and depressive symptoms is the quality of maternal attachment. Attachment theory proposes that infants develop 'internal working models' of relationships that serve as a psychological blueprint for interpersonal functions with others in childhood and later life. There are differential effects of such early relationships in developing components of social competence, feeling sympathy with others and exerting regulatory controls on how to respond at times of interpersonal conflict. This is the first experience during life which can increase or decrease genetic vulnerability. Inevitably, these views are based on the experience of people who have had very depriving experiences during the first few months of life, and from animals separated from their mothers for trial periods during neonatal life. What is required now is to ascertain individuals with known specific genetic vulnerability variables (even if the size of effect remains unknown) and determine prospectively how maternal environments influence development. For example, we could follow the development of infants with 's' allelic variants in the serotonin transporter and note individual differences in the development of known cognitive vulnerabilities for affective disorders such as the bias for rumination. We could also type such infants for other genes of interest, for example, allelic variations in the steroid receptor. Such variations might alter the receptor sensitivity to steroids and thereby the rate of transcription of proteins. These studies would require large samples, and the more genes measured and considered to work in combination with each other, the larger the samples would have to be.

A wealth of evidence, both human and animal, shows that early deprivation causes changes in the sensitivity of the HPA axis. In humans, maternal separation is followed by disruptions of attachment and delayed development. Loss of maternal care through separation leads to a potential change in the chemical signalling processes between the limbic system and the frontal and pre-frontal cortex.

A human infant with 'disorganised attachment' does not seek close contact with its caregiver, and may look confused as its mother displays gaze avoidance. This predicts social competence during childhood and social withdrawal in adolescence. Other varieties of poor attachment may show indifference or anger towards their caregiver. This leads to poor social development with a tendency to more anti-social behaviour and displays of negative emotion. If poor attachment is followed by persistent negative experiences this leads to anxious and behaviour disorders in middle childhood. Severe deprivation during infancy is associated with changes in the sensitivity of the HPA axis with cortisol hypersecretion. A prospective study of adolescents exposed to maternal postnatal depression and difficult early experiences as a result showed significant increases in morning cortisol levels at 13 years of age.

Maternal separation in rats causes the HPA system to be hyper-responsive, so that adult exposure to social defeat leads to anxious behaviour and long-lasting raised cortisol. Loss of maternal care through separation leads to a potential change in the chemical signalling processes between the limbic system and the frontal and pre-frontal cortex. Other studies with rats show that good maternal behaviours ('high licking and grooming') lead to a less labile HPA axis in later life. Cross-fostering designs show that this is an environmental effect, not mediated by genes. Loss of maternal care through separation leads to a potential change in the chemical signalling processes between the limbic system and the frontal and pre-frontal cortex. When females (from low LGN mothers) who have experienced high LGN mothering have their own litters, they continue to manifest high LGN behaviours. Good mothering is being transmitted without the presence of altered genes, but which alter subsequent gene expression. Their offspring will have increased hippocampal glucocorticoid receptor mRNA expression, higher central benzodiazepine receptor levels in the amygdala, and lower corticotropin releasing factor mRNA in the paraventricular nucleus of the hypothalamus.

Childhood

Severe chronic privations, such as being brought up in an orphanage since birth, are also associated with changes in the sensitivity of the HPA axis – with cortisol hypersecretion frequently reported. Many studies have demonstrated that these privation experiences are associated with an increase in common emotional and behavioural disorder in the school-age years.

It has become increasingly apparent that maltreatment of children (physical and sexual abuse) has significant biological consequences for neural systems and chemical codes for behaviour. Child maltreatment is associated with cortisol hypersecretion in some studies but also with hyposecretion in others. Girls are at greater risk than boys for sexual abuse.

In contrast to the effects of poor attachment, the effects of poor parenting practices are less dramatic. Poor parenting, whether overinvolved or depriving, both carry increased risks of common mental disorders later, but each can occur without the other. Marital discord, often associated with separations and violence, exerts an effect on common mental disorders in the children independent of the effects of parenting. Children who have experienced parental divorce and parental death also have higher rates of common mental disorders in adult life. Concepts of self-worth, peer popularity and social competence develop during childhood and have important later consequences for common mental disorders. Of these, the development of friends is the most important non-family activity. Those who do not develop friendships may have difficulties handling negative life events in later life.

Different infant temperaments relate to different disorders later: shy, tearful and easily upset to later depression. Children subjected to physical or sexual abuse display a wide range of common mental disorders in adolescence – not only much higher rates of depression, but self-harm behaviours and eating disorders, as well as problems in obtaining satisfactory sexual relationships.

It is only during middle childhood that children begin to adjust their self-perceptions as a result of failure at key tasks, with the first emergence of feelings of shame, helplessness and hopelessness. It is at this stage that the germs of later depressive illness become manifest as early cognitive changes occur especially in those who have a tendency to persistently ruminate and perseverate about real or supposed shortcomings.

Adolescence

The most common emotional disorder that emerges during the adolescent years is depression. This in part relates to tendencies to nervousness in childhood, partly due to the negative thoughts about the self that may have become habitual due to repeated failures in friendships or discouragement from parents or teachers, and which may be accompanied by physiological arousal. Girls who are unpopular with their peers and who have few friends are at high risk, boys somewhat less so.

We have described sequences of events which commonly lead to later depressive illnesses in Chapter 8. Chronic social difficulties are associated with higher rates of onset of all common mental disorders. We know that genetic vulnerabilities for depression referred to are more potent in the adolescent compared with the childhood years. By contrast it may be that genetic vulnerabilities for conduct disorder are more potent in the childhood years and associated with persistent life course anti-social behaviour and personality disorder in adult life.

Adult life

Childhood traumas are remembered by fewer people as age progresses, but among those remembering them there is a consistently higher rate of common mental disorders throughout the life cycle. A mutually satisfying relationship with a partner in whom one can confide, and the presence of social support in one's immediate environment, are both helpful in producing resilience to later stress.

One longitudinal study shows that those who have experienced divorce or separation during adult life are also more likely to develop disorders. As age advances, some sorts of stressful event (death of close family member, injury or onset of serious physical illness) become more likely, and this causes an increased rate of onsets of common disorders. However, there is no overall increase in rates of onset, since many other sorts of stressful life event (divorce or separation, problems at work, legal and financial problems) become less common.

Destabilisation

Most but not all onsets of depressive or anxious symptoms are preceded by stressful life events or major social difficulties. There is a moderate relationship between loss events and depression, and events signalling threat or danger with anxious symptoms. The superimposition of cognitive changes on an underlying anxious diathesis makes depressive symptoms more likely. The experience of failure and a sense of shame encourage depressive thoughts. Features such as low self-confidence, adverse social circumstances and having no intimate confidant also make depression more likely.

However, many events cannot be so neatly categorised, and mixtures of the two kinds of symptom are more common than either set of symptoms on their own. There is fairly good evidence for a stress-sensitisation hypothesis, where those who have experienced various kinds of childhood adversity will have lower thresholds for developing symptoms – with that threshold being roughly proportional to the severity of the childhood adversity. However, with a severe enough stress, symptoms can develop in the absence of earlier adversity.

It has been shown that there is an abnormality in serotonin function in vulnerable women in the community with a new onset of major depression that has been brought about by recent life events and difficulties. These findings support the theoretical proposition that a particular set of the serotonin receptors in the brain are activated by social adversity and mediate the syndromes of anxiety and depression. Serotonin activation of the neural system relating to peri-ventricular and peri-aqueductal grey matter inhibits inborn fight/flight reactions to impending danger, pain, or asphyxia. It has been proposed that depletion of serotonin provides a unitary explanation for impairments in the two key coping systems processes: loss of sensitivity to fearful stimuli and blunted flight/fight reactions. It has been established that morning cortisol hypersecretion precedes and predicts the onset of major depression in both adult women and adolescents of both sexes. Since morning, but not evening cortisol levels are under a high degree of genetic control, this suggests a marked genetic influence on cortisol vulnerability for the later onset of depression.

Occupancy of steroid receptors in the hippocampus and the amygdala triggers a complex cascade of cellular events in the serotonin (and other) systems in the pre-frontal and orbito-frontal cortex, leading to cognitive controls and behavioural actions. Serotonin vulnerable individuals will react poorly to the corticoid driven affective signals arising from deeper in the brain. High cortisol will therefore not be adequately responded to and may lead to abnormal psychological processes and psychiatric disorders.

Restitution

Restitution is here referred to in the sense of a return to the status quo ante, so that the individual no longer possesses the critical number of symptoms used to define a 'case'. A substantial number of episodes of anxiety or depression will respond without treatment, although many will relapse later. Low self-confidence strongly predicts recurrence of depression. About a quarter will be resistant to first line treatments.

Nevertheless, with moderate or severe depression there is evidence for the efficacy of both drug treatment and specific psychological treatments over the effects of placebos. More severe illnesses take longer to recover, and are less likely to improve spontaneously. Life changes involving either a 'fresh start' or a reduction of social difficulties improve speed of recovery, as does the availability of support from an intimate confidant during the episode. Factors delaying recovery include disability caused by physical illness limiting daily activities, having to care for a sick relative and advancing age.

Vulnerability to anti-social behaviour (ASB)

Vulnerability factors for behavioural disorders are less clear-cut than those for emotional disorders. It is not that we do not know about significant correlates between genes, environments and abnormal behaviour, rather there appears a much more direct set of associations between chronic social adversities and the formation of behavioural disorders, at least in childhood. The processes that activate anti-social episodes either between the index person and another, or within groups, remains unclear. Thus what collection of processes results in a child, adolescent or adult to commit at that moment an act of violence to another person or destruction of property or steal is not clear. There may be activating processes in the environment or within the individual that remain to be clearly elucidated. That they are different from emotional disorders is apparent.

Genetics

Genetic factors are much more important in the early child onset forms of anti-social behaviour than in the later adolescent forms. This may be related to levels of aggression associated with the form of conduct disorder but the developmental findings are rather equivocal as aggression does not change much within individuals over the first two decades of life. The precise gene–behaviour characteristics are likely to be complex. For example, there are important genetic contributions to anti-social behaviour mediated by psychological characteristics such as (lack of) constraint and novelty seeking. These are under major (about four-fifths) genetic control, and a significant genetic contribution to overall vulnerability to anti-social behaviour.

A G×E interaction relevant to behavioural disorders is the observation that maltreated children with a genotype conferring high levels of MAOA expression were less likely to develop anti-social problems. In this example of a G×E interaction there is a potential for genetic resilience in the face of environmental adversity. Vulnerable children would be those without high levels of MAO expression in the brain.

There are also clear-cut reductions in the grey matter of the brain in adults diagnosed with psychopathic disorders and with a childhood history of conduct disorder. All these findings support a genetically mediated brain-based difference to explain responses to social adversity being different in behaviourally disordered individuals compared with the population at large over the lifespan.

There are also changes in the serotonin system in severe psychopaths who show low serotonin function correlated with increased impulsivity compared with controls. This impaired serotonin and increased impulsivity response, combined with low or flat cortisol levels at times of stress, has important implications for ASB. Cortisol is part of the chemical coding pathway that 'accesses' personally salient emotional related memories. Low sensitivity to fearfulness may impair the mobilisation of a fear response through loss of retrieval of fear-related memories. Such memories may not even be 'kept in memory' by behaviour disordered individuals. This will blunt any signalling processes to cognitive centres in the cortex and serotonin vulnerable individuals will be at risk for disinhibited, impulsive non-socially adaptive behavioural responses following adverse experiences.

Infancy

As in anxiety and depression, the quality of maternal attachment is also important in anti-social behaviour. A poorly attached infant does not seek close contact with its caregiver, and may show indifference or anger. This leads to poor social development with a tendency to more anti-social behaviour and displays of negative emotion. If insecure attachment is followed by persistent negative experiences this leads to anxious and behaviour disorders in middle childhood. There may be biological consequences of this not explained by genetic predispositions. Thus children, adolescents and adults with *severe* conduct disorders and a history of early onset have been shown to have remarkably suppressed cortisol levels compared with controls at times of frustration. Severe privation experiences in infancy may diminish steroid receptor sensitivity in genetically vulnerable individuals. This may down-regulate the infant's ability to emotion process and regulate emotion-related behaviours.

Different infant temperaments relate to different disorders later. In the case of anti-social behaviour, impulsivity, restlessness and distractibility increase the liability to anti-social personality. Since these are highly heritable it may be that these infants are most at risk for difficult attachment experiences.

Childhood

Parents of children with anti-social behaviour have an increased rate of insensitive, harsh parenting, and tend not to set limits on their child's behaviour. Having said this, many children with anti-social behaviours during childhood do not become anti-social adults, but others have the life course persistent form of the disorder.

Abused and neglected children are more likely to develop anti-social behaviour, but many do not do so. A G×E interaction could well be important here, but this is not yet known. Children with anti-social behaviour are more likely to have soft CNS signs, undercontrolled temperaments and hyperactivity and poor performance on intelligence tests. These disorders are substantially more common among boys. The experience of parental divorce increases the rates for conduct disorder and anti-social behaviour.

Children with low empathy for others, particularly if associated with high activity and low sociability levels, are also more likely to develop conduct disorder. Unlike emotional disorders, the internal components of vulnerability do not appear mood sensitive. Thus low empathy and blunted emotion recognition are conscious processes regardless of the child's own mood state. Thus conduct disordered children do not have to be angry to be difficult or to commit anti-social acts.

Adolescence

Adolescent onset conduct disorders are relatively common in the teenage years. These occur in the main via deviant friendship groups and are not markedly associated with chronic adversities beginning in childhood. Such cases do not show the cognitive and affective deficits seen in child onset cases or anti-social adults. Early sexual maturation is advantageous for boys, with increases in popularity, self-esteem and intellectual abilities but an increased risk for delinquent behaviour. Behavioural disorders that persist through into adolescence do so because of chronic unremitting family adversities and the underlying genetic vulnerabilities and their associated cognitive deficits. Delinquency and severe violent behaviour may arise during adolescence in those with minor or no childhood difficulties closely associated with membership of a changing and often deviant peer group. Some personality types – in particular, those indicating behavioural under-control, impulsivity and risk taking – are at special risk of drug and alcohol disorders.

Destabilisation

Although it is probable that episodes of drug and alcohol dependence take their onset at times of stress in people's lives – the much higher prevalence of drug dependence among disadvantaged, unemployed adolescents and the occurrence of a move from heavy alcohol use to dependence at times of life crises in adult males (after separation or divorce, for example) – there is less evidence on this point, and in any case 'first use' of either agent takes place many years beforehand. There is little or no evidence that anti-social behaviour occurs mainly at times of major life stress. More likely is that minor everyday hassles result in greater perturbations in conduct vulnerable individuals.

Gender differences in common mental disorders

Exposure to testosterone masculinises the foetal brain. Consistent behavioural differences between male and female infants can be observed from birth onwards, and are related to levels of testosterone that the foetus is exposed to. On the first day of life, males will stare longer at a mobile, but females stare longer at a human face. Later, there are consistent differences in the play behaviours of the pre-school toddler. The male superiority in throwing is seen in toddlers only 2 years old, so cannot be due to practice at school. Males show a higher preference for playing alone, with toy cars, aeroplanes and tractors or with constructional toys. Boys like to ascend dominance hierarchies and use less subtle techniques than girls to do so.

Girls show a preference for co-operative play with teddy bears and dolls. These may be related to differences in cerebral laterality, occurring in the developing foetal and early infant brain related in part to testosterone. These developmental differences between the sexes have been related to the greater tendency of females to 'empathise' – or greater capacity to imagine what others are feeling, and better language skills – and the greater tendency of males to 'systematise' – or greater interest in how things work and better spatial skills. It must be emphasised that these are dimensional constructs and there is considerable overlap between the distributions for the two genders. So much so that there are females who are predominant systematisers and males who mainly empathise. But overall, the two qualities are normally distributed, with a clear female superiority in empathising and a male superiority in systematising.

A marked social difference is also apparent in friendship behaviours which may be connected to these psychological differences. Having few friends is characteristic of depressed boys as well as depressed girls, but we need to understand how many friendless boys escape depression.

As noted in Chapter 6 on childhood there are considerable changes in friendship behaviour over the child and adolescent period. There are sex-differentiated components to these. Both sexes show a preference for same-sex friendships in childhood with increasing growth for between-sex friendships occurring over adolescence. Female friendship networks in childhood are dominated by verbal communications with emotional language, males by performance language. Translated into everyday language, this means that emotions, both positive and negative, are more characteristic of girls' friendship patterns, while boys are more reserved. Where girls may make critical and personal remarks to another girl who has become unpopular (e.g. about her looks), boys are more likely to make performance remarks (e.g. about abilities). Females show high turnover of close one-to-one friendships within a relatively stable network; in contrast males show a relatively low turnover of close friends but also within a relatively stable network. Thus compared to males, females throughout childhood and adolescence are more exposed to intercurrent disappointing experiences than are boys within their friendship framework. This suggests that females are more exposed overall to one of the risks for emotional disorders, namely acute disappointments in confiding relationships. Such acute disappointments are however potent risks for depression for both sexes in first episode depressions in adolescents (Goodyer et al. 2000a). Empathising, being a female trait, may increase the liability for emotional symptoms in the presence of acute disappointments. Conversely, systematising may confer a certain degree of protection for an unpopular boy, who can still develop and derive satisfaction from some of the solitary interests of systematisers, like computing, model building, bird-watching, collecting stamps or the numbers of trains. To the extent that these are behaviours more often seen among males, and provide a degree of satisfaction, a friendless boy has a theoretical advantage over a friendless girl. It seems highly likely that these sexually differentiated processes embedded in the notions of empathising and systematising will contribute to distinctive clinical characteristics of anxiety and depression in females and behavioural disorders in males.

This would be a difference observed in children as well as adolescents, but the emergence of the female excess in depression is a postpubertal event. Thus compared to males more females may become depressed in adolescence as a result of an interaction between acute close friendship disappointments, high empathising and hormone changes post puberty. This leaves unanswered what the distinctive features of puberty are that may add to the bias in females being more likely to be depressed compared to males. Given that the increased liability for affective disorders in girls is best indexed by sex hormones and not observable physical change, it is likely that the additional risk reflects these postpubertal psycho-endocrine changes rather than the external changes of physical development. Further research is needed to determine what these additional risks might be.

One set of additional features that may add to the female risk for depression is the higher level of ruminations and negative automatic thoughts found in girls compared to boys. There is clear-cut evidence that ruminations are a major proximal risk factor for depression. Dwelling or perseverating on self-devaluative thoughts induces greater levels of dysphoria and increase the risk of clinical depression.

Overall it appears likely that the sex-differentiated risk is about an additive process of risks more likely to be found in female than male brains. Of course behaviours and their related neurobiology associated with being a male or a female occur in both sexes. In this way it is possible that a smaller proportion of males will be vulnerable to depression and perhaps emotional disorders in general.

This speculative model will necessarily have caveats. One already established is that very high systematisers, at the extreme end of the distribution, appear more likely to experience depression in adolescence. These patients are predominantly male with Asperger's syndrome or high functioning autism. Research has shown that there is an increased rate of depression and obsessive compulsive disorders in these relatives not explained by the burden of raising a disabled child (Smalley et al. 1995; Bolton et al. 1998). This uncommon group demonstrates that at the extreme ends of the distribution for systematising the mechanisms for affective disorder may be different and not apply to the population at large.

Adult life

The lowest rates for mental disorder are found in married people of both sexes. Cohabitation is associated with higher rates for mental disorders in women, but not in men. Unmarried mothers have very high rates. In both sexes, separation, divorce and widowhood signal higher rates. Among adults, there is by now a heavy male preponderance for such externalising disorders seen in childhood such as drug dependency, alcohol dependence and anti-social behaviour, and an equally strong female preponderance for internalising disorders, of which depression and anxiety are the most common.

We do not as yet know if there is an additive vulnerability model for externalising disorders for males as there is for females. Theoretically it seems highly likely. Males with low empathy, low cortisol levels at times of 'stress', low ruminative thinking, high neuropsychological deficits and high deprivation experiences in childhood may constitute one such set of vulnerability factors. As with female vulnerability for depression, the liability for crossing the threshold for anti-social behaviour may depend on the patterning of these factors as well as their number. This will become clearer with further prospective research into gender differences.

Take-home messages

- The origins of externalisng disorders are quite distinct from those of internalising disorders.
- While insecure attachment is more common in both, the influence of shared family environment is more important in the externalising disorders.
- We discuss in this chapter reasons why males display more external-ising disorders, and females more internalising disorders, through-out the life cycle.
- The two groups of disorders are associated with different genetic origins, with different temperamental and personality character-istics, and styles of parental discipline are relatively more important in externalising disorders.
- Vulnerability processes are characterised by the interactions between several variables not by the effects of a single factor.
- Vulnerability profiles are most likely to be found 'vertically' involv-ing social, psychological and neurochemical processes.
- Although some sections of this chapter are necessarily speculative, we have attempted to give the outlines of these very different origins.

Chapter 12

Prevention of common mental disorders

Resilience

It follows from the previous chapter that a child without a family history of common mental disorder, who has been securely attached to its caregiver, whose parents have a happy marriage, and who has not experienced parental neglect or physical or sexual abuse, is likely to have a low neuroticism score and a corresponding resistance to later life stress. If it experiences a sense of achievement and self-confidence at school and goes on to make a successful partnership in adult life, the risk of illness is decreased still further. This is fairly obvious and hardly leads to a preventive programme.

A resilient individual has a sense of self-confidence and high self-esteem; a repertoire of social problem-solving approaches; a secure stable affectionate relationship with another person, and experience of success and achievement. Even someone with a poor start in life may achieve a more resilient position by achieving one of these aims. For example, Rutter (1985b) has shown that someone reared in a depriving institution who obtains marital support in early adult life will achieve a better adjustment than someone who cannot achieve that objective. A good marriage is indeed a potent protective factor, in that it reduces the rate of stressful life events and enables people to cope with stressful random life events (Notarius and Pellegrini 1984).

Masten and others (1999) studied 205 inner city children for a period of 10 years after baseline observations in elementary school. The investigators studied the three domains of academic achievement, conduct and peer social competence and found that higher intelligence and good parenting appeared to have a specific protective role where anti-social behaviour was concerned, and were associated with good outcomes in all three domains. Resilient adolescents were said to be those who had adequate functioning in all domains despite high adversity. They differed from their maladaptive peers by having more resources and less negative emotionality (see Chapter 1).

Styles of functioning that may have protective value include the use of emotional 'distancing' to deal with a situation which cannot be avoided, and the ability to generate humour (Garmezy 1985). They also include traits not normally considered desirable, like callous indifference to others. Men who score low on empathising, as well as abnormally psychopathic individuals, may be relatively spared anxiety and depression.

Kinds of preventive programmes

The genes that an individual is born with cannot (yet) be altered. Early lack of attachment cannot be remedied. Childhood experiences cannot be modified retrospectively and random life stresses cannot be prevented. Prevention of disorders may not be easy, but it can be done.

Preventive programmes aim to improve the lot of future children, and remedy those features of present adjustment that can still be modified. For economic reasons, these strategies are often aimed at high risk groups. They do this by trying to improve parenting practices including encouraging attachment and reducing child abuse, by arranging for mothers either to avoid puerperal depression altogether or to have it treated early, and by improving friendships and the establishment of self-confidence. Adult life styles which may improve general functioning and a sense of well-being, include taking regular exercise, ensuring that time is available for leisure activities and improving the quality of relationships with partners. Some of these are easier to achieve than others!

It is customary to divide preventive activities into *primary prevention*, which seeks to prevent a disorder occurring at all, and *secondary prevention*, which seeks to bring early and effective treatment to those who have developed a disorder. Finally, *tertiary prevention* seeks to reduce disability that has developed already. We will give examples of each of these.

Primary prevention

Primary prevention refers to measures which can be taken to prevent disorders occurring at all. These can be divided into *universal measures*, which are applied to the whole population, and *selective measures*, which refer to measures applied to subpopulations thought to be at higher risk of developing the disorder that is to be prevented.

Universal measures

Some have argued that it makes better sense in public health terms to prevent morbidity by lowering the general level of symptoms in the entire population (Anderson *et al.* 1993). This argument certainly applies to political actions to improve the health of a community such as making physical punishment of children illegal, limiting alcohol use by taxation and licensing hours, or improving the housing stock and leisure facilities available to a population. While we may approve such actions, one can observe that although we are a more affluent society in the UK than we were 100 years ago, it is difficult to demonstrate any reduction in prevalence.

One of the few interventions to produce a reduction in suicide rates by limiting the way suicide is reported in the media was seen during a newspaper strike in Detroit (Motto 1970) and when Viennese newspapers agreed to report railway deaths in a less sensational way (Etzerdorfer *et al.* 1992).

Prevention programmes in schools aimed at reducing drug use have been shown to be effective. White and Pitts (1998) carried out a meta-analysis of 10 RCTs. Donaldson and others (2000) report modest success (7 to 10 per cent reduction) in the proportion of adolescents using alcohol in their early teens.

Encouraging results have been reported for school-based programmes aimed at reducing anti-social behaviour – starting with the Good Behaviour Game in primary school (Kellam and Rebok 1992) and going on to Olweus' work in Scandinavia, in which victimisation and bullying were tackled in whole-school interventions that included the creation of environments characterised by warmth, positive interest and involvement with adults combined with the use of firm limits and non-hostile sanctions when rules were broken (Olweus 1991).

An unusual brief intervention by GPs aimed at improving parenting skills by fostering positive parent–child interactions and promoting maternal self-esteem has reported remarkable long-term results. At age 28, the children whose mothers had received the intervention reported lower rates of neurotic symptoms, tobacco use and better academic achievement, with females reporting fewer depressive symptoms (Cullen and Cullen 1996).

Clarke and others (1993) report two small evaluations of an intervention for depression based on CBT administered by teachers using a manual. This has been used in schools by Shochet and others (2001), who found that the incidence of depression in the index group had been halved over ten months. Spence and others (2003) trained school teachers to deliver a 'problem solving for life' programme aimed at preventing depression in adolescence with 45-minute sessions spread over 8 weeks. This consisted of positive problem solving, optimistic thinking styles, life problem skills and cognitive restructuring. While the programme produced impressive results in the short term, the index group and the controls were not different one year later.

The bottom level of Sanders's (1999, 2000) 'Triple P Parenting Programme' is designed for the entire population and consists of a set of television programmes that were shown on national television in New Zealand to improve parenting skills. Evaluation was carried out with a group of Australian volunteers with children aged 2 to 8 years in Australia. They were allocated to watch the programmes on video at home, or were allocated to a waiting list. Evaluation was by questionnaire only and showed an effect size of 0.4–0.5 SD in anti-social behaviour, increased sense of parenting competence, and no loss at 6-month follow-up.

Selective measures

Many programmes have been described which give optimistic accounts of various programmes which it is hoped will have preventive value. Here we will confine ourselves to relatively successful programmes which have produced evidence for their efficacy.

Holden and others (1989) carried out one of the first well-controlled preventive study of home visits by a health visitor aimed at preventing postnatal depression. Of 174 mothers screened, those scoring over 13 on a short depression scale were interviewed by a psychiatrist and 60 were found to be depressed and randomised to usual care or regular home visits during which 'therapeutic listening' occurred in addition to the usual tasks of a health visitor. Only 38 per cent of the controls recovered, compared with 69 per cent of those receiving regular visits.

David Olds arranged for women who were pregnant for the first time and had one or more of the following high risk characteristics – aged <19, single parents, or low socio-economic status – to be visited at home by a trained nurse on nine occasions during their pregnancy, with continued visits after the child was born until the baby was 2 years old (Olds et al. 1998a, 1998b). There was an 80 per cent reduction in state-verified cases of child abuse in addition to numerous other benefits of the programme: smoking during pregnancy reduced, fewer pre-term deliveries, fewer subsequent pregnancies and children with a higher IQ. This is one of the few preventive studies to show a reduction in sexual abuse of children.

Sanders's and others (2000) 'Triple P Parenting Programme' has four further stages – for those consulting their family doctors, and for those requiring more intensive assistance. The primary care intervention consists of one or two 20-minute sessions at 'level 2', either with a trained primary health care worker consisting of individual counselling, backed by videotapes and 'tip-sheets'. A training programme for family physicians describes a brief training programme completed on a single workshop (Sanders and McFarland 2000). 'Level 3' consists of further sessions in primary care. Only in 'level 4' do the parents receive, either individually or in a group, an intensive programme spread over 10 weeks. Level 5, enhanced, is a further 10-week programme added on to the individually administered clinic programme that comprises addressing in an individualised way parental factors that obstruct effective parenting, and addresses marital communication, mood management and stress coping skills.

Evaluation of the different ways of delivering the standard level 4 programme has been carried out in a trial with 3 year olds. Participants were volunteers screened to meet criteria that included having an elevated score on the Eyberg Child Behaviour Inventory and at least one index of family adversity; parents were predominantly lower class. They were allocated to receive the standard basic clinician administered 10-week programme, self-administered, or an abbreviated version of the enhanced programme. The results showed that on direct observation only the enhanced condition reduced anti-social behaviour (effect size 0.5 SD) compared to waiting list controls. However, on the Eyberg questionnaire all treatment conditions produced an improvement, with a trend towards a larger effect in the enhanced (enhanced 1.0 SD, basic 0.7 SD, self-administered 0.5 SD). One-year follow-up showed further improvements in all three treatment groups (Sanders and McFarland 2000).

Youths at high risk of offending because a sibling had offended have been targeted in an eight-hour behavioural family intervention, producing a fall in reoffending rates to 20 per cent in those who had received family therapy, to be compared with 63 per cent in controls (Klein *et al.* 1977). McCambridge and Strang (2004) report a study with 200 young people currently using illegal drugs, who were assigned either to an intervention using motivational interviewing or to a simple didactic talk about drugs. The index condition produced a reduction in drug use with an effect size of 0.34 for alcohol and 0.75 for cannabis.

Cheadle and others (1995) describe a multi-level programme aimed at preventing excessive alcohol use by adolescents living in an American Indian reservation, where the alcohol use was very high. The intervention took place over five years and included individual counselling as well as work with the whole community and in schools. Onset of drinking was delayed and the rates of binge drinking were halved.

Secondary prevention

Secondary prevention is subdivided into: *indicated interventions*, given to those already displaying some symptoms of the disorder, stopping short of diagnosis; and *clinical interventions*, where the intervention is given to a disorder known to be related to the disorder. Thus, to prevent suicide one can aim an intervention at depression.

Indicated interventions

Dadds and others (1999) randomised schoolchildren between the ages of 7 and 14 who had high scores on an anxiety scale to 10 sessions of a group CBT-based intervention, or to a waiting list. Of 1786 children screened, only 128 were admitted to the study and randomised. Of these, 24 dropped out of treatment. In this study great improvement had occurred in the control group, but improvement was greater in the index group. At two-year follow-up, there were 20 per cent anxious children in the intervention group, as opposed to 39 per cent in the controls. Andrews and Wilkinson (2002) describe eight other similar RCTS.

Clarke and others (1995) attempted to prevent depression in high risk adolescents at school. Students were selected who had high scores on depression inventories which fell short of the severity needed to justify a diagnosis. The high risk children were given 15 sessions after school by a psychologist and a counsellor aimed at dealing with negative thoughts and developing better coping strategies. One year later, the students who had received the sessions had a lower incidence of depression or dysthymia than controls – 14.5 per cent, against 25.7 per cent. A later paper (Clarke *et al.* 2001) was concerned with children whose parents were depressed and used a similar programme with 15 sessions of group CBT spread over 2 years. They managed to reduce the prevalence of depression to 9.3 per cent in those who had received the intervention, as against 28.8 per cent in the controls. Measures begin to converge after two years, so the preventive effect may be short term.

Babor and Grant (1992) tried four different interventions in primary care for people who were drinking heavily. To be recruited they had to satisfy at least one of the following criteria: a man had to be drinking >300gr, and a woman >180gr of alcohol; they had to have had two or more episodes of intoxication a month; experience of alcohol-related harm in the past month. They were offered one of four interventions: advice and extended counselling (40 mins over 2 or 3 sessions); advice and 20 minutes of counselling; simple advice; no treatment. At follow-up, the controls had not altered their alcohol intake but simple advice or the 20-minute session both achieved a reduction of nearly 30 per cent. Only the extended counselling did better than this; they had reduced their intake by 38 per cent. The finding that a mere 5-minute session with advice achieved an almost 30 per cent reduction in intake is certainly arresting.

Clinical interventions

An effective treatment for conduct disorder is important because a proportion of these children will grow up to become anti-social adults. Thus, any effective treatment has considerable preventive value. Webster-Stratton and Hammond (1997) devised an intervention based upon training parents to manage their conduct-disordered children more effectively, using a structured sequence of topics, introduced in set order over 8 to 12 weeks, and involving play, praise, incentives, setting limits and discipline. The emphasis is on promoting sociable, self-reliant child behaviour and calm parenting, with constant reference to parent's own experience and predicament. Scott and others (2001) have adapted this approach to the UK. In an RCT with 141 children above the ninety-seventh percentile on anti-social behaviour aged 3 to 8 they show a large (1.06 SDs) effect size of their intervention. They stress that the problems become less and do not completely resolve, and that other treatment is frequently needed for associated problems.

Another approach with encouraging results is Multi-Systemic Training (MST) for juvenile offenders, in which elements of family therapy are combined with parent-management training, producing increased family cohesion, reduction of conflict and lower rates of rearrest and incarceration that was maintained for four years (Henggeler *et al.* 1998).

The problem with all these RCTs is that all they tell us is that an intervention has a preventive value in certain cases: but efficacy is not efficiency, and we need to know what their effects will be when applied in general, without the inevitable exclusions that occur in RCTs. In the case of high risk studies, the intervention is typically only offered to a tiny proportion of the population screened. The main limitation in applying methods based on CBT on a large scale is that psychologists and others trained in CBT are a very scarce resource, and the general use of such techniques may not be practicable in the forseeable future.

This is where computerised treatments, in particular computerised cognitive behaviour therapy (CCBT), come into their own. Programmes such as 'Beating the Blues' have been shown to be effective in both depression and anxiety when administered by computer in general medical clinics, and are effective both in those taking antidepressants and those not doing so (Proudfoot *et al.* 2003, 2004). More recently, versions of both CCBT and educational programmes can be downloaded from the internet and there is some evidence of their efficacy (Christensen *et al.* 2002).

Tertiary prevention

Just over a quarter of cases of depression do not respond to simple measures like single antidepressants or problem-solving therapy. It is these patients whose needs should be prioritised, and selectively referred to mental illness services able to give CBT by experienced psychologists, often in combination with various antidepressant drugs, supervised by psychiatrists. In practice, many of these patients suffer in silence and scarce CBT time is devoted to uncomplicated cases of depression that would respond to much simpler strategies.

Despite the general reluctance of politicians to invest much money in preventive programmes, and the disinclination of many teachers to find time for preventive programmes in already crowded school timetables, there is reason to hope that much more could be done if the will was there and the resources were provided. Measures taken to improve the health of the whole population are often taken by politicians by improving standards of living and passing laws such as requiring seatbelts and taxing alcohol and tobacco; less often by professionals, such as iodising table salt, fluoridising toothpaste and improving obstetric care. Yet all these are highly effective in preventing disorders.

Take-home messages

- *Resilient people* have low neuroticism and high self-confidence. They have generally experienced good parenting and have stable affectionate relationships with another person.
- *Universal primary prevention* involves measures given to everyone. Success has been reported for reducing bullying in schools, reducing anti-social behaviour and limiting drug use.
- *Selective primary prevention* is offered to high risk groups only. Success has been reported for home visits by nurses for young mothers and improving parenting skills.
- *Indicated secondary preventive* measures are offered to those who already have symptoms. Success has been reported for anxious and depressed school children, limiting alcohol and drug use in schools.
- *Clinical interventions* aim to reduce a disorder by tackling another behaviour. Success has been reported for improving conduct disorder in children by offering parent training and therapy for persistent juvenile offenders.

References

Abramson, L., Seligman, M., et al. (1978) 'Learned helplessness in humans: critique and reformulation', *Journal of Abnormal Psychology* 87: 49–74.

Ainsworth, M. D. and Bell S. M. (1970) 'Attachment, exploration, and separation: illustrated by the behavior of one-year-olds in a strange situation', *Child Development* 41: 49–67.

Albach, F. and Everaerd, W. (1992) 'Post-traumatic stress symptoms in victims of childhood incest', *Psychotheraphy and Psychosomatics* 57, 4: 143–51.

Alloy, L. B., Abramson, L. Y., et al. (1999) 'Depressogenic cognitive styles: predictive validity, information processing and personality characteristics, and developmental origins', *Behavior Research and Therapy* 37, 6: 503–31.

Alloy, L. B., Abramson, L. Y., et al. (2000) 'The Temple-Wisconsin Cognitive Vulnerability to Depression Project: lifetime history of axis I psychopathology in individuals at high and low cognitive risk for depression', *Journal of Abnormal Psychology* 109, 3: 403–18.

Amato, P. R. (1994) 'Life-span adjustment of children to their parents' divorce', *Future Child* 4, 1: 143–64.

American Psychiatric Association (1994) *Diagnostic and Statistical Manual For Mental and Behavioural Disorders*, Washington, DC: American Psychiatric Association.

Anderson, J., Huppert, F. and Rose, G. (1993) 'Normality, deviance and minor psychiatric morbidity in the community', *Psychological Medicine* 23, 2: 475–86.

Andrews, G. and Wilkinson, D. D. (2002) 'The prevention of mental disorders in young people', *Medical Journal of Australia* 177: S97–S99.

Andrews, G., Neilson, M., Hunt, C., Stewart, G. and Kiloh, L. (1990a) 'Diagnosis, personality & long term outcome of depression', *British Journal of Psychiatry* 157: 13–18.

Andrews, G., Stewart, G., Morris-Yates, A., et al. (1990b) 'Evidence for a general neurotic syndrome', *British Journal of Psychiatry* 157: 13–18.

Andrews, G., Henderson, S. and Hall, W. (2001) 'Prevalence, comorbidity, disability in the Australian National Mental Health Survey', *British Journal of Psychiatry* 178: 145–53.

Angold, A. and Costello, E. J. (2001) 'The epidemiology of depression in children and adolescents', in I. Goodyer (ed.) *The Depressed Child and Adolescent*, 2nd edn, Cambridge: Cambridge University Press, pp. 143–78.

Angold, A., Costello, E. J., Erkanli, A. and Worthman, C. M. (1999) 'Pubertal changes in hormone levels and depression in girls', *Psychological Medicine* 29, 5: 1043–53.

Angold, A., Erkanli, A., et al. (2002) 'Depression scale scores in 8–17-year-olds: effects of age and gender', *Journal of Child Psychology and Psychiatry* 43, 8: 1052–63.

Angst, J. (1990) *Depression and Anxiety: A Review of Settings*, Bern: Hogrefe-Huber.

Angst, J. and Dobler-Mikola, A. (1984) 'The Zurich Study II – the continuum from depressive to pathological depressive mood swings', *European Archives of Psychiatry and Neurological Science* 234: 21–9.

Angst, J. and Dobler-Mikola, A. (1985) 'The Zurich study VI. A continuum from depression to anxiety disorders', *European Archives of Psychiatry and Neurological Science* 235: 179–86.

Angst, J. and Preisig, M. (1995) 'Course of a clinical cohort of unipolar, bipolar and schizoaffective patients. Results of a prospective study from 1959 to 1985', *Schweizer Archiv für Neurologie und Psychiatrie* 146, 1: 5–16.

Angst, J. and Vollrath, M. (1991) 'The natural history of anxiety disorders', *Acta Psychiatrica Scandinavica* 84, 5: 446–52.

Arnett, J. J. (2000) 'Emerging adulthood. A theory of development from the late teens through the twenties', *American Psychologist* 55, 5: 469–80.

Arseneault, L., Cannon, M., et al. (2003) 'Childhood origins of violent behaviour in adults with schizophreniform disorder', *The British Journal of Psychiatry* 183: 520–5.

'Assessment of neuropsychological function through use of the Cambridge Neuro-psychological Testing Automated Battery: performance in 4- to 12-year-old children', *Journal of Child Psychology and Psychiatry* 45, 1: 109–34.

Attenburrow, M. J., Williams, C., et al. (2003) 'Acute administration of nutritionally sourced tryptophan increases fear recognition', *Psychopharmacology* 169, 1: 104–7.

Babor, T. F. and Grant, M. (1992) *Project on Identification and Management of Alcohol Related Problems: An RCT of Brief Interventions in Primary Health Care*, Geneva: World Health Organisation.

Babor, T. F., dela Fuente, J. R., Saunders, J., et al. (1989) *Audit: The Alcohol Use Disorders Identification*, Geneva: World Health Organisation.

Bamber, D. J., Cockerill, I. M., Rodgers, S. and Carroll, D. (2003) 'Diagnostic criteria for exercise dependence in women', *British Journal of Sports Medicine* 37, 5: 393–400.

Baron-Cohen, S. (2003) *The Essential Difference: Men Women and the Extreme Male Brain*, London: Lane.

Bartels, M., de Geus, E. J., et al. (2003) 'Heritability of daytime cortisol levels in children', *Behavior Genetics* 33, 4: 421–33.

Bartrop, R. W., Luckhurst, E., Lazarus, L., Kiloh, L. G. and Penny, R. (1977) 'Depressed lymphocyte function after bereavement', *Lancet* 1, 8016: 834–6.

Bassarath, L. (2001) 'Neuro-imaging studies of anti-social behaviour', *Canadian Journal of Psychiatry* 46, 8: 728–32.

Baulieu, E. E., Schumacher, M., et al. (2004) *Neurosteroids: A New Regulatory Function in the Nervous System*, New Jersey USA: Humana Press.

Baumrind, D. (1996) 'The discipline controversy revisited' *Family Relations* 45: 405–14.

Beardslee, W. R., Versage, E. M., et al. (1998) 'Children of affectively ill parents: a review of the past 10 years', *Journal of the American Academy of Child and Adolescent Psychiatry* 37, 11: 1134–41.

Beardslee, W. R., Gladstone, T. R., et al. (2003) 'A family-based approach to the prevention of depressive symptoms in children at risk: evidence of parental and child change', *Pediatrics* 112, 2: e119–31.

Beatty W. (1992) 'Gonadal hormones and sex differences in non-reproductive behaviours', in A. Gerall, H. Molz and I. Ward (eds) *Handbook of Behavioural Neurobiology, Vol. 11: Sexual Differentiation*, London: Plenum Press.

Bebbington, P., Meltzer, H., Brugha, T. S., Farrell, M., Jenkins, R., Ceresa, C. and Lewis, G. (2000a) 'Unequal access and unmet need: neurotic disorders and the use of primary care services', *Psychological Medicine* 30: 1359–67.

Bebbington, P., Meltzer, H., Brugha, T. S., Farrell, M., Jenkins, R., Ceresa, C. and Lewis, G. (2000b) 'Neurotic disorders and the receipt of psychiatric treatment', *Psychological Medicine* 30: 1359–67.

Beck, A. (1967) *Depression: Clinical Experiments with a Theoretical Aspect*, New York: Harper and Row.

Bell, C., Abrams, J., et al. (2001) 'Tryptophan depletion and its implications for psychiatry', *British Journal of Psychiatry* 178: 399–405.

Bennett, A. J., Lesch, K. P., Heils, A., Long, J. C., et al. (2002) 'Early experience and serotonin transporter gene variation interact to influence primate CNS function', *Molecular Psychiatry* 7: 118–22.

Berg, M. D., van den, Oldehinkel, A. J., Bouhuys, A. L., Brilman, E. I., Beekman, A. T. F. and Ormel, J. (2001) 'Depression in later life: three etiologically different subgroups', *Journal of Affective Disorders* 65: 19–26.

Berman, R. M., Sanacora, G., et al. (2002) 'Monoamine depletion in unmedicated depressed subjects', *Biological Psychiatry* 51, 6: 469–73.

Bhagwagar, Z., Whale, R., et al. (2002) 'State and trait abnormalities in serotonin function in major depression', *British Journal of Psychiatry* 180: 24–8.

Bhagwagar, Z., Hafizi, S., et al. (2003) 'Increase in concentration of waking salivary cortisol in recovered patients with depression', *American Journal of Psychiatry* 160, 10: 1890–1.

Bhutta, A. T., Cleaves, M. and Casey, P. H. (2002) 'Cognitive and behavioural outcome of school-aged children who were born pre-term: a meta-analysis', *JAMA* 288: 728–37.

Bifulco, A., Brown, G. W. and Adler, Z. (1991) 'Early sexual abuse and clinical depression in adult life', *British Journal of Psychiatry* 159: 115–22.

Bifulco, A., Brown, G. W., Moran, P., Ball, C. and Campbell, C. (1998) 'Predicting depression in women: the role of past and present vulnerability', *Psychological Medicine* 28, 1: 39–50.

Bifulco, A., Moran, P. M., Baines, R., Bunn, A. and Stanford, K. (2002) 'Exploring psychological abuse in childhood: II. Association with other abuse and adult clinical depression', *Bulletin of the Menninger Clinic*, 66, 3: 241–58.

Bijl, R. V., Ravelli, A., van Zessen, G. (1998) 'Prevalence of psychiatric disorder in the general population: results of the Netherlands Mental Health Survey and Incidence Study (NEMESIS)', *Social Psychiatry & Psychiatric Epidemiology* 33: 587–95.

Billig, J. P., Hershberger, S. L., Iacono, W. G., McGue, M. (1996) 'Life events and personality in late adolescence: genetic and environmental relations', *Behavioral Genetics* 26, 6: 543–54.

Birtchnell, J., Masters, N. and Deahl, M. (1988) 'Depression and the physical environment', *British Journal of Psychiatry* 153: 56–64.

Black, J., Humphrey, J. and Niven, J. (1963) 'Inhibition of Mantoux reaction by direct suggestion under hypnosis', *British Medical Journal* 1: 1649–52.

Blair, C. (2003) 'Behavioral inhibition and behavioral activation in young children: relations with self-regulation and adaptation to preschool in children attending Head Start', *Developmental Psychobiology* 42, 3: 301–11.

Blair, R. J., Colledge, E., Murray, L., et al. (2001) 'A selective impairment in the processing of sad and fearful expressions in children with psychopathic tendencies', *Journal of Abnormal Child Psychology* 29: 491–8.

Blalock, J. (1984) 'The immune system as a sensory organ', *Journal of Immunology* 132: 1067–70.

Blazer, D., Swartz, M., Woodbury, M., et al. (1988) 'Depressive symptoms and depressive diagnoses in a community sample', *Archives of General Psychiatry* 45: 1078–84.

Boehm, U., Klamp, T., Groot, M., et al. (1997) 'Cellular response to interferon gamma', *Annal Review of Immunology* 15: 749–95.

Boer, F. and Lindhout, I. (2001) 'Family and genetic influences: is anxiety "all in the family"?', in W. Silverman and P. Treffers (eds) *Anxiety Disorders in Children and Adolescents*, Cambridge: Cambridge University Press, pp. 235–55.

Boivin, M. and Begin, G. (1989) 'Peer status and self-perception among early elementary school children: the case of the rejected children', *Child Development* 60, 3: 591–6.

Boivin, M. and Hymel, S. (1997) 'Peer experiences and social self-perceptions: a sequential model', *Developmental Psychology* 33, 1: 135–45.

Bolton, P. F., Pickles, A., Murphy, M. and Rutter, M. (1998) 'Autism, affective and other psychiatric disorders: patterns of familial aggregation', *Psychological Medicine* 28, 2: 385–95.

Bond, L., Carlin, J. B., Thomas, L., Rubin, K. and Patton, G. (2001) 'Does bullying cause emotional problems? A prospective study of young teenagers', *British Medical Journal* 323: 480–84.

Booij, L., Van der Does, W., et al. (2002) 'Predictors of mood response to acute tryptophan depletion. A reanalysis', *Neuropsychopharmacology* 27, 5: 852–61.

Booij, L., Van der Does, A. J., et al. (2003) 'Monoamine depletion in psychiatric and healthy populations: review', *Molecular Psychiatry* 8, 12: 951–73.

Bouchard, T. J. (1994) 'Genes, environment and personality', *Science* 264: 1700–01.

Bowlby, J. (1981) *Attachment and Loss: Vol 1. Attachment*, New York: Basic Books.

Brame, B., Nagin, D. S., et al. (2001) 'Developmental trajectories of physical aggression from school entry to late adolescence', *Journal of Child Psychology and Psychiatry* 42, 4: 503–12.

Breslau, N., Davis, G. C., Andreski, P. and Peterson, E. (1991) 'Traumatic events and PTSD in an urban population of young adults', *Archives of General Psychiatry* 48: 216–22.

Bridges, K. and Goldberg, D. P. (1985) 'Somatic presentations of DSM III psychiatric disorders in primary care', *Journal of Psychosomatic Research* 29, 6: 563–9.

Brilman, E. I., and Ormel, J. (2001) 'Life events, difficulties and onset of depressive episodes in later life', *Psychological Medicine* 31: 859–69.

Brodaty, H. and Andrews, G. (1983) 'Brief psychotherapy in general practice: a randomised controlled prospective intervention trial', *British Journal of Psychiatry* 143: 11–19.

Brody, G. H., Kim, S., et al. (2003) 'Longitudinal direct and indirect pathways linking older sibling competence to the development of younger sibling competence', *Developmental Psychology* 39, 3: 618–28.

Broidy, L. M., Nagin, D. S., Tremblay, R. E., Bates, J. E., Brame, B., Dodge, K. A., Fergusson, D., Horwood, J. L., Loeber, R., Laird, R., Lynam, D. R., Moffitt, T. E., Pettit, G. S. and Vitaro, F. (2003) 'Developmental trajectories of childhood disruptive behaviors and adolescent delinquency: a six-site, cross-national study', *Developmental Psychology*, 39, 2: 222–45.

Brown, G. W. and Harris, T. (1978) *Social Origins of Depression: A Study of Psychiatric Disorder in Women*, London: Tavistock.

Brown, G. W. and Harris, T. (1986) 'Stress, vulnerability and depression: a question of replication', *Psychological Medicine* 16: 739–44.

Brown, G. W. and Harris, T. (1989) *Life Events*, London: Unwin Hyman, pp. 49–94.

Brown, G. W., and Harris, T. (1993) 'Aetiology of anxiety and depressive disorders in an inner city population. 1 Early adversity', *Psychological Medicine* 23: 143–54.

Brown, G. W., Bifulco, A. and Harris, T. (1987) 'Life events, vulnerability and the onset of depression: some refinements', *British Journal of Psychiatry* 150: 30–42.

Brown, G. W., Adler, Z. and Bifulco, A. (1988) 'Life events, difficulties and recovery from chronic depression', *British Journal of Psychiatry* 152: 487–98.

Brown, G. W., Lemyre, L. and Bifulco, A. (1992) 'Social factors and recovery from anxious and depressive disorders', *British Journal of Psychiatry* 161: 44–54.

Brown, G. W., Moran, P. (1994) 'Clinical and psychosocial origins of chronic depressive episodes. I. A community survey', *British Journal of Psychiatry* 165, 4: 447–56.

Brown, G. W., and Moran, P. M. (1997) 'Single mothers, poverty and depression', *Psychological Medicine* 27: 21–33.

Brown, G. W., Harris, T. O., Hepworth, C. and Robinson, R. (1994a) 'Clinical and psychosocial origins of chronic depressive episodes. II. A patient enquiry', *British Journal of Psychiatry* 165, 4: 57–65.

Brown, G. W., Harris, T. O. and Hepworth, C. (1995) 'Loss humiliation and entrapment among women experiencing depression: a patient and non-patient comparison', *Psychological Medicine* 25: 7–21.

Brunner, H. G., Nelen, M., Breakefield, X. O., et al. (1993) 'Abnormal behavior associated with a point mutation in the structural gene for monoamine oxidase A', *Science* 262: 568.

Buchanan, C., Eccles, J. and Becker, J. (1992) 'Are adolescents victims of raging hormones: evidence for activational effects of hormones on moods and behaviour at adolescence', *Psychological Bulletin* 111, 1: 62–107.

Buck, N. (1990) *The British Household Panel Survey*, Swindon: ESRC Data Archive Bulletin, no. 46.

Bukowski, W., Newcomb, A., et al. (eds) (1996) *The Company They Keep: Friendships in Childhood and Adolescence*, Cambridge: Cambridge University Press.

Cairns, R., Leung, M.-C., et al. (1995) 'Friendships and social networks in childhood and adolescence: fluidity, reliability and interrelations', *Child Development* 66: 1330–45.

Calder, A., Lawrence, A. D., et al. (2001) 'Neuropsychology of fear and loathing', *Nature* 2: 351–63.

Caldji, C., Francis, D., Sharma, S., et al. (2000) 'The effects of early rearing environment on the development of GABAA and central benzodiazepine receptor levels and novelty-induced fearfulness in the rat', *Neuropsychopharmacology* 22: 219–29.

Cannon, W. B. (1929) *Bodily Changes in Pain, Hunger, Fear and Rage*, New York, Appleton.

Carter, A. S., Briggs-Gowan, M. J., et al. (2004) 'Assessment of young children's social-emotional development and psychopathology: recent advances and recommendations for practice', *Journal of Child Psychology and Psychiatry* 45, 1: 109–34.

Casey, B. J. (1999) 'Images in neuroscience. Brain development. XII. Maturation in brain activation', *American Journal of Psychiatry* 156, 4: 504.

Caspi, A., Henry, B., McGee, R. O., Moffitt, T. E. and Silva, P. A. (1995) 'Temperamental origins of child and adolescent behavior problems: from age three to age fifteen', *Child Development* 66, 1: 55–68.

Caspi, A., Moffitt, T. E., Newman, D. L., et al. (1996) 'Behavioral observations at age 3 years predict adult psychiatric disorders. Longitudinal evidence from a birth cohort', *Archives of General Psychiatry* 53: 1033–9.

Caspi, A., Taylor, A., Moffitt, T. E., et al. (2000) 'Neighborhood deprivation affects children's mental health: environmental risks identified in a genetic design', *Psychological Science* 11: 338–42.

Caspi, A., McClay, J., Moffitt, T. E., et al. (2002) 'Role of genotype in the cycle of violence in maltreated children', *Science* 297: 851–4.

Caspi, A., Sugden, K. Moffitt, T., et al. (2003) Influence of life stress on depression. Polymorphism in the 5-HTT gene', *Science* 301: 386–9.

Challis, B. G., Luan, J., et al. (2004) 'Genetic variation in the corticotrophin-releasing factor receptors: identification of single-nucleotide polymorphisms and association studies with obesity in UK Caucasians', *International Journal of Obesity Related Metabolic Disorders* 28, 3: 442–6.

Chalmers, D. T., Kwak, S. P., et al. (1993) 'Corticosteroids regulate brain hippocampal 5-HT1A receptor mRNA expression', *Journal of Neuroscience* 13, 3: 914–23.

Champoux, M., Bennett, A., Shannon, C., Higley, J. D., et al. (2002) 'Serotonin transporter gene polymorphism, differential early rearing, and behaviour in rhesus monkey neonates', *Molecular Psychiatry* 7: 1058–63.

Cheadle, A., Prearson, D., Wagner E., et al. (1995) 'A community based approach to preventing alcohol abuse among adolescents on an American Indian reservation', *Public Health Reports* 110: 439–47.

Christensen, H., Griffiths, K. M., and Korten, A. E. (2002) 'Web-based cognitive behaviour therapy (CBT) analysis of site usage and changes in anxiety and depression scores', *Journal of International Medical Research* 4: e3.

Cicchetti, D. and Carlson, V. (eds) (1989) *Child Maltreatment: Theory and Research on the Causes and Consequences of Child Abuse and Neglect*, Cambridge: Cambridge University Press.

Clark, L. A. (1993) *Manual for the Schedule for Non-adaptive and Adaptive Personality (SNAP)*, Minnesota: University of Minnesota Press.

Clark, L. A., and Watson, D. (1991) 'Tripartite model of anxiety and depression – psychometric evidence and taxonomic implications', *Journal of Abnormal Psychology* 100: 316–36.

Clarke, G. N., Hawkins, W., Murphy, M., et al. (1993) 'School-based primary prevention of depressive symptomatology in adolescents', *Journal of Adolescent Research* 8: 183–204.

Clarke, G. N., Hawkins, W., Murphy, M., et al. (1995) 'Targeted prevention of unipolar depressive disorder in an at risk sample of high school adolescents: a RCT of cognitive interventions', *Journal of American Academy of Child and Adolescent Psychiatry* 34, 3: 312–21.

Clarke, G. N., Hornbrook, M., Lynch, F., et al. (2001) 'A randomised trial of group cognitive intervention in adolescent offspring of depressed parents', *Archives of General Psychiatry* 56: 1127–34.

Cloninger, R. F. (1987) 'A systematic method for clinical description and classification of personality', *Archive of General Psychiatry* 44: 573–88.

Cole, D. A., Martin, J. M., et al. (1997) 'A competency-based model of child depression: a longitudinal study of peer, parent, teacher, and self-evaluations', *Journal of Child Psychology and Psychiatry* 38, 5: 505–14.

Cole, D. A., Peeke, L., et al. (1999) 'A longitudinal study of negative affect and self-perceived competence in young adolescents', *Journal of Personality and Social Psychology* 77, 4: 851–62.

Combrink-Graham, L. and Fox, G. (2002) 'Development in school-age children', *Child and Adolescent Psychiatry*, Philadelphia: Lippincott Williams and Williams.

Connellan, J., Baron-Cohen, S., Wheelwright, S., Batki, A. and Ahluwalia, J. (2001) 'Sex differences in human neonatal social perception', *Infant Behaviour and Development* 23: 113–8.

Cooke, D. and Hole, D. (1983) 'The aetiological importance of stressful life events', *British Journal of Psychiatry* 143: 397–400.

Cooper, B. (1964) 'A study of 100 chronic psychiatric patients identified in general practice', *British Journal of Psychiatry* 111: 595–605.

Cooper, P. J. and Goodyer, I. M. (1993) 'A community study of depression in adolescent girls. 1. Estimates of symptom and syndrome prevalence', *British Journal Of Psychiatry* 163: 369–74.

Coppen, A. (1967) 'The biochemistry of affective disorders', *British Journal of Psychiatry* 113, 504: 1237–64.

Coryell, W., Akiskal, H., Leon, A. C., et al. (1994) 'The time course of untreated major depression; uniformity across episodes and samples', *American Journal of Psychiatry* 51: 405–10.

Costello, E. J., Angold, A., et al. (1996) 'The Great Smoky Mountains Study of Youth. Functional impairment and serious emotional disturbance', *Archives of General Psychiatry* 53, 12: 1137–43.

Costello, E. J., Keeler, G. P., et al. (2001) 'Poverty, race/ethnicity, and psychiatric disorder: a study of rural children', *American Journal of Public Health* 91, 9: 1494–8.

Costello, E. J., Erkanli, A., et al. (2002) 'The prevalence of potentially traumatic events in childhood and adolescence', *Journal of Trauma Stress* 15, 2: 99–112.

Costello, E. J., Compton, S. N., et al. (2003) 'Relationships between poverty and psychopathology: a natural experiment', *JAMA* 290, 15: 2023–9.

Cox, A. D., Puckering, C., Pound, A., et al. (1987) 'The impact of maternal depression in young children', *Journal of Child Psychology and Psychiatry* 28: 917–28.

Craig, T. (1989) 'Abdominal pain', in G. W. Brown and T. Harris (eds) *Life Events*, London: Unwin Hyman, pp. 233–60.

Creed, F. (1989) 'Appendectomy', in G. W. Brown and T. Harris (eds) *Life Events*, London: Unwin Hyman, pp. 213–32.

Croft, C., O'Connor, T. G., Keaveney, L., et al. (2001) 'Longitudinal change in parenting associated with developmental delay and catch-up. English and Romanian Adoption Study Team', *Journal of Child Psychology and Psychiatry* 42: 649–59.

Cui, X. J. and Vaillant, G. E. (1997) 'Does depression generate negative life events?', *Journal of Nervous Mental Disorders* 185, 3: 145–50.

Cullen, K. J. and Cullen, A. M. (1996) 'Long term follow-up of the Brusselton six-year controlled trial of prevention of children's behaviour disorders', *Journal of Paediatrics* 129: 136–9.

Cyranowski, J. M., Frank, E., Young, E. and Shear, M. K. (2000) 'Adolescent onset of the gender difference in lifetime rates of major depression: a theoretical model', *Archives of General Psychiatry* 57, 1: 21–7.

Dadds, M. R., Holland, D. E., Laurens, K. R., Mullins, M., Barrett, P. M., Spence, S. H. (1999) 'Early intervention and prevention of anxiety disorders in children: results at 2-year follow-up', *Journal of Consulting and Clinical Psychology* 67, 1: 145–50.

Daley, S. E., Hammen, C., Davila, J. and Burge, D. (1988) 'Axis II symptomatology, depression, and life stress during the transition from adolescence to adulthood', *Journal of Consulting and Clinical Psychology* 66, 4: 595–603.

DaMasio, A. R. (1995) *Descartes' Error*, London: Picador.

Davies, P. T. and Windle, M. (1997) 'Gender-specific pathways between maternal depressive symptoms, family discord, and adolescent adjustment', *Developmental Psychology* 33, 4: 657–68.

Davies, P. T. and Cummings, E. M. (1998) 'Exploring children's emotional security as a mediator of the link between marital relations and child adjustment', *Child Development* 69: 124–39.

Davies, P. T. and Windle, M. (2001) 'Interparental discord and adolescent adjustment trajectories: the potentiating and protective role of intrapersonal attributes', *Child Development* 72, 4: 1163–78.

Deakin, J. F. (1988) '5-HT2 receptors, depression and anxiety', *Pharmacology, Biochemistry and Behaviour* 29: 819–20.

Deakin, J. F. (1998) 'The role of serotonin in panic, anxiety and depression', *International Clinical Psychopharmacology* 13, suppl 4: S1–5.

Denham, S. A., Blair, K. A., et al. (2003) 'Preschool emotional competence: pathway to social competence?', *Child Development* 74, 1: 238–56.

Department of Health (2003) Information downloaded from the DoH website.

DeRijk, R., Schaaf, M., et al. (2002) 'Glucocorticoid receptor variants: clinical implications', *Journal of Steroid Chemistry and Molecular Biology* 81: 103–22.

Dinwiddie, S., Heath, A. C., Dunne, M. P., et al. (2000) 'Early sexual abuse and lifetime psychopathology: a co-twin case control study', *Psychological Medicine* 30: 41–52.

Dolan, M., Deakin, W. J., et al. (2002) 'Serotonergic and cognitive impairment in impulsive aggressive personality disordered offenders: are there implications for treatment?', *Psychological Medicine* 32, 1: 105–17.

Donaldson, S. I., Thomas, D. W., Graham, J. W., et al. (2000) 'Verifying drug use prevention program effects using reciprocal best-friend reports', *Journal of Behavioural Medicine* 23: 595–601.

Drevets, W. C. (1998) 'Functional neuro-imaging studies of depression: the anatomy of melancholia', *Annual Revue of Medicine* 49: 341–61.

Drevets, W. C. (1999) 'Prefrontal cortical-amygdalar metabolism in major depression', *Annals of New York Academy of Science* 877: 614–37.

Drewett, R. F., Corbett, S. S. and Wright, C. M. (1999) 'Cognitive and educational attainments at school age of children who failed to thrive in infancy: a population based study', *Journal of Child Psychology and Psychiatry* 40: 551–61.

Duggan C., Lee, A. and Murray, R. (1990) 'Does personality predict long term outcome in depression?', *British Journal of Psychiatry* 157: 19–24.

Duncan-Jones, P., Grayson, D. and Moran, P. A. P. (1986) 'The utility of latent trait models in psychiatric epidemiology', *Psychological Medicine* 16: 391–405.

Dunn, J. (1988) 'Sibling influences on childhood development', *Journal of Child Psychology and Psychiatry* 29, 2: 119–27.

Dunn, J. and Plomin, R. (1991) 'Why are siblings so different? The significance of differences in sibling experiences within the family', *Family Process* 30, 3: 271–83.

Dunn, J., Deater-Deckard, K., et al. (1998) 'Children's adjustment and prosocial behaviour in step-, single-parent, and non-stepfamily settings: findings from a community study. ALSPAC Study Team. Avon Longitudinal Study of Pregnancy and Childhood', *Journal of Child Psychology and Psychiatry* 39, 8: 1083–95.

Dunn, J., Deater-Deckard, K., et al. (1999) 'Siblings, parents, and partners: family relationships within a longitudinal community study. ALSPAC study team. Avon Longitudinal Study of Pregnancy and Childhood', *Journal of Child Psychology and Psychiatry* 40, 7: 1025–37.

Dweck, C. S., Davidson, W., et al. (1978) 'Sex differences in learned helplessness: II. Contingencies of evaluative feed-back in the classroom and III. An experimental analysis', *Developmental Psychology* 14: 268–76.

Dworkin, S., Vonkorff, M. and LeResche, L. (1990) 'Multiple pains, psychiatric and psychosocial disturbance: an epidemiologic investigation', *Archives of General Psychiatry* 47: 239–45.

Eaton, W. and Ritter, C. (1988) 'Distinguishing anxiety from depression with field survey data', *Psychological Medicine* 18: 155–166.

Edelson, J. L. (1999) 'The overlap between child maltreatment and woman battering', *Violence and Women* 5: 134–54.

Ehrhardt, A. A. and Baker, S. W. (1974) 'Foetal androgens, human CNS differentiation, and behaviour differences', in R. C. Friedman, R. M. Richart and R. L. Vande Wiele (eds) *Sex Differences in Behaviour*, New York: Wiley.

Eichenbaum, H. (1999) 'The hippocampus and mechanisms of declarative memory', *Behavior and Brain Research* 103, 2: 123–33.

Eisenberg, L. (1995) 'Social construction of the human brain', *American Journal of Psychiatry* 152, 11: 1563–75.

Eisenberg, L. (1999) 'Whatever happened to the faculty on the way to the agora?', *Archives of International Medicine* 159: 2251–6.

Eisenberg, L. (2002) 'Is biology destiny? Is it all in our genes?', *Journal of Psychiatric Research* 8: 337–48.

Elbert, T., Pantev, C., Wienbruch, C., Rockstroh, B. and Taub, E. (1995) 'Increased cortical representation of the fingers of the left hand in string players', *Science* 270: 305–7.

Eley, T. (1997) 'General genes: a new theme for developmental psychopathology', *Current Directions in Psychological Science* 6, 4: 90–95.

Eley, T. C. and Plomin, R. (1997) 'Genetic analyses of emotionality', *Current Opinions in Neurobiology* 7, 2: 279–84.

Eley, T. and Stevenson, J. (1999a) 'Exploring the co-variation between anxiety and depression symptoms: a genetic analysis of the effects of age and sex', *Journal of Child Psychology and Psychiatry* 40, 8: 1273–82.

Eley, T. and Stevenson, J. (1999b) 'Using genetic analysis to clarify the distinction between anxious and depressive symptoms', *Journal of Abnormal Child Psychology* 27, 2: 105–14.

Eley, T. and Deater-Deckhard, K., Fombonne, E., Fulker, D. and Plomin, R. (1998) 'An adoption study of depressive symptoms in middle childhood', *Journal of Child Psychology and Psychiatry* 39, 3: 337–45.

Eley, T. C., Lichtenstein, P. and Stevenson, J. (1999c) 'Sex differences in aetiology of aggressive and non-aggressive anti-social behaviour: results from 2 twin studies', *Child Development* 70: 155–68.

Eley, T. C., Lichtenstein, P., et al. (2003) 'A longitudinal behavioral genetic analysis of the etiology of aggressive and nonaggressive anti-social behavior', *Developmental Psychopathology* 15, 2: 383–402.

Emery, R. and Laumann-Billings, L. (2003) 'Child abuse', in M. Rutter and E. Taylor *Child and Adolescent Psychiatry: Modern Approaches*, Oxford: Blackwell, pp. 325–39.

Etzerdorfer, E., Sonneck, G. and Nagel-Kuess, S. (1992) 'Newspaper reports and suicide', *New England Journal of Medicine* 327: 502–3.

Evans, J. D. and Wheeler, D. E. (2001) 'Gene expression and the evolution of polyphenisms', *BioEssays* 23: 62–8.

Eysenck, H. J. (1947) *Dimensions of Personality*, London: Kegan Paul.

Ezquiaga, E., Garcia, A., Bravo, F. and Pallares, T. (1998) 'Factors associated with outcome in major depression: a 6-month prospective study', *Social Psychiatry and Psychiatric Epidemiology* 33, 11: 552–7.

Farmer, A., Harris, T., Redman, K., Sadler, S., Mahmood, A. and McGuffin, P. (2000) 'Cardiff depression study. A sib-pair study of life events and familiality in major depression', *British Journal of Psychiatry* 176: 150–5.

Fergusson, D. M. and Horwood, L. J. (1987) 'Vulnerability to life event exposure', *Psychological Medicine* 17: 739–49.

Finlay-Jones, R. and Brown, G. W. (1981) 'Types of stressful life events and the onset of anxiety and depressive disorders', *Psychological Medicine* 11: 803–16.

Fleming, J., Mullen, P. E., et al. (1999) 'The long-term impact of childhood sexual abuse in Australian women', *Child Abuse and Neglect* 23, 2: 145–59.

Foley, D. L., Neale, M. C. and Kendler, K. S. (1996) 'A longitudinal study of stressful life events assessed at interview with an epidemiological sample of adult twins: the basis of individual variation in event exposure', *Psychological Medicine* 26: 1239–52.

Ford, T., Goodman, R., et al. (2003) 'The British Child and Adolescent Mental Health Survey 1999: the prevalence of DSM-IV disorders', *Journal of American Academy of Child and Adolescent Psychiatry* 42, 10: 1203–11.

Francis, R., Diorio, J., Li, U. D. and Meany, M. J. (1999) 'Nongenomic transmission across generations of maternal behavior and stress response in the rat', *Science* 286, 5442: 1155–8.

Francis, D. D., Diorio, J., Plotsky, P. M., et al. (2002) 'Environmental enrichment reverses the effects of maternal separation on stress reactivity', *Journal of Neuroscience* 22: 7840–43.

Friedman, R. J. and Chase-Lansdale, P. L. (2003) 'Chronic adversities', in M. Rutter and E. Taylor *Child Psychiatry: Modern Approaches*, Oxford: Blackwell, pp. 261–86.

Gabe, J. and Williams, P. (1987) 'Is space bad for your health?', *International Journal of Health Service Research* 17: 667–9.

Garmezy, N. (1985) 'Stress-resistant children: in search for protective factors', in J. E. Stevenson (ed.) *Recent Research in Developmental Psychopathologies*, Oxford: Pergamon.

Gater, R. and Goldberg, D. P. (1991) 'Pathways to psychiatric care in South Manchester', *British Journal of Psychiatry* 159: 90–96.

Gater, R., de Almeida de Sousa, R., Caraveo, J., et al. (1991) 'Pathways to psychiatric care: a cross cultural study', *Psychological Medicine* 21: 761–74.

Ge, X., Kim, I. J., Brody, G. H., Conger, R. D., Simons, R. L., Gibbons, F. X. and Cutrona, C. E. (2003) 'It's about timing and change: pubertal transition effects on symptoms of major depression among African American youths', *Developmental Psychology* 39, 3: 430–39.

Geschwind, N. and Galaburda, A. M. (1985) 'Cerebral lateralisation, biological mechanisms, associations and pathology', *Archives of Neurology* 42: 428–59.

Ghaziuddin, M., Ghaziuddin, N. and Stein, G. S. (1990) 'Life events and the recurrence of depression', *Canadian Journal of Psychiatry* 35, 3: 239–42.

Giedd, J. N., Snell, J. W., Lange, N., Rajapakse, J. C., Casey, B. J., Kozuch, P. L., Vaituzis, A. C., Vauss, Y. C., Hamburger, S. D., Kaysen, D. and Rapoport, J. L. (1996) 'Quantitative magnetic resonance imaging of human brain development: ages 4–18', *Cerebral Cortex* 6, 4: 551–60.

Giedd, J. N., Blumenthal, J., Jeffries, N. O., Rajapakse, J. C., Vaituzis, A. C., Liu, H., Berry, Y. C., Tobin, M., Nelson, J. and Castellanos, F. X. (1999) 'Development of the human corpus callosum during childhood and adolescence: a longitudinal MRI study', *Progress in Neuro-Psychopharmacology and Biological Psychiatry* 23, 4: 571–88.

Giel, R., Koeter, M. and Ormel, J. (1990) 'Detection and referral of primary care patients with mental health problems', in D. Goldberg and D. Tantam (eds) *The Public Health Impact of Mental Disorders*, Basel: Hogrefe Huber.

Gilbert, P., Gilbert, J. and Irons, C. (2004) 'Life events, entrapments and arrested anger', *Journal of Affective Disorders* 79: 149–60.

Gill, B., Meltzer, H., Hinds, K., et al. (1996) *Psychiatric Morbidity among Homeless People*. OPCS Survey Report 7. London: HMSO.

Gold, P. W., Goodwin, F. K. and Chrousos, G. P. (1988) 'Clinical and biochemical manifestations of depression: relation to the neurobiology of stress', *New England Journal of Medicine* 319: 348–419.

Goldberg, D. P. (1991) 'Cost effectiveness studies in the treatment of schizophrenia', *Schizophrenia Bulletin* 17: 453–60.

Goldberg, D. P. (1995) 'Epidemiology of mental disorders in primary care settings', *Epidemiologic Reviews* 17, 1: 182–90.

Goldberg, D. P. and Bridges, K. (1988) 'Somatic presentations of psychiatric illness in primary care settings', *Journal of Psychosomatic Research* 132: 137–44.

Goldberg, D. P. and Huxley, P. J. (1980) *Mental Illness in the Community – The Pathway to Psychiatric Care*, London: Tavistock.

Goldberg, D. P. and Huxley, P. J. (1992) *Common Mental Disorders – A Biosocial Model*, London: Routledge.

Goldberg, D. P. and Williams, P. (1988) *A User's Guide to the GHQ*, Windsor: NFER-Nelson.

Goldberg, D. P., Bridges, K., Duncan-Jones, P. and Grayson, D. (1987) 'Dimensions of neurosis seen in primary care settings', *Psychological Medicine* 17: 461–71.

Goldberg, D. P., Bridges, K., Cook, D., et al. (1990) 'The influence of social factors on common mental disorders destabilisation and restitution', *British Journal of Psychiatry* 156: 704–13.

Goldberg, D. P., Jenkins, L., Millar, T. and Farragher, B. (1991) 'The ability of general practitioners to identify emotional distress among their patients', *Psychological Medicine* 23: 185–93.

Goldberg, D. P., Privett, M., Ustun, B., et al. (1998) 'The effects of detection and treatment on the outcome of major depression in primary care: a naturalistic study in 15 cities', *British Journal of General Practice* 48: 1840–44.

Goodman, R. (1995) 'The relationship between normal variation in IQ and common childhood psychopathology: a clinical study', *European Child and Adolescent Psychiatry* 4, 3: 187–96.

Goodyer, I. M. and Altham, P. M. E. (1991) 'Lifetime exit events in anxiety and depression in school age children I', Journal of Affective Disorders 21: 219–28.

Goodyer, I. M., Cooper, P. J., et al. (1993) 'Depression in 11 to 16 year old girls: the role of past parental psychopathology and exposure to recent undesirable life events', *Journal of Child Psychology and Psychiatry* 34: 1103–17.

Goodyer, I. M., Herbert, J., Tamplin, A. and Altham, P. M. (2000a) 'First-episode major depression in adolescents. Affective, cognitive and endocrine characteristics of risk status and predictors of onset', *British Journal of Psychiatry* 176: 142–9.

Goodyer, I. M., Herbert, J., Tamplin, A. and Altham, P. M. (2000b) 'Recent life events, cortisol, dehydroepiandrosterone and the onset of major depression in high-risk adolescents', *British Journal of Psychiatry* 177: 499–504.

Goodyer, I. M., Park, R. J., et al. (2001a) 'Possible role of cortisol and dehydroepiandrosterone in human development and psychopathology', *British Journal of Psychiatry* 179: 243–9.

Goodyer, I. M., Herbert, J., et al. (2003) 'Psychoendocrine antecedents of persistent first-episode major depression in adolescents: a community-based longitudinal enquiry', *Psychological Medicine* 33, 4: 601–10.

Goodyer, I. M., Park, R. J., et al. (2001b) 'Psychosocial and endocrine features of chronic first-episode major depression in 8–16 year olds', *Biological Psychiatry* 50, 5: 351–7.

Gove, W. R. (1972) 'The relationship between sex roles, marital status and mental illness', *Social Forces* 51: 34–44.

Graber, J. A., Lewinsohn, P. M., Seeley, J. R. and Brooks-Gunn, J. (1997) 'Is psychopathology associated with the timing of pubertal development?', *Journal of American Academy of Child and Adolescent Psychiatry* 36, 12: 1768–76.

Graeff, F. G., Guimaraes, F. S., et al. (1996) 'Role of 5-HT in stress, anxiety, and depression', *Pharmacological and Biochemical Behaviour* 54, 1: 129–41.

Grant, I., McDonald, I., Patteron, T. and Trimble, M. (1989) 'Multiple sclerosis', in G. W. Brown and T. Harris (eds) *Life Events*, London: Unwin.

Grasby, P. M. (1999) 'Imaging strategies in depression', *Journal of Psychopharmacology* 13, 4: 346–51.

Grayson, D., Bridges, K., Cook, D. and Goldberg, D. P. (1990) 'The validity of diagnostic systems for common mental disorders: a comparison between ID-Catego and DSM-3 systems', *Psychological Medicine* 20: 209–18.

Green, J. and Goldwyn, R. (2002) 'Annotation: attachment disorganisation and psychopathology: new findings in attachment research and their potential implications for developmental psychopathology in childhood', *Journal of Child Psychology and Psychiatry* 43: 835–46.

Guazzo, E. P., Kirkpatrick, P. J., et al. (1996) 'Cortisol, dehydroepiandrosterone (DHEA), and DHEA sulfate in the cerebrospinal fluid of man: relation to blood levels and the effects of age', *Journal of Clinical Endocrinology and Metabolism* 81: 3951–60.

Gunnar, M. R. (1998) 'Quality of early care and buffering of neuroendocrine stress reactions: potential effects on the developing human brain', *Preventive Medicine* 27: 208–11.

Gunnar, M. R. and Donzella, B. (2002) 'Social regulation of the cortisol levels in early human development', *Psychoneuroendocrinology* 27, 1–2: 199–220.

Gunnar, M. R., Morison, S. J., et al. (2001) 'Salivary cortisol levels in children adopted from Romanian orphanages', *Developmental Psychopathology* 13, 3: 611–28.

Gunnell, D., Middleton, N., et al. (2003) 'Why are suicide rates rising in young men?', *Journal of Child Psychology and Psychiatry* 34: 1103–17.

Halligan, S. L., Herbert, J., et al. (2004) 'Exposure to postnatal depression predicts elevated cortisol in adolescent offspring', *Biological Psychiatry* 55, 4: 376–81.

Hamarman, S., Pope, K. H., et al. (2002) 'Emotional abuse in children: variations in legal definitions and rates across the United States', *Child Maltreatment* 7, 4: 303–11.

Hammen, C., Burge, D., Burney, E., et al. (1990) 'Longitudinal study of diagnoses in children of women with unipolar and bipolar affective disorder', *Archives of General Psychiatry* 47: 1112–17.

Hammen, C., Henry, R. and Daley, S. (2000) 'Depression and sensitization to stressors among young women as a function of childhood adversity', *Journal of Consulting and Clinical Psychology* 68: 782–7.

Hariri, A. R., Mattay, V. S., Tessitore, A., et al. (2002) 'Serotonin transporter genetic variation and the response of the human amygdala', *Science* 297: 400–403.

Harmer, A. L., Sanderson, J. and Mertin, P. (1999) 'Influence of negative childhood experiences on psychological functioning, social support, and parenting for mothers recovering from addiction', *Child Abuse and Neglect* 23: 421–33.

Harris, A. W., Zaia, A. F., Bates, J. E., et al. (1997) 'Subtypes of social withdrawal in early childhood: sociometric status and social-cognitive differences across four years', *Child Development* 68: 278–94.

Harris, J. R. (1998) *The Nurture Assumption: Why Children Turn Out the Way They Do*, New York: Free Press.

Harris, T. O. (1989) 'Disorders of menstruation', in G. W. Brown and T. Harris (eds) *Life Events*, London: Unwin Hyman.

Harris, T. O. (2000) 'Introduction to the work of George Brown', in T. Harris (ed.) *Where Inner and Outer Worlds Meet*, London: Routledge, pp. 1–52.

Harris, T. O., Brown, G. W. and Robinson, R. (1999) 'Befriending as an intervention for chronic depression among women in an inner city. 1: Randomised controlled trial', *British Journal of Psychiatry* 174: 219–24.

Harris, T. O., Borsanyi, S., et al. (2000) 'Morning cortisol as a risk factor for subsequent major depressive disorder in adult women', *British Journal of Psychiatry* 177: 505–10.

Hart, J. T. and Dieppe, P. (1996) 'Caring effects', *Lancet* 347: 1606–8.

Hartup, W. W. (1996) 'The company they keep: friendships and their developmental significance', *Child Development* 67, 1: 1–13.

Heady, B. and Waring, A. (1989) 'Personality, life events and subjective well-being', *Journal of Personality Social Psychology* 57: 731–9.

Heim, C. and Nemeroff, C. B. (1999) 'The impact of early adverse experiences on brain systems involved in the pathophysiology of anxiety and affective disorders', *Biological Psychiatry* 46: 1509–22.

Heim, C., Ehlert, U., Hanker, J. P. and Hellhammer, D. H. (1998) 'Abuse-related post-traumatic stress disorder and alterations of the hypothalamic-pituitary-adrenal axis in women', *Psychosomatic Medicine* 60, 3: 309–18.

Henggeler, S. W., Cunningham, P. B., Pickrel, S. G., et al. (1998) 'Multi-systemic therapy: an effective prevention approach for serious juvenile offenders', *Journal of Adolescence* 19: 47–61.

Herman-Giddens, M. E., Slora, E. J., Wasserman, R. C, Bourdony, C. J., Bhapkar, M. V, Koch, G. G. and Hasemeier, C. M. (1997) 'Secondary sexual characteristics and menses in young girls seen in office practice: a study from the Pediatric Research in Office Settings network', *Pediatrics* 99, 4: 505–12.

Hetherington, E. M., Bridges, M., et al. (1998) 'What matters? What does not? Five perspectives on the association between marital transitions and children's adjustment', *American Psychology* 53, 2: 167–84.

Hetherington, E. M. and Stanley-Hagan, M. (1999) 'The adjustment of children with divorced parents: a risk and resiliency perspective', *Journal of Child Psychology and Psychiatry* 40, 1: 129–40.

Hickie, I., Bennett, B., Lloyd, A., Heath, A. and Martin, N. (1999) 'Complex genetic and environmental relationships between psychological distress, fatigue and immune functioning: a twin study', *Psychological Medicine* 29, 2: 269–77.

Hill, J. and Maughan, B. (eds) (2001) *Conduct Disorders in Childhood and Adolescence*, Cambridge: Cambridge University Press.

HMSO (1986) *Morbidity Statistics from General Practice 1981–1982*, London: Her Majesty's Stationery Office.

Holden, J., Sagovsky, R. and Cox, J. (1989) 'Counselling in general practice settings: a controlled study of health visitor intervention in the treatment of postnatal depression', *British Medical Journal* 298: 223–6.

Huesman, L. R., Eron, L. D., Lefkowitz, M. M. and Walder, L. O. (1984) 'Stability of aggression over time and generations', *Developmental Psychology* 20: 1120–34.

Hughes, C. and Dunn, J. (1998) 'Understanding mind and emotion: longitudinal associations with mental-state talk between young friends', *Developmental Psychology* 34, 5: 1026–37.

Hughes, C., Dunn, J. and White, A. (1998) 'Trick or treat?: uneven understanding of mind and emotion and executive dysfunction in "hard-to-manage" preschoolers', *Journal of Child Psychology and Psychiatry* 39: 981–94.

Hughes, C., White, A., Sharpen, J., et al. (2000) 'Anti-social, angry, and unsympathetic: "hard-to manage" preschoolers' peer problems and possible cognitive influences', *Journal of Child Psychology and Psychiatry* 41, 2: 169–79.

Hughes, C., Oksanen, H., et al. (2002) ' "I'm gonna beat you!" SNap!: an observational paradigm for assessing young children's disruptive behaviour in competitive play', *Journal of Child Psychology and Psychiatry* 43, 4: 507–16.

Hunt, P. J., Gurnell, E. M., et al. (2000) 'Improvement in mood and fatigue after dehydroepiandrosterone replacement in Addison's disease in a randomized, double blind trial', *Journal of Clinical Endocrinology and Metabolism* 85, 12: 4650–56.

Huppert, F. A. and Van Niekerk, J. K. (2001) 'Dehydroepiandrosterone (DHEA) supplementation for cognitive function (Cochrane Review)', *Cochrane Database System Review* 2: CD000304.

Hutchings, B. and Mednick, S. A. (1975) 'Registered criminality in the adopted and biological parents of registered male adoptees', in S. A. Mednick, J. Schulsinger and J. Higgins (eds) *Genetics, Environment and Psychopathology*, Amsterdam: Elsevier.

Huxley, P. J. and Goldberg, D. P. (1975) 'Social versus clinical prediction in minor psychiatric morbidity', *Psychological Medicine* 5: 96–100.

Huxley, P. J., Goldberg, D. P., Maguire, G. P. and Kincey, V. (1979) 'The prediction of the course of minor psychiatric morbidity', *British Journal of Psychiatry* 135: 535–43.

Irwin, M. (1999) 'Immune correlates of depression', *Advances in Experimental Medicine and Biology* 461: 1–24.

Irwin, M., Daniels, M. and Bloom, E. T. (1987) 'Life events, depressive symptoms and immune function', *American Journal of Psychiatry* 144: 437–41.

Irwin, M., Patterson, T., Smith, T., Caldwell, C., Brown, S. and Gillin, J. (1990) 'Reduction in immune function in life stress and depression', *Biological Psychiatry* 27: 22–30.

Jackson, G., Gater, R., Goldberg, D., Tantam, D., Loftus, L. and Taylor, H. (1993) 'A new community mental health team based in primary care', *British Journal of Psychiatry* 162: 375–84.

Jang, K. L., Vernon, P. A. and Livesley, W. J. (2000) 'Personality traits, family environment and alcohol misuse', *Addiction* 95: 873–88.

Jasper, K. (1963) *General Psychopathology*, Manchester: Manchester University Press.

Johnson, M. H. (1997) *Developmental Cognitive Neuroscience*, Oxford: Blackwell.

Johnstone, A. and Goldberg, D. (1976) 'Psychiatric screening in general practice: a controlled trial', *Lancet* I: 605–8.

Joiner, T. E., Jr., Lewinsohn, P. M., et al. (2002) 'The core of loneliness: lack of pleasurable engagement – more so than painful disconnection – predicts social impairment, depression onset, and recovery from depressive disorders among adolescents', *Journal of Personality Assessment* 79, 3: 472–91.

Just, N., Abramson, L. Y., et al. (2001) 'Remitted depression studies as tests of the cognitive vulnerability hypotheses of depression onset: a critique and conceptual analysis', *Clinical Psychology of Review* 21, 1: 63–83.

Kaltiala-Heino, R., Kosunen, E. and Rimpela, M. (2003) 'Pubertal timing, sexual behaviour and self-reported depression in middle adolescence', *Journal of Adolescence* 26, 5: 531–45.

Kamins, M. L. and Dweck, C. S. (1999) 'Person versus process praise and criticism: implications for contingent self-worth and coping', *Developmental Psychology* 35, 3: 835–47.

Kanba, S., Manki, H., Shintani, F., Ohno, Y., Yagi, G. and Asai, M. (1998) 'Aberrant interleukin-2 receptor-mediated blastoformation of peripheral blood lymphocytes in a severe major depressive episode', *Psychological Medicine* 28, 2: 481–4.

Karishma, K. K. and Herbert, J. (2002) 'Dehydroepiandrosterone (DHEA) stimulates neurogenesis in the hippocampus of the rat, promotes survival of newly formed neurons and prevents corticosterone-induced suppression', *European Journal of Neuroscience* 16, 3: 445–53.

Kaufman, J., Plotsky, P. M., et al. (2000) 'Effects of early adverse experiences on brain structure and function: clinical implications', *Biological Psychiatry* 48, 8: 778.

Kedward, H. B. (1969) 'The outcome of neurotic illness in the community', *Social Psychiatry and Psychiatric Epidemiology* 4: 1–4.

Kellam, S. G. and Rebok, G. W. (1992) 'Building developmental and aetiological theory through epidemiologically based preventive intervention trials', in J. McCord and R. Tremblay (eds) *Preventing Antisocial Behaviour*, New York: Guilford Press, pp. 162–95.

Kelvin, R. G., Goodyer, I. M., et al. (1999) 'Latent negative self-schema and high emotionality in well adolescents at risk for psychopathology', *Journal of Child Psychology and Psychiatry* 40, 6: 959–68.

Kendler, K. and Prescott, C. (1999) 'A population based twin study of lifetime major depression in men and women', *Archives of General Psychiatry* 56: 39–44.

Kendler, K. and Karkowski-Shuman, L. (1997) 'Stressful life events and genetic liability to major depression: genetic control of exposure to the environment', *Psychological Medicine* 27: 539–47.

Kendler, K. and Gardner, C. O. (2001) 'Monozygotic twins discordant for major depression: a preliminary exploration of the role of environmental experiences in the aetiology and course of illness', *Psychological Medicine* 31: 411–24.

Kendler, K., Heath, A., Martin, N. G., et al. (1987) 'Symptoms of depression and anxiety: same genes, different environments?', *Archives of General Psychiatry* 44: 451–7.

Kendler, K. S., Neale, M. C., Kessler, R. C., Heath, A. C. and Eaves, L. J. (1992a) 'Generalised anxiety disorder in women, a population based twin study', *Archives of General Psychiatry* 49: 267–72.

Kendler, K. S., Neale, M. C., Kessler, R. C., Heath, A. C. and Eaves, L. J. (1992b) 'The genetic epidemiology of phobias in women, the inter-relationship of agoraphobia social phobia, situational phobia and simple phobia', *Archives of General Psychiatry* 49: 273–81.

Kendler, K. S., Neale, M. C., Kessler, R. C., Heath, A. C. and Eaves, L. J. (1992c) 'Major depression and generalized anxiety disorder: same genes, (partly) different environments?', *Archives of General Psychiatry* 49: 716–22.

Kendler, K., Neale, M. C., Kessler, R. C., et al. (1993a) 'A twin study of recent life events and difficulties', *Archives of General Psychiatry* 50: 789–96.

Kendler, K. S., Neale, M. C., Kessler, R. C., Heath, A. C. and Eaves, L. J. (1993b) 'Panic disorder in women, a population based twin study', *Psychological Medicine* 23: 297–406.

Kendler, K. S., Neale, M. C., Kessler, R. C., Heath, A. C. and Eaves, L. J. (1993c) 'Major depression and phobias: the genetic and environmental sources of comorbidity', *Psychological Medicine* 23: 361–71.

Kendler, K. S., Walters, E. E., Neale, M. C., Kessler, R. C., Heath, A. C. and Eaves, L. J. (1995) 'The structure of the genetic and environmental risk factors for six major psychiatric disorders in women. Phobia, generalised anxiety disorder, panic disorder, bulimia, major depression, and alcoholism', *Archives of General Psychiatry* 52: 374–83.

Kendler, K. S., Davis, C. G. and Kessler, R. C. (1997a) 'The familial aggregation of common psychiatric and substance use disorders in the National Co-morbidity study', *British Journal of Psychiatry* 170: 541–8.

Kendler, K. S., Walters, E. E. and Kessler, R. C. (1997b) 'The prediction of length of major depressive episodes: results from an epidemiological sample of female twins', *Psychological Medicine* 27, 1: 107–17.

Kendler, K. S., Karkovski, L. M. and Prescott, C. A. (1999) 'Hallucinogen, opiate, sedative and stimulant use and abuse in a population of female twins', *Acta Psychiatrica Scandinavica* 99: 368–76.

Kendler, K. S., Thornton, L. M. and Gardner, C. O. (2001) 'Genetic risk, numbers of previous episodes and stressful life events in predicting onset of major depression', *American Journal of Psychiatry* 158: 582–6.

Kendler, K. S., Gardner, C. O., et al. (2002) 'Toward a comprehensive developmental model for major depression in women', *American Journal of Psychiatry* 159, 7: 1133–45.

Kendler, K. S., Hettema, J. M., Butera, F., Gardner, C. O., Prescott, C. A. (2003) 'Life event dimensions of loss, humiliation, entrapment and danger in the prediction of onsets of major depression and generalised anxiety', *Archives of General Psychiatry* 60: 789.

Kessler, R., McGonagle, K. A., Zhao, S., et al. (1994) 'Lifetime and 12 month prevalence of DSM-3R psychiatric disorders in the United States: results from the National Comorbidity study', *Archives of General Psychiatry* 51: 8–10.

Kessler, R. C., Berglund, P., Demler, O., Jin, R., Koretz, D., Merikangas, K., Rush, J., Walters, E. and Wang, P. (2003) 'The epidemiology of major depressive disorder: results from the national comorbidity survey replication', *JAMA* 289: 3095–3105.

Kim-Cohen, J., Caspi, A., et al. (2003) 'Prior juvenile diagnoses in adults with mental disorder: developmental follow-back of a prospective-longitudinal cohort', *Archives of General Psychiatry* 60, 7: 709–17.

Kimonides, V. G., Khatibi, N. H., et al. (1998) 'Dehydroepiandrosterone (DHEA) and DHEA-sulfate (DHEAS) protect hippocampal neurons against excitatory amino acid-induced neurotoxicity', *Proceedings of National Academy of Sciences of the USA* 95, 4: 1852–7.

Kimonides, V. G., Spillantini, M. G., et al. (1999) 'Dehydroepiandrosterone antagonizes the neurotoxic effects of corticosterone and translocation of stress-activated protein kinase 3 in hippocampal primary cultures', *Neuroscience* 89, 2: 429–36.

King, R. (2002) 'Adolescence', in M. Lewis (ed.) *Textbook of Child and Adolescent Psychiatry*, New York: Macmillan.

Kinzl, J. and Biebl, W. (1992) 'Long-term effects of incest: life events triggering mental disorders in female patients with sexual abuse in childhood', *Child Abuse and Neglect* 16, 4: 567–73.

Klaassen, T., Riedel, W. J., et al. (2002) 'Mood congruent memory bias induced by tryptophan depletion', *Psychological Medicine* 32, 1: 167–72.

Klein, N. C., Alexander, J. F. and Parsons, B. V. (1977) 'Impact of family systems intervention on recidivism and sibling delinquency', *Journal of Consulting and Clinical Psychology* 45: 469–74.

Klein, R. G. and Pine, D. (2003) 'Anxiety disorders', in M. Rutter and E. Taylor (eds) *Child and Adolescent Psychiatry*, 4th edn. Oxford: Blackwell, pp. 486–509.

Kleinman, A. (1988) *Rethinking Psychiatry*, London: Plenum.

Kroboth, P. D., Salek, F. S., et al. (1999) 'DHEA and DHEA-S: a review', *Journal of Clinical Pharmacology* 39, 4: 327–48.

Kroboth, P. D., Amico, J. A., et al. (2003) 'Influence of DHEA administration on 24-hour cortisol concentrations', *Journal of Clinical Psychopharmacology* 23, 1: 96–9.

Krueger, R. F. and Finger, M. S. (2001) 'Using item response theory to understand comorbidity among anxiety and unipolar depressive disorders', *Psychological Assessment* 13: 140–51.

Krueger, R. F., Hicks, B. M., Patrick, C. J., et al. (2002) 'Etiologic connections among substance dependence, anti-social behaviour and personality', *Journal of Abnormal Psychology* 111: 411–23.

Krueger, R. F. and Tackett, J. L. (2003) 'Personality and psychopathology – working towards the bigger picture', *Journal of Personality Disorders* 17, 2: 109–28.

Krueger, R. F., Caspi, A., Moffitt, T. E. and Silva, P. A. (1998) 'The structure and stability of common mental disorders (DSM-III-R): a longitudinal-epidemiological study', *Journal of Abnormal Psychology* 107: 216–27.

Krueger, R. F., Chentsova-Dutton, Y. E., Markon, K. E., Goldberg, D. P. and Ormel, J. (2003) 'A cross-cultural study of the structure of comorbidity among common psychopathological syndromes in the general health care setting', *Journal of Abnormal Psychology* 112, 437–47.

Krueger, R. F., Nichol, P. E., Hicks, B. M., et al. (2004) 'Using latent trait modelling to conceptualize an alcohol problems continuum' (in press).

Kuan, C. Y., Roth, K. A., Flavell, R. A. and Rakic, P. (2000) 'Mechanisms of programmed cell death in the developing brain', *Trends Neuroscience* 23, 7: 291–7.

Kurstjens, S. and Wolke, D. (2001) 'Effects of maternal depression on cognitive development of children over the first 7 years of life', *Journal of Child Psychology and Psychiatry* 42: 623–36.

Labrie, F., Belanger, A., et al. (1997) 'Marked decline in serum concentrations of adrenal C19 sex steroid precursors and conjugated androgen metabolites during aging', *Journal of Clinical Endocrinology and Metabolism* 82, 8: 2396–402.

Laudenslager, M., Ryan, S., Drugan, R., Hyson, R. and Maier, S. (1983) 'Coping and immunosuppression: inescapable but not escapable shock suppresses lymphocyte proliferation', *Science* 221: 568–70.

Lee, A. and Murray, R. (1988) 'The long term outcome of Maudsley depressives', *British Journal of Psychiatry* 153: 741–52.

Leenstra, A. S., Ormel, J. and Giel, R. (1995) 'Positive life change and recovery from depression and anxiety. A three-stage longitudinal study of primary care attenders', *British Journal of Psychiatry* 166, 3: 333–43.

Leon, D. A. (2001) 'Getting to grips with fetal programming – aspects of a rapidly evolving agenda', *International Journal of Epidemiology* 30: 96–8.

Lewinsohn, P. M., Clarke, G. N., et al. (1994) 'Major depression in community adolescents: age at onset, episode duration, and time to recurrence', *Journal of the American Academy of Child and Adolescent Psychiatry* 33: 809–18.

Lewinsohn, P. M., Allen, N. B., Seeley, J. R. and Gotlib, I. H. (1999) 'First onset versus recurrence of depression: differential processes of psychosocial risk', *Journal of Abnormal Psychology* 108, 3: 483–9.

Lewinsohn, P. M., Joiner, T. E. Jr, et al. (2001) 'Evaluation of cognitive diathesis-stress models in predicting major depressive disorder in adolescents', *Journal of Abnormal Psychology* 110, 2: 203–15.

Lewis, A. (1934) 'Melancholia – a clinical survey of depressive states', *Journal of Mental Science* 80: 1–41.

Lieberman, A. F. and Van Horn, P. (1998) 'Attachment, trauma and domestic violence: implications for child custody', *Child and Adolescent Clinics of North America* 7: 423–33.

Linkowski, P., Van Onderbergen, A., et al. (1993) 'Twin study of the 24-h cortisol profile: evidence for genetic control of the human circadian clock', *American Journal of Physiology* 264, 2 pt 1: E173–81.

Linn, M. W., Linn, B. S. and Jensen, J. (1984) 'Stressful events, dysphoric mood, and immune responsiveness', *Psychological Reports* 54: 219–22.

Loeber, R. and Hay, D. (1997) 'Key issues in the development of aggression and violence from childhood to early adulthood', *Annual Review of Psychology* 48: 371–410.

Loeber, R. and Farrington, D. P. (2000) 'Young children who commit crime: epidemiology, developmental origins, risk factors, early interventions, and policy implications', *Developmental Psychopathology* 12, 4: 737–62.

Loeber, R., Green, S. M., et al. (2000) 'Findings on disruptive behavior disorders from the first decade of the Developmental Trends Study', *Clinical Child and Family Psychology Review* 3, 1: 37–60.

Lupien, S. J. and Lepage, M. (2001) 'Stress, memory, and the hippocampus: can't live with it, can't live without it', *Behavioural Brain Research* 127, 1–2: 137–58.

Lupien, S. J., King, S., et al. (2000) 'Child's stress hormone levels correlate with mother's socioeconomic status and depressive state', *Biological Psychiatry* 48, 10: 976–80.

Lupien, S. J., King, S., et al. (2001) 'Can poverty get under your skin? Basal cortisol levels and cognitive function in children from low and high socioeconomic status', *Development and Psychopathology* 13, 3: 653–76.

Lupien, S. J., Wilkinson, C. W., et al. (2002a) 'Acute modulation of aged human memory by pharmacological manipulation of glucocorticoids', *Journal of Clinical Endocrinology and Metabolism* 87, 8: 3798–807.

Lupien, S. J., Wilkinson, C. W., et al. (2002b) 'The modulatory effects of corticosteroids on cognition: studies in young human populations', *Psychoneuroendocrinology* 27, 3: 401–16.

Lutchmaya, S., Baron-Cohen, S. and Raggatt, P. (2002) 'Foetal testosterone and eye contact', *Infant Behaviour and Development* 24: 418–24.

McBurnett, K., Lahey, B. B., et al. (2000) 'Low salivary cortisol and persistent aggression in boys referred for disruptive behavior', *Archives of General Psychiatry* 57, 1, 38–43.

McCambridge, J. and Strang, J. (2004) 'The efficacy of a single-session motivational interviewing in reducing drug consumption', *Addiction* 99: 39–52.

Maccoby, E. (1966) *The Development of Sex Differences*, Stanford: Stanford University Press.

Maccoby, E. (1990) 'Gender and relationships, a developmental account', *American Psychologist* 45: 513–20.

Maccoby, E. (1998) *The Two Sexes, Growing Apart, Coming Together*, Cambridge, MA: Harvard University Press.

Maccoby, E. E. (2000) 'Parenting and its effects on children: on reading and misreading behavior genetics', *Annual Review of Psychology* 51: 1–27.

Maccoby, E. E. (2002) 'Gender and social exchange: a developmental perspective', *New Directions in Child and Adolescent Development* 95: 87–105.

McDonald, E., Mann, A. and Thomas, H. (1987) 'Interferons as mediators of psychiatric morbidity', *Lancet* 4: 1175–8.

McGuffin, P. and Gottesman, I. I. (1984) 'Genetic influences on normal and abnormal development', in M. Rutter and L. Hersov (eds) *Child Psychiatry: Modern Approaches*, London: Blackwell.

McGuffin, P. and Thapar, A. (1992) 'The genetics of personality disorder', *British Journal of Psychiatry* 160: 12–23.

McNeal, C. and Amato, P. R. (1998) 'Parent's marital violence', *Journal of Family Issues* 19: 123–39.

Maes, M., Meltzer, H. Y., et al. (1995) 'Effects of serotonin precursors on the negative feedback effects of glucocorticoids on hypothalamic-pituitary-adrenal axis function in depression', *Psychoneuroendocrinology* 20, 2: 149–67.

Magee, W. J. (1999) 'Effects of negative life experiences on phobia onset', *Social Psychiatry and Psychiatric Epidemiology* 34, 7: 343–51.

Mann, A., Jenkins, R. and Belsey, E. (1981) 'The 12 month outcome of patients with neurotic illness in general practice', *Psychological Medicine* 11: 535–50.

Manuzza, S., Klein, R. G., Bessler, A., Malloy, P., et al. (1993) 'Adult outcome of hyperactive boys', *Archives of General Psychiatry* 50: 565–76.

Marks, J., Goldberg, D. P. and Hillier, V. (1979) 'Determinants of the ability of general practitioners to detect emotional illness', *Psychological Medicine* 9: 337–53.

Marx, C., Petros, S., et al. (2003) 'Adrenocortical hormones in survivors and non-survivors of severe sepsis: diverse time course of dehydroepiandrosterone, dehydroepiandrosterone-sulfate, and cortisol', *Critical Care Medicine* 31, 5: 1382–8.

Masten, A. S. (2001) 'Ordinary magic. Resilience processes in development', *American Psychology* 56, 3: 227–38.

Masten, A. S., Hubbard, J. J., et al. (1999) 'Competence in the context of adversity: pathways to resilience and maladaptation from childhood to late adolescence', *Developmental Psychopathology* 11, 1: 143–69.

Mayberg, H. S. (1997) 'Limbic-cortical dysregulation: a proposed model of depression', *Journal of Neuropsychiatry and Clinical Neuroscience* 9, 3: 471–81.

Mayberg, H. S., Liotti, M., et al. (1999) 'Reciprocal limbic-cortical function and negative mood: converging PET', *American Journal of Psychiatry* 156, 5: 675–82.

Mayberg, H. S., et al. (2000) 'Regional metabolic effects of fluoxetine in major depression: serial', *Biological Psychiatry* 48, 8: 830–43.

Mayeux, L. and Cillessen, A. H. (2003) 'Development of social problem solving in early childhood: stability, change, and associations with social competence', *Journal of Genetic Psychology* 164, 2: 153–73.

Meaney, M. J., Stewart, J. and Beatty, W. W. (1985) 'Sex differences in social play: the socialisation of sex roles', *Advances in the Study of Behaviour* 15: 1–58.

Meikle, A. W., Stringham, J. D., et al. (1988) 'Heritability of variation of plasma cortisol levels', *Metabolism* 37, 6: 514–7.

Melzer, H., Gill, B., Petticrew, M., et al. (1995a) *OPCS Surveys of Psychiatric Morbidity in Great Britain. Report 1: The Prevalence of Psychiatric Morbidity among Adults Living in Private Households*, London: HMSO.

Melzer, H., Gill, B., Petticrew, M., et al. (1995b) *OPCS Surveys of Psychiatric Morbidity in Great Britain. Report 2: Physical Complaints, Service Use and Treatment of Adults with Psychiatric Disorder*, London: HMSO.

Meltzer, H., Bebbington, P., Brugha, T. S., Farrell, M., Jenkins, R. and Lewis, G. (2000) 'The reluctance to seek treatment for neurotic disorders', *Journal of Mental Health* 9: 319–27.

Menkes, D. B. and MacDonald, J. A. (2000) 'Interferons, serotonin and neurotoxicity', *Psychological Medicine* 30: 259–68.

Meyer, A. (1955) *Psychobiology – A Science of Illness*, Springfield: Charles Thomas.

Millar, T. and Goldberg, D. P. (1991) 'Determinants of the ability of general practitioners to manage common mood disorders', *British Journal of General Practice* 41: 357–9.

Miller, P. and Ingham, J. (1983) 'Dimensions of experience', *Psychological Medicine* 13: 417–29.

Miller, P. and Ingham, J. (1985) 'Dimensions of experience and psychopathology', *Journal of Psychiatric Research* 29: 475–88.

Miller, P. M. and Surtees, P. G. (1995) 'Partners in adversity. V: Support, personality and coping behaviour at the time of crisis', *European Archives of Psychiatry and Clinical Neuroscience* 245, 4–5: 245–54.

Mizruchin, A., Gold, I., Krasnov, I., Livshitz, G., Shahin, R. and Kook, A. I. (1999) 'Comparison of the effects of dopaminergic and serotonergic activity in the CNS on the activity of the immune system', *Journal of Neuro-immunology* 101, 2: 201–4.

Modestin, J., Oberson, B. and Erni, T. (1998) 'Possible antecedents of DSM-III-R personality disorders', *Acta Psychiatrica Scandinavica* 97, 4: 260–66.

Moffitt, T. E. and Caspi, A. (2001) 'Childhood predictors differentiate life-course persistent and adolescence-limited antisocial pathways among males and females', *Developmental Psychopathology* 13, 2: 355–75.

Moffitt, T., Caspi, A., Rutter, M. and Silva, P. (2001) *Sex Differences in Antisocial Behaviour*, Cambridge: Cambridge University Press.

Moffitt, T. E., Caspi, A., Harrington, H. and Milne, B. J. (2002) 'Males on the life-course-persistent and adolescence-limited antisocial pathways: follow-up at age 26 years', *Developmental Psychopathology* 14, 1: 179–207.

Monroe, S. M., Rohde, P., Seeley, J. R. and Lewinsohn, P. M. (1999) 'Life events and depression in adolescence: relationship loss as a prospective risk factor for first onset of major depressive disorder', *Journal of Abnormal Psychology* 108, 4: 606–14.

Motto, J. A. (1970) 'Newspapers influence on suicide. A controlled study', *Archives of General Psychiatry* 23: 143–8.

Mullen, P. E., Martin, J. L., et al. (1993) 'Childhood sexual abuse and mental health in adult life', *British Journal of Psychiatry* 163: 721–32.

Mullen, P. E., Martin, J. L., et al. (1994) 'The effect of child sexual abuse on social, interpersonal and sexual function in adult life', *British Journal of Psychiatry* 165, 2: 35–47.

Murphy, E. (1982) 'Social origins of depression in old age', *British Journal of Psychiatry* 141: 135–42.

Murphy, E. and Brown, G. W. (1980) 'Life events, psychiatric disturbance and physical illness', *British Journal of Psychiatry* 136: 326–38.

Murphy, F. C., Smith, K. A., et al. (2002) 'The effects of tryptophan depletion on cognitive and affective processing in healthy volunteers', *Psychopharmacology* 163, 1: 42–53.

Murray, K. T. and Sines, J. O. (1996) 'Parsing the genetic and nongenetic variance in children's depressive behavior', *Journal of Affective Disorders* 38, 1: 23–34.

Murray, L. (1992) 'The impact of postnatal depression on infant development', *Journal of Child Psychology and Psychiatry* 33: 543–61.

Murray, L. and Cooper, P. J. (2003) 'Intergenerational transmission of affective and cognitive processes associated with depression-infancy and the pre-school years', in I. M. Goodyer (ed.) *Unipolar Depression – A Lifespan Perspective*, Oxford: Oxford University Press, pp. 17–35.

Murray, L., Kempton, C., Woolgar, M., et al. (1993) 'Depressed mothers' speech to their infants and its relation to infant gender and cognitive development', *Journal of Child Psychology and Psychiatry* 34: 1083–1101.

Murray, L., Fiori-Cowley, A., Hooper, R., et al. (1996) 'The impact of postnatal depression and associated adversity on early mother–infant interactions and later infant outcome', *Child Development* 67: 2512–26.

Murray, L., Woolgar, M., Cooper, P. and Hipwell, A. (2001a) 'Cognitive vulnerability to depression in 5-year-old children of depressed mothers', *Journal of Child Psychology and Psychiatry* 42, 7: 891–9.

Murray, L., Woolgar, M., Cooper, P., et al. (2001b) 'Cognitive vulnerability to negative feedback effects of glucocorticoids on hypothalamic-pituitary-adrenal axis negative mood: converging PET', *American Journal of Psychiatry* 156, 5: 675–82.

Nagin, D. S., Pagani, L., Tremblay, R. E. and Vitaro, F. (2003) 'Life course turning points: the effect of grade retention on physical aggression', *Developmental Psychopathology* 15, 2: 343–61.

Nazroo, J. Y., Edwards, A. C. and Brown, G. W. (1997) 'Gender differences in the onset of depression following a shared life event: a study of couples', *Psychological Medicine* 27: 9–20.

Neeleman, J., Oldehinkel, A. and Ormel, J. (2003) 'Positive life change and remission of non-psychotic mental illness', *Journal of Affective Disorders* 76: 69–78.

Neilsen, E., Brown, G. W. and Marmot, M. (1989) 'Myocardial infarction', in G. W. Brown and T. Harris (eds) *Life Events*, London: Unwin Hyman.

Nelson, C. and Bloom, F. E. (1997) 'Child development and neuroscience', *Child Development* 68: 970–97.

Nemeroff, C. B. (2002) 'New directions in the development of antidepressants: the interface of neurobiology and psychiatry', *Human Psychopharmacology* 17 (suppl 1): S13–6.

Newcomer, J. W., Selke, G., et al. (1999) 'Decreased memory performance in healthy humans induced by stress-level cortisol treatment', *Archives of General Psychiatry* 56, 6: 527–33.

Nolen-Hoeksema, S. (2000) 'The role of rumination in depressive disorders and mixed anxiety/depressive symptoms', *Journal of Abnormal Psychology* 109, 3: 504–11.

Notarius, C. and Pellegrini, D. (1984) 'Marital processes as stressors and stress mediators: implications for marital repair', in S. Duck (ed.) *Personal Relationships 5: Repairing Relationships*, London: Academic Press.

O'Connor, T. G. and Rutter, M. (2000) 'Attachment disorder behavior following early severe deprivation: extension and longitudinal follow-up. English and Romanian Adoptees Study Team', *Journal of American Academy of Child and Adolescent Psychiatry* 39: 703–12.

O'Connor, T. G., McGuire, S., Reiss, D., Hetherington, D. M. and Plomin, R. (1998) 'Co-occurrence of depressive symptoms and ASB in adolescents – a common genetic liability', *Journal of Abnormal Psychology* 107: 27–37.

O'Connor, T. G., Thorpe, K., Dunn, J. and Golding, J. (1999) 'Parental divorce and adjustment in adulthood: findings from a community sample. The ALSPAC Study Team. Avon Longitudinal Study of Pregnancy and Childhood', *Journal of Child Psychology and Psychiatry* 40, 5: 777–89.

Oldehinkel, A. J., Ormel, J. and Neeleman, J. (2000) 'Predictors of time to remission from depression in primary care patients: do some people benefit more from positive life change than others?', *Journal of Abnormal Psychology* 109: 299–307.

Oldehinkel, A. J., Berg, M. D. van den, Bouhuys, A. L. and Ormel, J. (2003) 'Do depressive episodes lead to accumulation of vulnerability in the elderly?', *Depression and Anxiety* 18: 67–75.

Olds, D., Henderson, C. J., Kitzman, H., Eckenrode, J., et al. (1998a) 'The promise of home visitation: results of two randomised trials', *Journal of Community Psychology* 26, 1: 5–21.

Olds, D., Henderson, C. R., Tatelbaum, R., et al. (1998b) 'Improving the life course development of socially disadvantaged mothers: an RCT of home visits', *American Journal of Public Health* 78: 1436–44.

Olsen, K. (1992) 'Genetic influences on sexual behaviour differentiation', in A. Gerall, H., Molz, and I. Ward (eds) *'Handbook of Behavioural Neurobiology, Vol. 11: Sexual Differentiation*, London: Plenum Press.

Olweus, D. (1991) 'Bully/victim problems among schoolchildren', in K. Rubin, and P. Pepler (eds) *The Development and Treatment of Childhood Aggression*, Hillsdale, NJ: Lawrence Erlbaum Associates, Inc.

Ono, Y., Ando, J., Onoda, N., Yoshimura, K., Momose, T., Hirano, M. and Kanba, S. (2002) 'Dimensions of temperament as vulnerability factors in depression', *Molecular Psychiatry* 7, 9: 948–53.

Ormel, J. and Costa e Silva, J. (1995) 'The impact of psychopathology on disability and health', in B. Ustun and N. Sartorius (eds) *Mental Illness in General Health Care*, Chichester: Wiley.

Ormel, J. and Wohlfarth, T. (1991) 'How neuroticism, long-term difficulties and life situation change influence psychological distress: a longitudinal model', *Journal of Personality and Social Psychology* 60: 744–55.

Ormel, J., von Korff, M., van den Brink, W., et al. (1993) 'Depression, anxiety and social disability show synchrony of change in primary care patients', *American Journal of Public Health* 83: 385–90.

Ormel, J., Oldehinkel, A. J., Goldberg, D. P., Hodiamont, P. P. G., Wilmink, F. W. and Bridges, K. (1995) 'The structure of common psychiatric symptoms: how many dimensions of neurosis?', *Psychological Medicine* 25: 520–1.

Ormel, J., Kempen, G. I. J. M., Penninx, B. W. J. H., Brilman E. I., Beekman, A. T. F. and Sonderen, E. van (1997) 'Chronic medical conditions and mental health in older people: disability and psychosocial resources mediate specific mental health effects', *Psychological Medicine* 27: 1065–77.

Ormel, J., Oldehinkel, A. J. and Brilman, E. I. (2001) 'The interplay and etiological continuity of neuroticism, difficulties and life events in the etiology of major and subsyndromal, first and recurrent depressive episodes in later life', *American Journal of Psychiatry* 158: 885–91.

Ormel, J., Oldehinkel, A. J., Nolen, W. A. and Vollebergh, W. (2004) 'Psychosocial disability before, during, and after a major depressive episode. A three-wave population-based study of state, scar and trait effects, *Archives of General Psychiatry* [in press].

Osborn, D. P., Fletcher, A. E., Smeeth, L., et al. (2003) 'Factors associated with depression in a representative sample of 14,217 people aged over 75 in the United Kingdom', *International Journal of Geriatric Psychiatry* 18: 623–30.

Overbeek, G., Volleberg, W., Engels, C. M. and Meeus, W. (2003) 'Young adults relationship transitions and the incidence of mental disorders – a three wave, longitudinal study', *Social Psychiatry and Psychiatric Epidemiology* 38: 669–76.

Paikoff, R. L., Brooks-Gunn, J. and Warren, M. P. (1991) 'Predictive effects of hormonal change on affective expression in adolescent females over the course of one year', *Journal of Youth and Adolescence* 20: 191–214.

Pajer, K., Gardner, W., et al. (2001) 'Decreased cortisol levels in adolescent girls with conduct disorder', *Archives of General Psychiatry* 58, 3: 297–302.

Pantev, C., Oostenveld, R., Engelien, A., Ross, B., Roberts, L. E. and Hoke, M. (1998) 'Increased auditory cortical representation in musicians', *Nature* 392: 811–4.

Park, R. J., Goodyer, I. M., et al. (2004) 'Effects of induced rumination and distraction on mood and overgeneral autobiographical memory in adolescent major depressive disorder and controls', *Journal of Child Psychology and Psychiatry* 45, 5: 996–1006.

Parker, C. R. Jr. (1999) 'Dehydroepiandrosterone and dehydroepiandrosterone sulfate production in the human adrenal during development and aging', *Steroids* 64, 9: 640–7.

Patton, G. C., Coffey, C., Posterino, M., et al. (2003) 'Life events and early onset depression: cause or consequence?', *Psychological Medicine* 33: 1203–10.

Patton, G. C., Coffey, C., Carlin, J. B., Olsson, C. A. and Morley, R. (2004) 'Prematurity at birth and adolescent depressive disorder', *British Journal of Psychiatry* 184: 446–7.

Paykel, E. S. (1974) 'Life stress and psychiatric disorder. Stressful life events: their nature and effects', Chichester: Wiley, pp. 42–51.

Petterson, S. M. and Albers, A. B. (2001) 'Effects of poverty and maternal depression on early child development', *Child Development* 72: 1794–1813.

Pettito, J. M., Lewis, M. H., Lysle, D. T., Gariepy, J.-L., Huag, Z., McCarthy, D. B. and Evans, D. L. (2000) 'Behavioural states and immune responsiveness', in K. Goodkin and A. P. Visser (eds) *Psychoneuroimmunology*, Washington, DC: American Psychiatric Press.

Pevalin, D. and Goldberg, D. P. (2003) 'Social precursors to onset and recovery from episodes of common mental illness', *Psychological Medicine* 33, 2: 299–306.

Phillips, D. I. (2001) 'Fetal growth and programming of the hypothalamic-pituitary-adrenal axis', *Clinical and Experimental Pharmacology and Physiology* 28, 11: 967–70.

Plomin, R. (1990) 'The role of inheritance on behaviour', *Science* 248: 183–8.

Plomin, R., Asbury, K., et al. (2001) 'Why are children in the same family so different? Non-shared environment a decade later', *Canadian Journal of Psychiatry* 46, 3: 225–33.

Plotsky, P. M., Owens, M. J., et al. (1998) 'Psychoneuroendocrinology of depression. Hypothalamic-pituitary-adrenal axis', *Psychiatric Clinics of North America* 21, 2: 293–307.

Posternak, M. A. and Miller, I. (2001) 'Untreated short-term course of major depression: a meta-analysis of outcomes from studies using wait-list control groups', *Journal of Affective Disorders* 66: 139–46.

Poulin, F. and Boivin, M. (2000) 'Reactive and proactive aggression: evidence of a two-factor model', *Psychological Assessment* 12, 2: 115–22.

Poulton, R. G. and Andrews, G. (1992) 'Personality as a cause of adverse life events', *Acta Psychiatrica Scandinavica* 85, 1: 35–8.

Prescott, C. A., Aggen, S. H., Kendler, K. S. (2000) 'Sex-specific genetic influences on the comorbidity of alcoholism and major depression in a population-based sample of US twins', *Archives of General Psychiatry* 57: 803–11.

Prince, M., Harwood, R. H., Blizard, R. A., et al. (1997) 'Social support deficits, loneliness and life events as risk factors for depression in old age. Gospel Oak V', *Psychological Medicine* 27: 323–32.

Prince, M. J., Harwood, R. H., Blizard, R. A., Thomas, A. and Mann, A. (1998) 'Impairment, disability and handicap as risk factors for late life depression. Gospel Oak V', *Psychological Medicine* 27: 311–21.

Prince, M., Beeckman, A. J., Deeg, D. J., et al. (1999) 'Depressive symptoms of late life assessed by the EURO-D scale: effects of age, gender and marital status in 14 European centres', *British Journal of Psychiatry* 174: 339–45.

Proudfoot, J., Goldberg, D. P., Mann, A., et al. (2003) 'Computerised. Interactive, multi-media cognitive-behavioural program for anxiety and depression in general practice', *Psychological Medicine* 33, 2: 217–28.

Proudfoot, J., Ryden, C. and Everitt, B. (2004) 'Clinical efficacy of computerised cognitive-behavioural therapy for anxiety and depression in primary care', *British Journal of Psychiatry* 185: 46–54.

Puckering, C., Pickles, A., Skuse, D., et al. (1995) 'Mother–child interaction and the cognitive and behavioural development of four-year-old children with poor growth', *Journal of Child Psychology and Psychiatry* 36: 573–95.

Putnam, F. W. (2003) 'Ten-year research update review: child sexual abuse', *Journal of American Academy of Child and Adolescent Psychiatry* 42, 3: 269–78.

Quintana, J. (1992) 'Platelet serotonin and plasma tryptophan decreases in endogenous depression', *Journal of Affective Disorders* 24: 55–62.

Raine, A., Venables, P. H., et al. (1997) 'Low resting heart rate at age 3 years predisposes to aggression at age 11 years: evidence from the Mauritius Child Health Project', *Journal of American Academy of Child and Adolescent Psychiatry* 36, 10: 1457–64.

Raine, A., Reynolds, C., et al. (1998) 'Fearlessness, stimulation-seeking, and large body size at age 3 years as early predispositions to childhood aggression at age 11 years', *Archives of General Psychiatry* 55, 8: 745–51.

Raine, A., Lencz, T., Bihrle, S., LaCasse, L. and Colletti, P. (2000) 'Reduced prefrontal gray matter volume and reduced autonomic activity in anti-social personality disorder', *Archives of General Psychiatry* 57, 2: 119–27.

Rasch, G. (1960) *Probabilistic Models for some Intelligence and Attainment Tests*, Copenhagen: Danish Institute for Educational Research.

Reinisch, J. M. (1977) 'Prenatal exposure of human foetuses to synthetic progestin and oestrogen affects personality', *Nature* 266: 561–2.

Reinisch, J. M. and Saunders, S. A. (1981) 'Prenatal gonadal steroid influences on gender related behaviours', in G. J. DeVries *Progress in Brain Research*, Amsterdam: Elsevier.

Rhee, S. H., Waldman, I. D., Hay, D. and Levy, F. (1999) 'Sex differences in genetic and environmental influences on DSM 3R attention deficit hyperactivity disorder', *Journal of Abnormal Psychology* 108: 24–41.

Rice, F., Harold, G. and Thapar, A. (2002) 'The genetic aetiology of childhood depression: a review', *Journal of Child Psychology and Psychiatry* 43, 1: 65–79.

Richards, M., Hardy, R. and Wadsworth, M. (1997) 'The effects of divorce and separation on mental health in a national UK birth cohort', *Psychological Medicine* 27, 5: 1121–8.

Richters, M. M. and Volkmar, F. R. (1994) 'Reactive attachment disorder of infancy or early childhood', *Journal of American Academy of Child and Adolescent Psychiatry* 33: 328–32.

Riedel, W. J. (2004) 'Cognitive changes after acute tryptophan depletion: what can they tell us?', *Psychological Medicine* 34, 1: 3–8.

Riggs, N. R., Blair, C. B., et al. (2003) 'Concurrent and 2-year longitudinal relations between executive function and the behavior of 1st and 2nd grade children', *Neuropsychology Development and Cognition Sect C Child Neuropsychology* 9, 4: 267–76.

Rijsdijk, F. V., Snieder, H., Ormel, J., Sham, P., Goldberg, D. P. and Spector, T. D. (2003) 'Genetic and environmental influences on psychological distress in the population: General Health Questionnaire analyses in UK twins', *Psychological Medicine* 33: 793–801.

Roberts, S. B. and Kendler, K. S. (1999) 'Neuroticism and self-esteem as indices of the vulnerability to major depression in women', *Psychological Medicine* 29, 5: 1101–9.

Roberts, A. C., Robbins, T. W., et al. (2000) *The Prefrontal Cortex: Executive and Cognitive Functions*, Oxford: Oxford University Press.

Robins, L. N. (1978) 'Sturdy childhood predictors of adult anti-social behaviour: replications from longitudinal studies', *Psychological Medicine* 8: 611–22.

Robins, L. N., Wing, J. K., Wittchen, H.-U., et al. (1988) 'The composite international diagnostic interview – an epidemiologic instrument suitable for use in conjunction with different diagnostic systems and in different cultures', *Archives of General Psychiatry* 45: 1069–77.

Rodgers, B. (1994) 'Pathways between parental divorce and adult depression', *Journal of Child Psychology and Psychiatry* 35, 7: 1289–1308.

Roiser, J., Rubinsztein, J. S., et al. (2003) 'Cognition in depression', *Psychiatry* 1: 43–7.

Roisman, G. L., Padron, E., Sroufe, L. A., et al. (2002) 'Earned-secure attachment status in retrospect and prospect', *Child Development* 73: 1204–19.

Rolls, E. T. (2000) 'The orbitofrontal cortex', in A. C. Roberts, T. W. Robbins and L. Weiskrantz. *The Pre-frontal Cortex: Executive and Cognitive Functions*, Oxford: Oxford University Press, pp. 67–86.

Romans, S. E., Gendall, K. A., et al. (2001) 'Child sexual abuse and later disordered eating: a New Zealand epidemiological study', *International Journal of Eating Disorders* 29, 4: 380–92.

Romeo, R. D. (2003) 'Puberty: a period of both organizational and activational effects of steroid hormones on neurobehavioural development', *Journal of Neuroendocrinology* 15, 12: 1185–92.

Ronalds, C., Creed, F. H., Webb, S. and Tomenson, B. (1997) 'The outcome of anxiety & depression in primary care', *British Journal of Psychiatry* 171: 427–33.

Rosmond, R., Chagnon, Y. C., et al. (2000a) 'A glucocorticoid receptor gene marker is associated with abdominal obesity, leptin, and dysregulation of the hypothalamic-pituitary-adrenal axis', *Obesity Research* 8, 3: 211–8.

Rosmond, R., Chagnon, Y. C., et al. (2000b) 'A polymorphism of the 5′-flanking region of the glucocorticoid receptor gene locus is associated with basal cortisol secretion in men', *Metabolism* 49, 9: 1197–9.

Rosmond, R., Chagnon, M., et al. (2001) 'A polymorphism in the regulatory region of the corticotropin-releasing hormone gene in relation to cortisol secretion, obesity, and gene-gene interaction', *Metabolism* 50, 9: 1059–62.

Rowe, R., Maughan, B., Worthman, C. M., Costello, E. J. and Angold, A. (2004) 'Testosterone, antisocial behavior, and social dominance in boys: pubertal development and biosocial interaction', *Biological Psychiatry* 55, 5: 546–52.

Rudolph, K. D., Hammen, C., Burge, D., et al. (2000) 'Toward an interpersonal life-stress model of depression: the developmental context of stress generation', *Development and Psychopathology* 12, 2: 215–34.

Rueter, M. A., Scaramella, L., et al. (1999) 'First onset of depressive or anxiety disorders predicted by the longitudinal course of internalizing symptoms and parent–adolescent disagreements', *Archives of General Psychiatry* 56, 8: 726–32.

Rutter, M. (1985a) 'Resilience in the face of adversity', *British Journal of Psychiatry* 147: 598–611.

Rutter, M. (1985b) 'Psychosocial resilience and protective mechanisms', in J. Rolf, M. Masten, D. Cicchetti, K. Nuechterlein and S. Weintraub *Risk and Protective Factors in the Development of Psychopathology*, Cambridge: Cambridge University Press, pp. 181–214.

Rutter, M. (1994) 'Stress research: accomplishments and the tasks ahead', in R. Haggert, L. Sherrod, N. Garmezy and M. Rutter *Stress, Risk and Resilience in Children and Adolescence*, Cambridge: Cambridge University Press, pp. 354–86.

Rutter, M. (1995) 'Clinical implications of attachment concepts: retrospect and prospect', *Journal of Child Psychology and Psychiatry* 36: 549–71.

Rutter, M. (2000) 'Psychosocial influences: critiques, findings, and research needs', *Development and Psychopathology* 12, 3: 375–405.

Rutter, M. (2002) 'The interplay of nature, nurture, and developmental influences: the challenge ahead for mental health', *Archives of General Psychiatry* 59, 11: 996–1000.

Rutter, L. Taylor, M. and Hersov, L. (2002) *Child Psychiatry: Modern Approaches*, Oxford: Blackwell.

Rutter, M. and Sroufe, L. A. (2000) 'Developmental psychopathology: concepts and challenges', *Developmental Psychopathology*, 12, 3: 265–296.

Rutter, M., Dunn, J., Plomin, R., et al. (1997) 'Integrating nature and nurture: secretion in men', *Metabolism* 49, 9: 1197–9.

Rutter, M. L., Kreppner, J. M. and O'Connor, T. G. (2001) 'Specificity and heterogeneity in children's responses to profound institutional privation', *British Journal of Psychiatry* 179: 97–103.

Sandberg, S., McGuinness, D., et al. (1998) 'Independence of childhood life events and chronic adversities: a comparison of two patient groups and controls', *Journal of American Academy of Child and Adolescent Psychiatry* 37, 7: 728–35.

Sandberg, S., Rutter, M., Pickles, A., McGuinness, D. and Angold, A. (2001) 'Do high-threat life events really provoke the onset of psychiatric disorder in children?', *Journal of Child Psychology and Psychiatry* 42, 4: 523–32.

Sanders, M. R. (1999) 'Triple P-Positive Parenting Program: towards an empirically validated multilevel parenting and family support strategy for the prevention of behavior and emotional problems in children', *Journal of Clinical Child and Family Psychology Review* 2, 2: 71–89.

Sanders, M. R. and McFarland, M. T. (2000) 'Treatment of depressed mothers with disruptive children: a controlled evaluation of cognitive behavioral family intervention', *Behaviour Therapy* 31: 89–112.

Sanders, M. R., Montgomery, D. T., Brechman-Toussaint, M. L. (2000) 'The mass media and the prevention of child behavior problems: the evaluation of a television series to promote better child and parenting outcomes', *Journal of Child Psychology and Psychiatry* 41: 939–948.

Sargent, P. A., Kjaer, K. H., et al. (2000) 'Brain serotonin1A receptor binding measured by positron emission tomography with [11C]WAY-100635: effects of depression and antidepressant treatment', *Archives of General Psychiatry* 57, 2: 174–80.

Saudino, K. J., Pedersen, N. L., McGlearn, G. E. et al. (1997) 'Can personality explain genetic influence on life events?', *Journal of Personality and Social Psychology* 72: 196–206.

Schleifer, S., Keller, S., Camerino Thornton, J. and Stein, M. (1983) 'Suppression of lymphocyte stimulation after bereavement', *Journal of American Medical Association* 250: 374–7.

Schleifer, S. J., Keller, S. E. and Bartlett, J. A. (1999) 'Depression and immunity: clinical factors and therapeutic course', *Psychiatry Research* 85, 1: 63–9.

Schwab-Stone, M. E., Ayers, T. S., Kasprow, W., et al. (1995) 'No safe haven: a study of violence exposure in an urban community', *Journal of American Academy of Child and Adolescent Psychiatry* 34: 1343–52.

Schwartz, C. E., Foley, F. W., Rao, S. M., Bernardin, L. J., Lee, H. and Genderson, M. W. (1999) 'Stress and course of disease in multiple sclerosis', *Behavioural Medicine* 25, 3: 110–16.

Scott, S., Spender, Q., Doolan, M., Jacobs, B. and Aspland, H. (2001) 'Multicentre controlled trail of parenting groups for child anti-social behaviour in clinical practice', *British Medical Journal* 323: 194–7.

Segal, Z. V. and Ingram, R. (1994) 'Mood priming and construct activation in tests of cognitive vulnerability to unipolar depression', *Clinical Psychology Review* 14, 7: 663–95.

Shekelle, R. B., Raynor, W. J. and Ostfeld, A. M. (1981) 'Psychological depression and 17 year risk of cancer', *Psychosomatic Medicine* 43: 117–25.

Shepherd, M., Fisher, N., Kessel, N. and Stein, L. (1959) 'Psychiatric morbidity in an urban practice', *Proceedings of the Royal Society of Medicine* 52: 269–74.

Shepherd, M., Cooper, B., Brown, A. C., et al. (1966) *Psychiatric Illness in General Practice*, Oxford: Oxford University Press.

Shepherd, M., Wilkinson, G. and Williams, P. (1986) *Mental Illness in Primary Care Settings*, London: Routledge.

Shochet I. M., Dadds M. R., Holland D., Whitefield K., Harnett P. H., Osgarby S. M. (2001) 'The efficacy of a universal school-based program to prevent adolescent depression', *Journal of Clinical Child Psychology* 30, 3: 303–15.

Sidebotham, P., Heron, J., et al. (2002) 'Child maltreatment in the "Children of the Nineties": deprivation, class, and social networks in a UK sample', *Child Abuse and Neglect* 26, 12: 1243–59.

Simon, G., Goldberg, D. P., Von Korff, M. and Ustun, T. B. (2002) 'Understanding cross-national differences in depression prevalence', *Psychological Medicine* 32, 4: 585–94.

Sims, A. (1975) 'Factors predictive of outcome in neurosis', *British Journal of Psychiatry* 127: 54–62.

Skuse, D. H., Gill, D. Reilly, S., et al. (1995) 'Failure to thrive and the risk of child abuse: a prospective population survey', *Journal of Medical Screening* 2: 145–9.

Smalley, S. L., McCracken, J. and Tanguay, P. (1995) 'Autism, affective disorders, and social phobia', *American Journal of Medical Genetics* 60, 1: 19–26.

Smith, C. A. and Farrington, D. P. (2004) 'Continuities in anti-social behavior and parenting across three generations', *Journal of Child Psychology and Psychiatry* 45, 2: 230–47.

Smith, G., McKenzie, J., Marner, D. and Steele, R. (1985) 'Psychological modulation of the human immune response', *Archives of Internal Medicine* 145: 2110–12.

Smoller, J. W., Rosenbaum, J. F., et al. (2003) 'Association of a genetic marker at the corticotropin-releasing hormone locus with behavioral inhibition', *Biological Psychiatry* 54, 12: 1376–81.

Sowell, E. R., Thompson, P. M., Holmes, C. J., Jernigan, T. L. and Toga, A. W. (2000) 'In vivo evidence for post-adolescent brain maturation in frontal and striatal regions', *Nature Neuroscience* 2, 10: 859–61.

Spasojevic, J. and Alloy, L. B. (2001) 'Rumination as a common mechanism relating depressive risk factors to depression', *Emotion* 1, 1: 25–37.

Spear, L. P. (2000) 'The adolescent brain and age related behavioural manifestations', *Neuroscience and Behavioural Reviews* 24, 24: 417–63.

Spence, S. H., Sheffield, J. K. and Donovan, C. L. (2003) 'Preventing adolescent depression: an evaluation of the problem solving for life program', *Journal of Consulting and Clinical Psychology* 71, 1: 3–13.

Sroufe, L. A., Carlson, E. A., Levy, A. K., et al. (1999) 'Implications of attachment theory for developmental psychopathology', *Developmental Psychopathology* 11: 1–13.

Stein, J. A., Leslie, M. B., et al. (2002) 'Relative contributions of parent substance use and childhood maltreatment to chronic homelessness, depression, and substance abuse problems among homeless women: mediating roles of self-esteem and abuse in adulthood', *Child Abuse and Neglect* 26, 10: 1011–27.

Steinberg, L. and Morris, A. S. (2001) 'Adolescent development', *Annual Review of Psychology* 52: 83–110.

Stevens, D., Charman, T. and Blair, R. J. (2001) 'Recognition of emotion in facial expressions and vocal tones in children with psychopathic tendencies', *Journal of Genetic Psychology* 162: 201–11.

Stevenson, J., Richman, N. and Graham, P. (1985) 'Behaviour problems and language abilities at three years and behavioural deviance at eight years', *Journal of Child Psychology and Psychiatry* 26, 2: 215–30.

Stewart, S. M., Kennard, B. D., et al. (2004) 'A cross-cultural investigation of cognitions and depressive symptoms in adolescents', *Journal of Abnormal Psychology* 113, 2: 248–57.

Stone, A. A., Schwartz, J. E., et al. (2001) 'Individual differences in the diurnal cycle of salivary free cortisol: a replication of flattened cycles for some individuals', *Psychoneuroendocrinology* 26, 3: 295–306.

Strickland, P. L., Deakin, J. F., et al. (2002) 'Bio-social origins of depression in the community. Interactions between social adversity, cortisol and serotonin neurotransmission', *British Journal of Psychiatry* 180: 168–73.

Strous, R. D., Maayan, R., et al. (2003) 'Dehydroepiandrosterone augmentation in the management of negative, depressive, and anxiety symptoms in schizophrenia', *Archives of General Psychiatry* 60, 2: 133–41.

Surtees, P. G. and Wainwright, N. W. (1996) 'Fragile states of mind: neuroticism, vulnerability and the long-term outcome of depression', *British Journal of Psychiatry* 169, 3: 338–47.

Surtees, P., Dean, C., Ingham, J. C., et al. (1983) 'Psychiatric disorders in women in an Edinburgh community: association with demographic factors', *British Journal of Psychiatry* 1422: 238–46.

Swanston, H. Y., Tebbutt, J. S., O'Toole, B. I. and Oates, R. K. (1997) 'Sexually abused children 5 years after presentation: a case-control study', *Pediatrics* 100, 4: 600–8.

Tavares, J. V., Drevets, W. C., et al. (2003) 'Cognition in mania and depression', *Psychological Medicine* 33, 6: 959–67.

Teasdale, J. D. and Barnard, P. J. (1993) *Affect, Cognition and Change: Remodelling Depressive Thought* Hillsdale, NJ: Lawrence Erlbaum Associates, Inc.

Teasdale, J. and Dent, J. (1987) 'Cognitive Vulnerability to Depression: an investigation of two hypotheses', *British Journal of Clinical Psychology* 26: 113–26.

Tellegen, A. (2003) *Manual of the Multi-Dimensional Personality Questionnaire*, Minnesota: University of Minnesota Press.

Tennant, C., Bebbington, P. and Hurry, J. (1981) 'The short term outcome of neurotic disorders in the community: the relationship of remission to "neutralising" life events', *British Journal of Psychiatry* 139: 213–20.

Thapar, A. and McGuffin, P. (1997) 'Anxiety and depressive symptoms in childhood – a genetic study of comorbidity', *Journal of Child Psychology and Psychiatry* 38, 6: 651–6.

Tocharoen, A., Garrison, C., McKeown, R., Waller, J., Jackson, K., Addy, C. and Shoob, H. (2000) 'The longitudinal study of phobic disorder in a community sample from early to late adolescence', *Annals of Epidemiology* 10, 7: 483.

Torgerson, S. (1985) 'Developmental differentiation of anxiety and depressive neuroses', *Acta Psychiatrica Scandinavica* 71: 304–10.

Torgersen, S., Lygren, S., Oien A., Skre, I., et al. (2000) 'A twin study of personality disorders', *Comprehensive Psychiatry* 41: 416–25.

Tracy, R. L. and Ainsworth, M. D. (1981) 'Maternal affectionate behavior and infant-mother attachment patterns', *Child Development* 52: 1341–3.

Turner, J. E. Jr. and Cole, D. A. (1994) 'Developmental differences in cognitive diatheses for child depression', *Journal of Abnormal Child Psychology* 22, 1: 15–32.

Tyrer, P. and Alexander, J. (1979) 'Clasification of personality disorder', *British Journal of Psychiatry* 135: 163–7.

Ustun, T. B. and Sartorius, N. (1995) *Mental Illness in General Health Care*, Chichester: Wiley.

Ustun, T. B. and von Korff, M. (1995) 'Primary mental health services: access and provision of care', in T. B. Ustun and N. Sartorius *Mental Illness in General Health Care*, Chichester: Wiley.

Vaillancourt, T., Brendgen, M., et al. (2003) 'A longitudinal confirmatory factor analysis of indirect and physical aggression: evidence of two factors over time?', *Child Development* 74, 6: 1628–38.

Van den Brink, W., Koeter, M., Ormel, J., et al. (1990) 'Psychiatric diagnosis in an out-patient population', *Archives of General Psychiatry* 46: 369–72.

Van der Oord, E. J., Boomsma, D. I. and Verhulst, F. C. (1994) 'A study of problem behaviours in the 10 to 15 year old biologically related and unrelated international adoptees', *Behaviour Genetics* 24: 193–203.

van Goozen, S. H., Matthys, W., et al. (1998) 'Salivary cortisol and cardiovascular activity during stress in oppositional-defiant disorder boys and normal controls', *Biological Psychiatry* 43, 7: 531–9.

van Goozen, S. H., Matthys, W., et al. (2000) 'Hypothalamic-pituitary-adrenal axis and autonomic nervous system activity in disruptive children and matched controls', *Journal of American Academy of Child and Adolescent Psychiatry* 39, 11: 1438–45.

van IJzendoorn, M. H., Juffer, F. and Duyvesteyn, M. G. (1995) 'Breaking the inter-generational cycle of insecure attachment: a review of the effects of attachment-based interventions on maternal sensitivity and infant security', *Journal of Child Psychology and Psychiatry* 36: 225–48.

van Niekerk, J. K., Huppert, F. A., et al. (2001) 'Salivary cortisol and DHEA: associ-ation with measures of cognition and well-being in normal older men, and effects of three months of DHEA supplementation', *Psychoneuroendocrinology* 26, 6: 591–612.

Van Os, J. and Jones, P. B. (1999) 'Early risk factors and adult person – environment relationships in affective disorder', *Psychological Medicine* 29: 1055–68.

Verhulst, F. C. and van der Ende, J. (1997) 'Factors associated with child mental health service use in the community', *Journal of American Academy of Child and Adolescent Psychiatry* 36, 7: 901–9.

Volleberg, W. A., Iedema, J., Bilj, R. V., et al. (2001) 'The structure and stability of common mental disorders: the Nemesis study', *Archives of General Psychiatry* 58: 597–603.

Wade, T. D. and Kendler, K. S. (2000) 'The genetic epidemiology of parental disci-pline', *Psychological Medicine* 30: 1303–12.

Watson, D., Clark, L. A., Weber, K., et al. (1995) 'Testing a tripartite model: exploring the symptom structure of anxiety and depression in student, adult and patient samples', *Journal of Abnormal Psychology* 104: 15–25.

Weaver, S. A., Aherne, F. X., Meaney, M. J., et al. (2000) 'Neonatal handling perman-ently alters hypothalamic-pituitary-adrenal axis function, behaviour, and body weight in boars', *Journal of Endocrinology* 164: 349–59.

Webster-Stratton, C. and Hammond, M. (1997) 'Treating children with early-onset conduct problems: a comparison of child and parent training interventions', *Journal of Consulting and Clinical Psychology* 65, 1: 93–109.

Westergard, G. C., Suomi, S. J., Chavanne, T. J., Houser, L., et al. (2003) 'Physiological correlates of aggression and impulsivity in free ranging female primates', *Neuropsychopharmacology* 28: 1045–55.

White, D. and Pitts, M. (1998) 'Educating young people about drugs: a systematic review', *Addiction* 93: 1478–87.

WHO (1988) *International Classification of Disease*, Geneva: World Health Organization.

WHO (1994) *ICD-10 Classification of Mental and Behavioural Disorders*, Geneva: World Health Organization.

WHO (2004) *WHO Guide to Mental and Neurological Conditions in Primary Care*, 2nd edn, London: Royal Society of Medicine.

Widiger, T. A. and Costa, P. T. (2002) 'Five factor model of personality research', in T. A. Widiger and P. T. Costa (eds) *Personality Disorder and the Five Factor Model of Personality*, Washington, DC: American Psychological Association.

Widom, C. S. (1989) 'The cycle of violence', *Science* 244: 160–66.

Wills, T. A., Vaccaro, D. and McNamara, G. (1994) 'Novelty seeking, risk taking, and related constructs as predictors of adolescent substance use: an application of Cloninger's theory', *Journal of Substance Abuse* 6, 1: 1–20.

Wing, J. K. and Brown, G. W. (1970) *Institutionalism and Schizophrenia*, Cambridge: Cambridge University Press.

Wissink, S., Meijers, O., et al. (2000) 'Regulation of the rat serotonin-1A receptor gene by corticosteroids', *Journal of Biological Chemistry* 275: 1321–6.

Wolkowitz, O. M., Reus, V. I., et al. (1999) 'Double-blind treatment of major depression with dehydroepiandrosterone', *American Journal of Psychiatry* 156, 4: 646–9.

Yehuda, R., Halligan, S. L., et al. (2004) 'Effects of trauma exposure on the cortisol response to dexamethasone administration in PTSD and major depressive disorder', *Psychoneuroendocrinology* 29, 3: 389–404.

Young, A. H., Sahakian, B. J., et al. (1999) 'The effects of chronic administration of hydrocortisone on cognitive function in normal male volunteers', *Psychopharmacology* 145, 3: 260–6.

Young, S. E., Stallings, M. C., Corley, R. P., et al. (2000) 'Genetic and environmental influences on behavioural disinhibition', *American Journal of Medical Genetics* 96: 684–95.

Zeanah, C. H., Smyke, A. T. and Dumitrescu, A. (2002) 'Attachment disturbances in young children. II: Indiscriminate behavior and institutional care', *Journal of American Academy of Child and Adolescent Psychiatry* 41: 983–9.

Zimmermann, P. (1999) 'Structure and functions of internal working models of attachment and their role for emotion regulation', *Attachment and Humman Development* 1: 291–306.

Author index

Subject index